Counselors Finding Their Way

Jeffrey A. Kottler
Editor

5999 Stevenson Avenue
Alexandria, VA 22304
www.counseling.org

Counselors Finding Their Way

10 9 8 7 6 5 4 3 2 1

American Counseling Association
5999 Stevenson Avenue
Alexandria, VA 22304

Director of Publications
Carolyn C. Baker

Production Manager
Bonny Gaston

Copy Editor
Susan Harris

Cover design by Spot Color

Library of Congress Cataloging-in-Publication Data
Counselors finding their way / edited by Jeffrey A. Kottler.
    p. cm.
  ISBN 1-55620-192-3 (alk. paper)
  1. Counselors.   2. Counseling.   I. Kottler, Jeffrey A.
BF637.C6.C695 2001
361'.06—dc21   2001045822

Table of Contents

Part X   Finding Your Own Truth

Part XI   Making a Difference

About the Editor

Jeffrey A. Kottler is the author of over 50 books in counseling and related fields, including *Compassionate Therapy: Working With Difficult Clients* (1992), *On Being a Therapist* (1993), *Beyond Blame* (1994), *Travel That Can Change Your Life* (1997), *Introduction to Therapeutic Counseling* (2000), *Nuts and Bolts of Helping* (2000), *Doing Good: Passion and Commitment For Helping Others* (2000), *Making Changes Last* (2001), *Learning Group Leadership* (2001), and *Theories in Counseling and Therapy* (2002). For the past 10 years, he has been the editor of "Finding Your Way," a column that has appeared in *Counseling Today*.

Jeffrey is professor and chairperson of the Counseling Department at California State University, Fullerton. In the past several years, he has been finding his way by teaching counseling as a visiting professor in diverse cultures such as Peru, Hong Kong, Nepal, Australia, New Zealand, Iceland, Faroe Islands, and the Yakima Indian nation.

About the Authors

Cynthia Baldwin is Professor Emeritus at the University of Nevada, Reno.

Brent Bandhauer is an elementary school counselor in Las Vegas, Nevada.

Carol Becker is a counselor in Manchester, Missouri.

Fred Bemak is Professor and Chair of Counseling at George Mason University in Fairfax, Virginia.

Patricia A. Blecich is the program coordinator for Mercy Housing & Shelter Corporation in Hartford, Connecticut.

Sandra Lee Blood is a counselor in independent practice in Lake Zurich, Illinois.

Marielle Brandt is an assistant professor in the Department of Counselor Education at California State University, Sacramento.

Christine A. Breier is a counselor in Naperville, Illinois.

Leah Brew is a faculty member at California State University, Fullerton.

Ford Brooks is a faculty member in the Counseling Department of Shippensburg University in Pennsylvania.

Robert W. Brown was coordinator of the counseling program at Oakland University in Rochester, Michigan. He died in 1995.

Marj Burgess is a counselor and personal coach in Gardiner, Maine.

Laurie Carty is a professor of nursing at the University of Windsor, Ontario, Canada.

Linda Chassman is a family therapist and a lecturer at California State University, Fullerton.

Stuart F. Chen-Hayes is an assistant professor in the counselor education program at Lehman College of the City University of New York.

Rita Chi-Ying Chung is a faculty member at George Mason University in Fairfax, Virginia.

Dana Comstock is Associate Professor at St. Mary's University in San Antonio, Texas.

Robin Cook is a faculty member at Wichita State University, Kansas.

Jewel Dhuru practices spiritually based counseling in Milwaukee, Wisconsin.

Jason Eckert is a substance abuse and mental health counselor in New York City.

Brenda K. Garboos is a rehabilitation counselor at Mt. Sinai Hospital in New York City.

Richard Gariolo is a counselor in independent practice in Emerson, New Jersey.

Anne M. Geroski is an assistant professor in the counseling program at the University of Vermont.

Dan Gregerson is a mental health counselor in Kalispell, Montana.

Patricia Guest is a counseling supervisor for the District Attorney's Pre-Trial Diversion Program in Montgomery, Alabama.

Larry L. Gulick works as a career consultant in Grove City, Ohio.

Shannon Hodges is an assistant professor of counseling at Niagara University in Lewistown, New York.

Rafat Hussain is a senior lecturer in Health Management at the University of New England in Armidale, New South Wales, Australia.

Gary Koch is a faculty member at Olivet Nazarene University in Bourbonnais, Illinois.

Cary Kottler is a student at Rice University in Houston, Texas.

Jeffrey A. Kottler is Professor and Chair of Counseling at California State University, Fullerton.

Marva Larrabee is a retired faculty member from the University of South Carolina. She lives in West Columbia, South Carolina.

David Leary is the director of the "Come In" Youth Resource Center in the inner city of Sydney, New South Wales, Australia.

John McCarthy is a visiting assistant professor at Chatham College in Pittsburgh, Pennsylvania.

Helene McGlauflin is a counselor at Woodside Elementary School in Topsham, Maine.

Felicity Monk lives in New Zealand where she is currently pursuing a career in investigative journalism.

Gerald Monk is Associate Professor of Counseling at San Diego State University.

Smita Nagpal is a family counselor in Hudson, Michigan.

Kathy O'Byrne is Director of Experiential Learning at the University of California, Los Angeles.

Stephanie B. Palladino is a school counselor at Whately Elementary School, in Whately, Massachusetts.

Olive Poliks is a counselor at East Aurora High School in Aurora, Illinois.

Kathy Potter is a career consultant in Santa Clara, California.

Judy Provost is a faculty member at Rollins College in Winter Park, Florida.

Mary Read is a doctoral student at the University of Southern California and a counselor in independent practice.

Joe Roberts is doing research on virtual reality therapy in Jackson, Mississippi.

R. Terry Sack is a professor of human development and psychological counseling at Appalachian State University in Boone, North Carolina.

Wayne Schneider is the clinical director of Horizon Counseling in Syosset, New York.

David S. Shepard is a faculty member in the Department of Counseling at California State University, Fullerton.

Joan R. Sherman is a family therapist in Lancaster, Pennsylvania.

Beth Soucar is a doctoral student at Temple University in Philadelphia.

Ronald Strahl volunteers his time doing mental health triage in Sheboygan, Wisconsin.

Mary Lee Swickert is a faculty member at Central Michigan University.

M. K. Tailor holds a certification in school counseling in the state of Georgia.

Michael Taleff is a consultant and trainer and is involved in research on critical thinking and counselor effectiveness. He lives in Hollidaysburg, Pennsylvania.

Laura Vaccaro is founder and facilitator of a support group for women and works for a company as director of research and development.

Gudbjörg Vilhjálmsdóttir is an assistant professor of school counseling at the University of Iceland in Reykjavík, Iceland.

Laurie Williamson is an assistant professor in counselor education at Appalachian State University in Boone, North Carolina.

Sherrill Wiseman is a counselor in Calgary, Alberta, Canada.

Elizabeth Witherspoon is a counselor in independent practice in Lewisville, North Carolina.

Preface

Practicing counseling can be one of the most absolutely fun, exciting, and fulfilling jobs on Earth but also among the most frustrating and challenging. Every day we encounter people who are wracked with pain, who are confused, or who are very annoying to other people—and these are just our colleagues (just kidding!). Indeed the people who consult us for help are sometimes resistant, ornery, and uncooperative. The ones who are most highly motivated may also be so anxious, depressed, or dysfunctional that it is difficult for them to move along at the pace we might prefer.

On top of all these pressures, often compounded by the demands of the workplace, are the challenges we face in our own journeys as counselors and therapists. We are expected to act as guides for others in territory that we may not be totally familiar with ourselves. Moreover, we face our own demons in the struggle to find our way.

Our supervisors and teachers may have unrealistic expectations for what we can do, what *anyone* can do in our positions. The public has its own illusions and myths about the magic we can wield and the healing that is supposedly within our power. And our clients want instant cures, or at the very least, for us to convince others that they don't really have a problem in the first place. No wonder some of us feel so lost, even if it isn't altogether safe to admit this aloud.

For the past decade I have edited a column called "Finding Your Way," which appears in *Counseling Today*, a publication of the American Counseling Association. As originally intended, this space was designed to give newcomers to the field, as well as veterans, the opportunity to talk about their journeys as practicing counselors. It is so rare in the professional literature that we read about the very personal stories and struggles of counselors, especially with regard to their efforts to find their way through the maze of personal obstacles and professional challenges.

Over the years, the articles that have appeared in print have evolved to include other topics that have direct relevance to counselors and therapists—fears of failure and being a fraud, unresolved personal issues from the past that interfere with professional effectiveness, and so forth. Readers have said repeatedly that this column is the one place they look for inspiration, as well as to hear the authentic, honest voices of others who show the courage to speak their concerns out loud. Students from every part of the world have reported that the realistic portrayals of what it's like to be a counselor in the trenches has eased their transitions to professional practice.

I am pleased to present to you the second volume of "Finding Your Way," which covers the 5-year period since the first book was published in 1997. In addition to the essays that have already appeared in *Counseling Today*, I have solicited more than a dozen new contributions that have never before appeared in print. Each of these chapters is consistent with the tone and style of those that have made these pieces so unique in the literature. All authors have been directed to avoid the use of citations, references, and a traditionally academic style and instead to write as personally as possible. It was reasoned that since there are so many other vehicles to advance the "science" and academic rigor of our profession, this would remain one place where practitioners could talk about what is in their hearts.

I believe that the essays contained in this book are indeed different from what is published elsewhere. In each case, the author has taken great pains to be as revealing, honest, and open as possible, talking about how his or her own life experiences have helped shape professional development. In addition to whatever theme the authors are discussing, they have shown great courage in talking about such personal issues in a public forum.

Many of the authors in this book are first time published writers. They not only struggled to tell their stories of finding their way but also faced their fears of critical judgment by peers. After all, these are not just ideas that have been presented, but their most precious, sacred stories. In some cases, they have been told out loud for the very first time.

This book would be useful to several different audiences. It is, of course, an excellent resource for students and prospective counselors as it shares the realities of practice in the most direct and honest way imaginable. Yet this is also an inspirational book for veteran practitioners. It is affirming precisely because the voices do speak the truth in a very personal way. Such explorations encourage readers to look more deeply at their own motives for doing this sort of work and to come to terms with their own journeys to find their way.

The sections of this book are organized according to several broad themes. In Part I we begin with Feeling Lost—the ways that counselors cope with feeling disoriented, confused, and filled with doubt. Part II on Facing Pain and Adversity, Part III on Transitions and Transformations, and Part IV on Learning From Failure all continue explorations of the dark, difficult side of helping others for a living and the personal costs that are paid by practitioners. Part V, Cultural Clashes, also contains a series of essays on facing difficult challenges, but these stories are specifically about experiences of oppression, racism, and prejudice. Part VI presents an international perspective as counselors From Around the World speak about some of their difficult adjustments.

In Part VII, Clients As Teachers, the focus shifts to the ways that counselors have learned and grown as a result of their interactions with clients. Part VIII, Refining Our Thinking, continues this theme by addressing the ways that seminal moments have led to dramatic shifts in the ways counselors view their lives and work. The next two sections on Personal and Professional Lives (Part IX) and Finding Your Own Truth (Part X) present a series of stories about the ways that clinicians have struggled to find their own voice and develop their own unique counseling styles. The last section, Making a Difference, includes narratives about the incredible joys and benefits that we enjoy as counselors as a result of our often challenging work.

—Jeffrey A. Kottler
Fullerton, California

Part I

Feeling Lost

1

Navigationally Challenged

Jeffrey A. Kottler

I find myself lost. Constantly. When in a strange city, I like to explore the area by going for a run, but I usually go much further than I ever anticipated as I try to find my way back to the starting point. Even in the local mall I walk in circles before I find what I'm looking for.

Since I am a counselor and educator, as well as a writer, I spend my life helping others who are lost to find their way. So do you. I wonder, though, how I can be a guide for our students, clients, and readers in one territory when I become so disoriented in another.

More than a few times I've tried to solve my problem of being navigationally challenged. I have faith in the power of experts, so I consulted the best: two burly sergeants from the Desert Warfare School who were teaching a course on orienteering. Finally, I would learn some sense of direction.

The instruction I received was everything I could have wanted. I learned how to use a compass and read a topographical map. I even became proficient in how to identify coordinates, within 15-meter grids, for calling in air support from Stealth bombers. Although this is not a skill that I would probably ever have to use, it did increase my sense of competence in my newfound navigational abilities.

I thought to myself that there is a metaphor in this, an object lesson of sorts (but then as a counselor I see metaphors in everything). I figured that if I could learn to overcome my geographical handicap, to face one of my greatest weaknesses, surely this would be a great story to model for my students and clients. "See," I would tell them, "even a lost soul like me can learn to find my way out of the wilderness."

I was filled with endless fantasies of other obstacles I could overcome. Maybe next I could learn to understand how my car works, or why heavy steel planes can fly and heavy boats don't sink, or how electricity works.

Nah. But I could dream. At the very least, now that I was navigationally competent, I could be even more powerful as a mentor for others. No longer would I walk around the world in a perpetual state of disorientation.

The very next weekend I set out on a field trip into the mountains. Equipped with my new compass and several sets of topographical maps of the area, not to mention a brand new pair of hiking books to celebrate my victory over disorientation, I set out to test my new skills. The night before I had studied my maps, planned my route, practiced with my compass to find my way around the house with no problem, and so I was ready.

I had a marvelous day climbing to the top of the highest peak, following my maps to guide me through canyons, over ridges, and up the perfect ascent to the top. No longer was I lost. I actually knew where I was, not to mention where I was going. I must tell you that this is a new experience for me—usually I only know where I've been, and even that is just an illusion.

As I ascended the last slope to the top of the mountain, my mind raced with all the ways I could use my newly developed talent to give even more accurate directions to lost souls, as well as to function even better as a guide in my teaching and counseling. This was just such a dynamite feeling, I couldn't help but feel proud about what I had accomplished. This was even more difficult than getting a doctorate, publishing my first book, or even learning to ride a bike without training wheels. I felt dizzy with the realization that I would never be lost again—as long as I carried my trusty compass.

I sat on the top of my mountain and reveled in the view of the valley below. It was a lovely day in the desert—blue sky, cooling breeze, a hawk floating in the distance. I found the perfect ledge to rest my back, letting my feet dangle over the edge. As I ate my lunch, savoring each bite, I reviewed the route I had taken to the top, just so I could give good directions to someone else searching for the pinnacle. Looking at the map, though, something didn't look quite right. There was a ridge in front of me that wasn't supposed to be where it was. That struck me as funny at the time, although I no longer had much appetite for my lunch.

I spread out the maps on the ground, took a compass reading, and discovered, much to my amazement, that I had climbed the wrong mountain! Sitting over to the left, right next to me, was the peak I had planned to scale.

So, what is the moral of this tale, I wondered to myself as I walked dejectedly down to the bottom. No matter how optimistic I tried to be, I had to accept the fact that even with an expensive compass, the best maps available, and the training of two burly sergeants from the Desert Warfare School, I was hopelessly lost. But then, I reminded myself with a glimmer of optimism, I couldn't really be lost since I knew I was in the wrong place. Okay, I was reaching for some sign of progress.

It seems that even though we don't always get to where we think we are going, the view is nevertheless gorgeous at the top, and the journey is still invigorating.

2
Do I Have What It Takes?

Sandra Lee Blood

I have been in private practice almost nine years, and I'm struggling to keep my practice afloat. When asked why this is the case, I glibly offer, "Oh, you know, managed care . . . " and trail off. But it is more than that. The answer seems to lie within myself, and so far it is elusive. It is difficult to watch the self-destruction, to "know that I have met the enemy, and she is me" as the comic strip character Pogo used to say.

If I look inside and I am fearlessly honest, I am responsible for the ups and downs in my practice. Sometimes I rail, "It's not fair." Bankers, scientists, and architects don't have their fortunes tied so intimately to their personalities. But that is just the nature of the beast, and I must accept it.

So when I look inside, what do I see? I see a person whose empathy wears thin. I answer with an eye toward "fixing" my clients rather than being with them or fully exploring their issues. Sometimes I am too direct and confrontational—I offer a book or suggest another professional, like a financial planner. I have too little patience. As my therapeutic ear is piecing together the big picture, I want my client to see it too, so I run ahead in my comments instead of staying back where they are. In all these things, somehow, I have emotionally pulled away and gone to the surface for air. When I am in that place, the impact on my practice is global and most clients seem to feel its effects. I see it in their eyes, if I am honest. Sometimes they don't come back. Then I get really discouraged.

I had a particularly difficult day a couple of weeks ago. It was the day before the fourth of July. No problem, I thought. At least I didn't have to reschedule because of the holiday. But I misjudged the holiday mood of my clients. Like dominoes, they fell. The first got caught in holiday traffic, as an accident backed up cars for miles. She made it through the door as her session time ended. She had been out of town, so I hadn't seen her at her other regularly scheduled session that week, and she usually needed to see me after a visit home, which this had been. If I had had a crystal ball, I could have suggested she wait and I could have rescheduled her appointment. However, my afternoon was full. So she headed home. Twenty minutes into the next session time, I get a call from my next client, telling me she has just that minute returned home from a doctor's appointment for her daughter. It had taken longer than she expected. A few minutes later, I got a page from my next client. A family crisis had arisen and she had to attend to it right away. I was torn between frustration at the cancellation and happiness at hearing the non-victimized resolve in her voice: She was taking action—progress!

As I sat alone in my office waiting for my last client, I allowed some self-pity about sitting around while everyone else was running to enjoy preholiday festivities. I wondered at the profession I'd chosen. None of my clients knew about the other and how with each cancellation the frustration mounted. I'm supposed to be the even-keeled one, always ready with a serene smile. That smile is also supposed to appear when my client sweetly announces, "Oh, by the way, I forgot my checkbook," or, "Oh my, I've used my last check," or "Can you hold this till Friday?"

These frustrations, though irritating, pale in comparison to the variety of resistances I have seen. If I have a chance to explore the resistance in session, we are fortunate; there is hope for working it through. It is when the client calls and cancels, not connecting his or her actions to the internal dynamics, and then hides behind voice mail, screening his or her calls, that the client is lost forever. I once had a client plead illness several weeks in a row, sitting in the bathtub trying to pass a kidney stone and "unable to come to the phone," until the therapeutic connection got too faint to be restored.

I lose focus. With all the modalities out there, it is confusing whether you're trying to be eclectic or follow one method exclusively. What is faddish, and what really works? It's so much easier to believe I've found "the way" than to struggle with the ambiguities of a human nature that will never be tamed. I think I'm most tempted to try something new and different when I'm feeling therapy isn't working and my anxiety increases and heightens my insecurity. Maybe bells and whistles will distract them and they won't notice I don't know what I'm doing.

Sometimes I lose my way by imposing my preconceptions as a template over the way I listen to my clients. As a client relates an incident, I draw on an experience I have had and whisper inwardly, "I know what that is like," as a bridge to empathy. Sometimes it may be true, but sometimes it may only superficially resemble my experience. It is an open invitation to countertransference.

Countertransference. Have you ever had your clients mirror your life? I once moved unknowingly into the identical apartment complex within a month of my client. One of my most difficult situations involved discovering a very dear friend of mine for whom I had hidden feelings was also the object of the affections of my client. I once saw the spouse of someone with a syndrome the same as a relative of mine. I have had a client who closely resembles in many ways someone I personally know. I think it would be beneficial for each to know the other, but I am unable to effect that meeting. Each of these situations is like a high wire circus act of therapeutic intricacy.

Perhaps the most painful aspect of losing my way is not knowing "the rest of the story," after clients leave. There is no way of knowing how they are doing. I saw a narcissistically vulnerable couple individually for several years early in my practice and made some mistakes. Finally they left. I heard from them once since then. The husband called; nothing appeared changed, but no, he didn't want to make another appointment. Then there was the girl with the Peter Pan complex who never wanted to grow up and take responsibility. She was a "happy ending," moved away, and then wrote a letter she would be in town and could she call? I wrote back affirmatively, but she never contacted me. I will always wonder why. And then my clients struggle with the "one-sided" nature of the relationship. Of course it is the "failures" that haunt more than the "successes." The therapeutic line can provide as much pain on one side as the other. There is a particular kind of sacrifice for a counselor who agrees to never be "friends" or more for the greater good of being in a position to be able to help, keeping therapeutic objectivity. I dare say few clients think of it.

I can also lose my way by forgetting why I'm a counselor in the first place. With all the twists and turns the profession takes with managed care, licensure/third party reimbursement battles, and tribal bickering, it's easy to think of looking for greener grass. I forget the plumb line, the North Star, which is the knowledge that I have a gift. Although it may not seem special, everyone truly does not possess it. I need to believe I have something to offer, if only my ability to come alongside and be with a person. I must reconnect with my strong desire to help people, to make a difference. A popular word these days is *calling*. If that was my beginning, that is what shapes my purpose in life.

But today I'm feeling vulnerable to one of the digressions. You're probably catching me on a bad day. I know I've been whining a lot. Of course I could tell you about times it's all been worthwhile, when growth is apparent, a client has an "aha" experience in session, or termination comes appropriately. But today, my way is cloudy. I still wonder if I have what it takes. And answers don't come easily.

3

Me? A Professor?

Christine A. Breier

It has been my honor to be a student of some outstanding educators in our counseling field. I grieve the nearing end of my formal education as I struggle to find my way into academia. Not only will I miss the honor of being a student in higher education, but I fear the honor of being a counselor educator. I fear that I do not have the "stuff" of which a "real professor" is made.

First of all, I have difficulty envisioning myself as a professor. Professors have always been *those* people to me. And now *me*? A *professor*? Ha! I've been contemplating this lately. Actually, I've probably been more like pathologically ruminating about it. What is it that seems not to fit for me? I feel so clumsy. I really don't fit the professor image. I'm not anything like the "real professor" image in my mind. I don't have that suave essence about me. I stumble on my words at times, and sometimes I even say "um." Professors have encyclopedia-like brains, all parts of which can be accessed spontaneously, even with multiple student eyeballs staring at once. They can look at research and know their ANOVAs from MANOVAs and chi squares and multiple regressions. I can recall what Type I and Type II errors are, but that's only because I made up a goofy song by which to remember them. A real professor would never do that.

There are two clowns that exemplify my current struggle. My image of the real professor is that of the "whiteface" clown. The whiteface clown has been described by a clownmaster as elegantly dressed, sophisticated, serious and proper in character. The whiteface is a "clown debonair" according to the French, and naturally, is highly cultured. I suppose the whiteface clown captures my image of a true professor: elegant, serious, proper, cultured, and socially graced.

In contrast, my image of myself is as an "auguste" clown. The clownmaster described the auguste clown as the "dumb dumb." The auguste clown stumbles on his or her own feet and seems to mess everything up. The auguste has been known to interrupt and bother the whiteface. The auguste finds even simple tasks and problems difficult but often uses his or her ingenuity and skillfulness to devise complex acrobatic solutions. In contrast to the whiteface's pomposity, the auguste clown is characterized by simplicity, stupidity, unpredictability, charm, and naïveté with exaggerated and absurd mannerisms.

While not yet a professor, I have had the opportunity to be a teaching apprentice on several occasions, and I completed an internship where I taught a practicum course on my own. In my first teaching apprenticeship, I truly felt like a dumb-dumb. In fact, looking back, I was. I was seeking to be the whiteface, when I had auguste-ness oozing from the core of my being. I was not the sophisticated whiteface with 20 or 30 years experience, and believing that I should be is what made me a true dumb-dumb.

But now I am back at this place of being a neophyte once again. I will soon enter my first years in academia. I will soon be a professor. A *real* professor. Me? I've finally become a master of studenthood. I've mastered the art of learning and learning how I learn. As a master of studenthood, I am able to profoundly question and rest comfortably amidst the dissonance. I have no answers. How could I now be ready to profess?

I think of myself as a professor and I chuckle, perhaps on behalf of future students in my classes. Goofy me? A professor? As I crank out the last drafts of my dissertation and finish up my internship, I wait for my advisor to ask me if I've considered clown school. Maybe I've been the $n = 1$ in another doctoral student's deceptive qualitative research project all along.

Me? A professor? After all, I still like to experiment with my hair. I like unpeeling oranges and seeing how long I can make the peel without it breaking. I like to walk on the curb to see if I can still balance like I used to. I still like to push, lean, and coast on the shopping cart in the grocery store. I prefer Chicken McNuggets over chicken cordon bleu and sometimes I even order a McDonald's Happy Meal just for the free toy. I even like *stickers*, for goodness sake!

On some deep level, I struggle, believing that *real* professors are of the whiteface sort (minus the pomposity). I am no professor debonair. I am of the auguste sort—heart and soul. At least for now I am. I haven't the brain of an encyclopedia, but I am clever. I am not very linear, but I am creative. I'm not a MANOVA master, but I can tell stories of my fear of the MANOVA monster. I'm not spontaneously brilliant, but I am highly resourceful. I don't have many answers, but I do have stimulating questions.

While I value my strengths, I fear that academia is only for professionals of the white-faced sort. Throughout these first years as a professor, I must let my character slowly evolve. I suppose that as a neophyte, I shall indeed innocently interrupt and bother my colleagues with my questions as well as my absurdity from time to time. I'll probably struggle with seemingly simple tasks. I shall let my auguste-ness ooze from my pores, stumbling and bumbling all the way, and perhaps I'll leave a smile or two in the process. Only when I do these things can I authentically develop my identity as a true clownselor educator. Oops . . . ummmm . . . .

4

Being Crazy

Laurie Carty

I have always wondered how much depression is considered normal. As a counselor and educator, this is a question I'm frequently asked by my clients and students. My struggle with this question began long before I became a counselor. When I was a child I believed I was crazy because I was almost always depressed. My mother disapproved of sadness and she would say, "You have nothing to be sad about." I hid in my room to avoid being judged.

There was a lot to be depressed about in my family. Our home was full of pain, anger, tension, and conflict. My parents would frequently lose control, and their arguments often escalated into physical violence. Feelings were secrets not to be shared. We were all very isolated from each other and also from the world outside.

I was the firstborn in a family of six children. Like many others in the helping professions, I learned my first lessons as a helper and caretaker in my family of origin. I cared for my younger siblings and often cared for my parents when they lost control.

I became very good at helping and this naturally led to a professional career. For the last 25 years I have been a nurse, counselor, and professor. I continue to reflect on the meaning of being crazy. And I know I'm not alone. "Am I crazy?" is the most frequently asked question by my students.

I experienced this fear of being crazy one day as I was returning to my office after lunch. I saw students running out of the building. This struck me as very strange. I picked up my pace and entered the building. I heard a man's voice screaming, "Help me! Help me! God help me! God help me!! The words sounded desperate, but it was the tone and depth of pain in his voice that made me shiver. The sound seemed to be coming from above in the stairwell. I stood frozen trying to decide if I should investigate alone. I was afraid and wanted to run away like the students I had seen running. I teach my students about self-safety and I knew what I would tell them to do in this situation. The man's moans were getting louder and louder. I took a deep breath and headed up the stairs.

When I got to the next landing, I saw the biggest guy I have ever seen. He must have been six and half feet tall, built like a slab of granite. He was slamming his fists against the wall, crying, "I can't stand it. I just can't stand it anymore." He was unaware of my presence.

I tried to think of something helpful to say to him. "Is something wrong?" I asked him, and then I groaned to myself. What a stupid thing to say! This guy is climbing the walls and I ask him if something might be wrong.

I was thinking about what I might do next when he turned to face me. I am small and this man towered over me. We locked eyes for what seemed to me forever but was only a few seconds. I will never forget how intense this contact felt. It felt like he was looking into my soul.

All of a sudden, he began crying and sobbing again. He slumped down on the stairs and I sat down next to him. I told him we were going to go together to get some help for his pain. He looked at me with this little boy expression, absolute trust in his eyes. I thought about the enormity of my responsibility as a counselor when clients give me their absolute trust like this. He stood up and followed me down the stairs, crying all the way.

On the way to the health center, he told me that he was on a student visa and he had some serious problems with his family back home. In between disjointed sobs, he also confided that he had just failed an important exam. I listened as best I could and calmed him down until we reached the clinic. The last I saw of him was when he was led from the reception room into the treatment area. This was the last glimpse I had of the guy and I never heard what happened to him afterwards. Did he stay in the country or go home? Did he graduate? Was he crazy? I doubt it.

It was my interest in being crazy that motivated me to become a counselor in the first place. I thought if I could study and learn about the brain and human behavior, perhaps I could understand myself and find the answers to heal my own depression. I now realize I'm not alone in this fantasy.

The road that I have traveled as a counselor has not been a straight one, as is so often the case with those of us who are lost trying to find our way. Many life experiences have influenced the directions in which I have gone. One experience occurred when I was a student nurse in a large psychiatric hospital. This institution was one big hiding place, even its location outside the city. Craziness, like death, is denied by our culture. We prefer that the mentally ill remain invisible. We want crazy people to go their rooms and hide and not make too much noise. What is not seen does not exist.

I had hoped that this experience would help me find answers that would fix me up. I never found these answers. In fact, the experience frightened and horrified me. It was difficult to know who were the patients and who were the staff. Who was crazy and who was normal? On my first day on the ward, patients and staff were doing an activity together. I was unable to identify a single staff member.

After this student internship, I felt disillusioned, depressed, and even more lost. Counseling was a career path that I wanted to follow, but I now seriously reconsidered whether I wanted to pursue that further. I considered moving into critical care nursing—at least they actually *do* something. They actually stop wounds from bleeding.

Following my graduation I married and went to work in an isolated community. The following year our son was born. At work I began to notice that I was worrying about doing everything perfectly with every patient. Some things in nursing do need to be perfect such as medication and patient identification, but I was generalizing this standard to everything. I obsessed about hand washing and all the rituals of aseptic technique. The most difficult part was that all the while I knew my thoughts were crazy, but I felt unable to stop them.

We decided to move to a new community hoping a change might help. It didn't, so I consulted a professional. The psychiatrist reassured me that I wasn't crazy and would not go crazy. I'm not sure if I was glad or sad about this pronouncement. Four months later I was hospitalized on the psychiatric ward. Maybe I was trying to prove the doctor wrong.

It's difficult to share this part of my life. I will never forget my arrival at the hospital. As I stood at the nurses station, I was filled with shame, guilt, feelings of being dirty, of doing something wrong. I felt like I was a bad person at my core. My brain raced with thoughts of needing to wash so that I wouldn't contaminate or hurt others. In those few moments I could recall my student experience in psychiatric care. I saw patients depersonalized and treated like objects. I saw them herded into the cafeteria to eat and lined up waiting for their zap of shock treatment. I remembered the hollow, vacant eyes of the staff and the complete absence of feeling in the patients.

I remained in the hospital for 12 weeks and had daily therapy sessions with the same psychiatrist who assured me I was fine. Most of the time he just yelled at me for seeing the world differently than he did. He threatened me that if I didn't subscribe to his ideas he would have no choice but to give me shock therapy. He ordered insulin injections to make me eat more. When none of these treatments worked he fired me as a patient. I was pronounced cured.

I learned so much from the experience being a patient. The care I received was not at all like what I had witnessed during my student days. The nurses were kind and they showed compassion. Their eyes were not dead. I especially enjoyed hanging out with some of the other patients. All in all, I had some positive experiences and learned more about doing counseling that I had in all my previous training.

After leaving the hospital I found a more supportive counselor who helped me to connect with my feelings. I went on for more graduate training, continuing to search for answers. I still haven't found those answers yet. I still wonder about how much depression is normal and what it means to be crazy.

Part II

Facing
Pain
and
Adversity

5

A Dangerous Journey

Patricia A. Blecich

The path we counselors walk can be treacherous, sometimes littered with large boulders—other times with small hidden slivers of glass. Along this path we see the wounds of others and gather our own. Yet we travel on because that is the nature of who we are and what we do. People are animate and must remain mobile. Those who tread lightly do not grow the calluses that make walking the path easier.

I have tread the treacherous path, as many others have. In my youth I experienced the pain of two divorces, and the alcoholism, drug addiction, and mental illness of some family and friends. As a child, I grew calluses that enabled me to stumble through my adolescent years, escaping the death of my spirit. Despite this, I have found dignity and purpose in my life through caring for those suffering from drug addictions and mental illness.

For 6 months after graduating from a rehabilitation counseling program, I walked along a bright path, content that I was now a "grown-up." I was a master's-level counselor now, with a pedigree. Despite the odds, I made a name for myself and carved a niche within the field in which I've always wanted to be. My first real counseling job was an excruciating and exhilarating combination of direct counseling and program management. I was in charge of a shelter serving the homeless, drug-addicted, mentally ill, and recently released prison population. Fresh out of school, I was as idealistic and fearless as I would ever be. The neighborhood I worked in was one of the roughest in the state, this I knew. The people I counseled were of the most gravely ill populations, many of them having an undiagnosed mental illness along with a host of other problems.

That the field of direct care to mentally ill persons can be dangerous is a given, yet most of us continue to believe that in the hearts of all humans is a basic desire to be good. In graduate school, I led the pack of "bleeding hearts," brazenly going into the toughest neighborhoods, giving my hand to anyone who needed help. Not a person or a place could scare me, and I believed the key to becoming an agent of change was to give all people the benefit of the doubt. Yeah, maybe you murdered someone years ago, but you are still human, still worthy of unconditional positive regard. Matter of fact, maybe I'd even invite you over for Christmas dinner.

I was so oblivious to my naïveté that I was settling into a dangerous comfort, forgetting where I was, what I was dealing with. On a warm September day last year I was joking with my colleagues in the staff dining room, discussing nonsense and enjoying their company as usual. Later that same day at precisely 2:40 p.m., I watched my colleague, Paul, take his last breath and die after he was brutally butchered by one of our clients, a man who suffered from paranoid schizophrenia. On that day, I began the hardest part of my journey yet. So I invite you to walk my path for a moment, as I confront the pain, anguish, and despair of losing a colleague and friend, of witnessing the brutality of the world in a way I never imagined, of wondering why I even bother to do what I do.

They say that what doesn't kill you makes you stronger. Within the week after my colleague's murder, so many emotions washed over me in so short a time that I could barely keep track of what I was feeling from one moment to the next. I still can't. But one theme emerged rather quickly. Even though Paul died horribly and tragically, we were all still alive, and we would heal and become stronger. I survived. The victim could have been any one of us. My heart was broken but my spirit was still alive. Paul died, perhaps so all who knew him would grow stronger and wiser. And such a legacy has been unparalleled by anyone I have met.

I no longer believe all people have a desire to be good, in society's terms. I do believe now that all people have an inner self, so complex and unique that no one will ever fully understand where people are coming from and why they do things. No behavior fits into the neat little paradigms of abnormal psychology, social work, and counseling psychology. People react and behave as they do on the basis of their own internal framework. If their framework commands them to kill, they will, because not to do so would be denying one's inner self. Moreover, people will continue to exhibit new "inner cores" that will be added to the *DSM-IV* eventually, and similarities will make us complacently believe that if we can name something, we can treat it.

I do believe that many incidents of violence can be prevented. I continue to wonder if there was something I could have done to help keep this client from reaching the destructive level he did. I think about him frequently, recall his dress, his mannerisms, anything that could have warned me. The client now charged with Paul's murder had been a fixture to the park bench near our shelter. He was never rude or threatening, yet we all knew instinctively that he was one with serious problems. Perhaps that day Paul had stepped into his territory, looked at him the wrong way or otherwise inadvertently instigated him. The client, feeling somehow threatened, decided "the enemy" must be destroyed. It was not an act of good versus evil, it was self-preservation. Self-preservation is instinctual and undeniable in all life forms. Paul was probably no more than someone who was in the wrong place at the wrong time. This client stabbed Paul over and over, enraged, vengeful, intent on self-preservation. To him, Paul was no mortal human, capable of being killed with one strategic blow—he may have represented a system to be eradicated, requiring the use of heavy artillery.

So where does this leave me? Watching my friend die so horrifically, I have responded mostly with blind anger. Anger at clients, each of whom now looks like a murderer to me. Anger at the administration who for years took our safety concerns too lightly. Anger at myself for being a member of that administration. As both a manager and a direct care staff member, I am fighting a two-sided battle. This should not have happened. This could have been prevented. How many schools should become graveyards? How many workplaces should be invaded by violent outbursts? How many more educators and human service providers must die in the line of duty? Will I be next? There is no simple answer.

I have not given up my commitment to the practice of counseling, as I had vowed I would the day my friend was murdered. Rather it has taken me to a new level of understanding that this work requires a constant redefining of one's sense of knowing, a perpetual challenge to what you thought was the answer. It is through the review and redefining of oneself that one can practice dynamic counseling. As scientists no longer heed that the world is flat, so must we constantly shift our paradigms and theories, not to solely reflect our personal beliefs but with the concept that what you learn—what you contribute today—is not an end product but a brick in the foundation of something we will never fully understand but cannot stop trying to understand.

I will never forget Paul, or the man who killed him. I will never forget that I was fortunate enough to not be his victim. I will never forget that I work in a dark and often violent world. I will also never look at my clients with the same trust and open empathy that I used to, and I will probably resign my position out of ethical consideration for my clients' well-being. But I will persevere; I have been on the front lines of battle. There are places for me besides the front lines now. Advocacy, research, and macro-level change beckon me. And in 6 months I have seen how much I have yet to learn. I have a long journey ahead.

6

Finding My Voice

Marielle Brandt

I t is early afternoon. We have all just returned to school from a morning field trip to Old Tucson Studios, a famous filming location in the desert where many Hollywood western movies are made. Both first-grade classes had been combined for the field trip and all 40 children are seated in Mrs. Martino's classroom, working individually on our "show and tell" assignment: Draw a picture of something or someone you liked at Old Tucson today.

I am sitting at a table in the far corner of the room with a few of the children. Lisa LaRue knew immediately what she wanted to draw and is working diligently on her picture, using a variety of colors, freely and spontaneously adding new things as she goes along. Chris Marnell has been accused of "hogging the brown" and is making a cowboy with a huge brown hat. Bobby Matz, a student I admire immensely for his confidence and abilities, is using a Number 2 pencil and eraser to carefully sketch and perfect a tiny drawing at the center of his paper. Others ask him, "What are you making?" He answers in a matter-of-fact tone, "Myself." Wow! He is just so bright. Why didn't I think of something like that? I hope I can come up with a clever idea too.

Hmmm. This assignment is tough for me. I didn't particularly enjoy the field trip this morning. The kids were noisy and rambunctious, and the teachers became cross with us several times. I get very uncomfortable when my teacher is angry. I wish those kids would all just listen to her and behave! Also, watching the cowboys fighting with their guns was scary to me. I became frightened several times, thinking that someone was going to get hurt or killed. Those guns were really loud and it sure seemed like that fighting was real!

Oh . . . Am I daydreaming again? What am I going to draw? Sigh. The mountains were so pretty today with all the blue and purple and . . . Hey! Maybe that is what I'll draw. I carefully place the tip of a blue crayon to the white paper and spend a few minutes tentatively making some light, wispy lines, delineating peaks and valleys and filling them in with some pastel colors. Shortly thereafter, the teachers announce that our time is almost up. Clinton Guthrie peeks over at my creation and says, "What is that? You're supposed to draw something from the field trip today, dummy!" Terribly embarrassed and afraid that I have done the assignment wrong, I frantically grab a red crayon, clumsily make three connected rectangles horizontally across my page and scribble two circles beneath each. I look down at my paper, disappointedly. What a boring, ugly train. My mountains looked so much nicer. Well, at least I've done something right and won't be noticed or stand out in any way. Now I can feel safe again.

Just then, Mrs. Martino announces, "In a little while it will be time for recess. Before we go, I'd like each one of you to stand, holdup your picture and describe it to the rest of the class."

After all of the other children have taken their turn, Mrs. Martino asks, "Has everyone had a chance to share? Did we miss anyone?" I am still nestled back in the corner of the room, hoping that she doesn't notice me. I don't think she is aware of my *problem*. One of the kids from the other class points directly at me and asserts, "That girl didn't go yet." I slowly sink back in my chair, as Mrs. Martino invites me to share my picture. Several seconds pass. I remain glued to my chair, silent, staring wide-eyed at the paper in front of me.

My homeroom teacher, Mrs. Erlandson, approaches me, extending her hand outward. I look to her with desperation, and I hope she is going to rescue me from this situation. She was also my kindergarten teacher last year and knows all about my problem. She leads me out of my chair, escorts me to the front of the room, lets go of my hand, and returns to her seat. At that very moment, I become aware of where I am standing and what I am expected to do. Without any warning, the torrent begins. Anxiety and intense fear sweep across my tiny body like an enormous tidal wave. My heart starts beating so rapidly and with such force that I feel its vibration throughout my neck and chest. A large knot twists and burns in my abdomen like a pool of boiling lava. My breaths are shallow and deliberate. Hairs on the back of my neck and shoulders begin to stand erect. The skin on my arms and legs is feeling cold and tingly, my palms sweating profusely. I stand there, staring out into the void. I see the faces and eyes of all 40 children and 2 teachers. This is the first time I've braved standing in front of the class in my 1½ years of attending school. I want so much to feel proud of myself—to make my classmates proud. I am not experiencing pride, however. I am terrified. I remember the expectation—*hold up your picture and describe it to the rest of the class.* I wish that words could flow from my mind and into my mouth, like they seem to for all the other kids. I can't think of any words. I am stuck. I feel my tongue pressing against the back of my teeth, my lips tightening, wanting to come together to form sentences. I hear voices of encouragement coming from some pals in my homeroom. "C'mon Marielle . . . just say 'train' . . . you can do it!" I want to do this for them. I don't want to let them down again. I am getting overstimulated. I am overwhelmed. Still, no words come from my mouth. My arms, with picture in hand, are paralyzed, dangling at my sides. I have failed again. I avert my gaze downward and become fixated on a spot in the carpet. I wish I could just disappear. I am deeply ashamed. I feel transparent. I am vulnerable. I shut down. I become numb.

Several children from the other first grade class are asking, "What is wrong with her?" "Why doesn't she say anything?" "Is she deaf?" I hear some whispers and soft replies in the background. "Marielle is just very shy. She doesn't talk."

I hadn't spoken a word outside my home since about 1971 —a year when my family was engulfed in loss, tragedy, grief, separation, and adjustment. From age 2 until I was about 3½, we endured the loss of three loved ones: my mother's brother, her mother, and lastly, her oldest son. (I list these from my mother's perspective because I believe, as her youngest child, I closely witnessed—and even, endured *with* her—her pain and suffering from losing three people of such close relation to her.) Also, interspersed within the same time period, were the marriages of two of my oldest siblings and the birth of my mother's first grandchild (my oldest niece). Celebration, loss, tragedy, and a multitude of changes had exploded upon us.

I can remember all of these events in detail, the full range and depth of feelings my family experienced in association with them, and especially, the tremendous impact it all had on my mother. From my very young perspective, the world seemed like a massive, overwhelming, unpredictable, and unsafe place. Just when it seemed okay to start feeling joyous about something, another tragedy or loss would occur. There wasn't enough time for recovery or assimilation between events. It was a period of confusion and hopelessness, and I felt extremely vulnerable. I started becoming a rather hypervigilant, highly anxious child. I began detaching from the overwhelming world around me. Consequently, and even though I learned to speak in full sentences at a younger age than any of the nine children in my family (as reported by my parents), I stopped talking at age 3. I lost my voice.

The 30 years that have followed illustrate an arduous process of overcoming for me. And despite having to endure many struggles, obstacles, and pains along the way, the aggregate of experiences, in many respects, symbolizes a stimulating and oftentimes highly rewarding journey of finding my voice again.

I first found my voice among my peers several months after the field trip to Old Tucson. Bobby Cook was the first child to whom I uttered words. I felt safe with him and sensed that he really understood and accepted me. He was my best friend. Thanks to good teachers and a caring and encouraging school environment, I eventually came out of my shell and spoke to just about anyone who initiated contact with me by the third grade; however, extreme shyness still pervaded throughout my school years, and all forms of verbal expression represented challenges for me. In high school and even well into college, written and oral assignments produced intense feelings of fear and inadequacy, and some resulted in failure. Although the fears had diminished to a certain degree, the feelings of anxiety were still present, just as they had been in the first grade.

Successfully completing undergraduate college, holding a variety of paid and volunteered jobs, serving in the military reserve, enduring the illness and loss of both parents while I was in college, investing myself in a 6-year marriage (and later divorce), and spending time moving around the United States and living in Europe all represent a sample of adulthood experiences which I believe have helped me to truly come to know myself, to intimately understand what it means to overcome, to better understand and relate to others, to wholeheartedly believe in our human potential for positive growth and change, and to want more than anything to hear others' voices and help them to find their way.

As a counselor, I do not require my clients to talk. They are allowed to be themselves and to utilize a variety of media to express themselves. They are free to choose what they wish to use as a voice. I found my voice as a counselor (and intend to always work toward improving its clarity) by making contact with clients and by learning to accurately convey my understanding of their emotional world via my words, my actions, and my very presence.

I first found my voice within my family. Then, I found my voice among peers. Next, I found my voice as a student in the classroom. Later, I found my voice as a counselor and supervisor. Most recently, I found my voice as a professor of counseling. And now, there is another important place where I wish to find my voice—that is professionally, as a *writer.*

So . . . I figure that a good place to start moving toward this next destination is right here: by reflecting on the distance I have traveled throughout my journey (over what was often some pretty rough terrain) and acknowledging mistakes and accomplishments made along the way; by recognizing the fear that still exists in me with respect to verbal/written expression and developing realistic expectations for myself; and importantly, by taking some kind of action (i.e., taking a risk and sharing a brief summary of this process, in *writing!*). In its own small way, this article represents a personal landmark on the journey of finding my voice.

7

The Initiation

Dana Comstock

About 5 years ago I was thrilled to discover I was pregnant. After a miscarriage, and a year of "trying," I couldn't wait to tell my husband. After all, it was our anniversary. Our families were delighted. Because of my previous miscarriage, the early weeks were the most frightening for me. I decided to get through the first trimester before I shared the good news with anybody else.

At my 12-week checkup, I heard my baby's heartbeat for the first time. This milestone brought me great relief. I finally began to accept that maybe, just maybe, my hopes and dreams were coming true. As the weeks passed, I grew more excited and more comfortable engaging in the customary baby preparations and nesting rituals. I felt a deep sense of peace knowing my life would soon go full circle. I could hardly contain my joy, and often thought I would explode. Happier than I'd ever been, I was consumed both physically and emotionally. I savored every moment of this life-giving experience and was constantly aware of my changing body and new beloved companion.

It was around this time that I attended a counseling conference. My pregnancy was no secret by now. I proudly showed off my bulging belly, and shared the news with anyone who would listen. It was during this conference that I felt my baby move for the first time one evening in my hotel room. Although I had anticipated that moment, it came suddenly and unexpectedly. Time stood still, and I sat quietly, in awe of this gift for a long time.

I had taken good care of myself and was now being rewarded with appreciative kicks, pokes, and flips. On my way home, I thought about how different things would be next year at the convention. I'd bring baby pictures, or maybe I'd just bring the baby, or maybe I'd be too busy to go.

Within days of returning home, I was horrified to discover I had serious complications with premature cervical dilation. In an instant, my hopes went into a dizzying tailspin. I was terrified, out of control, and completely unprepared. To cope, I mechanically followed the instructions of my doctor, who was working feverishly to correct the problem. In disbelief, I resolved to hold onto every encouraging statistic and success story.

After surgery to reverse the dilation, antibiotics, 2 weeks of strict bed rest, tears, and prayers, I developed an infection and went into labor. During labor, I was assigned a grief counselor who specialized in helping families cope with infant loss. Although this sounded good, I was guarded and somewhat irritated. After all, *I* was a counselor who helped people find their way all the time. I didn't need someone telling me about the stages of grief. I had other things on my mind and was certain I could get myself through this on my own.

Nevertheless, I needed a crash course in childbirth education, even if it was done in the shadow of impending sorrow. I was particularly afraid of the actual delivery and was grateful that she took the time to walk me through each step. She also explained how my baby would look, and made herself available to answer any questions. She checked in with me throughout my labor, and she also worked with my husband and our parents who were with us.

In the end, my daughter was born still and premature. She was named Samantha.

My grief counselor kept telling me I was going to be "okay." She knew this because I was "doing all the right things," like having held and named my daughter. I kept Samantha with me for a long time. I studied her face, and wondered what her life might have been like. I also wondered about the course of my own life. I had not once considered this path. I didn't know how to see past this moment when Samantha *was* my future.

We took care to get clear footprints and photographs, knowing this would be all we would have of her to take home. I watched despairingly as my husband and our families said their goodbyes. None of us had ever dealt with anything quite like this, or in this way. It was strange thinking I was doing something so well that felt so horrible. In fact, I was doing so well that my life came to a standstill. I abandoned all professional and academic responsibilities. I simply didn't know which way to go. I was emotionally raw, unsteady, and heartbroken.

As the reality of this loss settled in, I began to realize my plans for joining the "mommy club" had gone awry. I now found myself being unwillingly initiated into a club I didn't know, or want to know, existed, a club for grieving parents. In fact, this was a club I had never planned or wanted to join. I deeply resented having to "pay dues" when I felt my daughter had just been stolen from me.

After I returned home from the hospital, I tried to deal with both the emotional and physical aspects of her loss. My emotional pain competed with engorged breasts and a bleeding body. Exhausted from the trauma, I settled into a routine of sobbing and sleeping. I was alone with my experience most days, and was unable to leave the house because of my instability and constant crying. The pain was inescapable.

I had no sense of how I was doing this "grief thing" until one day I found myself immobile. I have a memory of sitting on the toilet, unable to do anything but sob and rock with my face buried in my hands. I was literally psychotic with grief when a voice inside my head mused: "this must be what it's like to just lose it, to *really* go crazy." I felt as if I was observing myself and, in that instant, I made a decision to get help. The Starbucks Java Chip ice cream wasn't working. I needed something stronger.

I went to see a psychiatrist friend of mine. Needing to share my experience, I showed her a photograph of me holding my daughter. She gazed at the picture and said, "That doesn't look like you." I secretly considered it wasn't me. Once again, reality. Like it or not, I *had* to redefine myself in the context of this loss and find my way back into a life I didn't want or care to live.

My healing process was wrought with complexities. I had a keen sense that I was a burden and a source of discomfort to others. On another level, I was deeply ashamed of my needs and vulnerabilities. I was supposed to know how to take care of myself. I was a counselor. A counselor who'd been told she was doing all the right things.

I was also feeling responsible for the pain I had seemingly caused my husband and our families. This was all accompanied by my disappointment in my body, which I felt had betrayed me. My sense of betrayal was not debatable, especially with a now-confirmed diagnosis of "*incompetent* cervix." I was, however, eventually talked out of feeling responsible for hurting my family. Experiencing myself as a source of discomfort to others was regularly reinforced. These experiences only served to exacerbate my sense of shame.

I responded quickly to medication and therapy. Although I still felt socially awkward, I was growing tired of my isolation and was hungry for companionship. One afternoon, my husband and I decided to go on an excursion to the neighborhood mall. After walking a bit, my eyes met with those of an acquaintance. As I sensed a genuine surge of excitement to see her, I noticed how horrified she seemed at our untimely meeting. We both survived an awkward exchange of well wishes and meaningless chat. I was unprepared for such a shift in my relationships.

During this time, I saw an interview of one of Katie Couric's colleagues. This person described her as "courageous" for having put her associates at ease on the day she returned to work after her husband died of colon cancer. I recall a sense of injustice that a person in so much pain should have to expend even one ounce of energy putting others at ease.

I have slowly grown into a deeper understanding of others and myself. As the days passed, I sorted through a growing collection of cards and letters. I was supported by family, friends, and people I only knew professionally. I was especially moved by the messages of love and healing I received from clients who were consumed with their own pain. I felt, and still feel, that this meant something *big* about the mutual healing that takes place in the counseling relationship.

My grief counselor called periodically. She even extended an invitation for me to come and speak at a local hospital to address the needs of obstetric patients experiencing infant loss. I accepted this invitation. In preparing for my talk, I reflected on what had been truly healing for me during my hospital stay. I remembered the student nurse who stayed an extra shift to be with me during delivery, the silent tears of my labor and delivery assistant, and the Sunday afternoon my doctor came to visit when he could have been home with his own family. It dawned on me that I had, all along, been loved back into life.

Having lost my way, I am more aware of my blind spots. I am also more accepting of my limitations and vulnerabilities. I have learned how I tend to manage these issues both personally and professionally. I now have a sense of what it means for me to negotiate personal adversity as a counselor. I have also experienced, and appreciate, the things that can happen only in the face of the counselor's adversity.

All told, there are many things in life I would rather not have to see or experience. I can't blame people for being uncomfortable; that's simply the nature of pain. I, too, avert my eyes. Quite frankly, I believe that with regard to some experiences, "ignorance *is* bliss." This is not, however, a mantra for counselors. My initiation into the "grieving club" enabled me to see more clearly. I was made an expert in infant loss, by default.

I now appreciate my club membership and all the amenities. Such benefits include the undeserved gift of compassion and the ability to feel and love more deeply.

I now bask in the company of other club members who unknowingly shape my sensitivity and understanding of the hurt in *all* people. I have become less afraid of my sense of helplessness. I had always struggled with a need to "do something," the *right* thing, and most of my therapeutic mishaps occurred during those times.

My experience is that healing comes through the joining with others in their pain, wherever or however they happen to be hurting. Having experienced fleeting psychotic grief, I am more open to the responses in my clients that I may not initially understand. I now know there is no "right way" to grieve. It took being broken to find a way to be more complete and present with others. In closing, I'd like to share that I attended the ACA Annual Conference this year as the proud mother of Samantha and 2 year-old Julianna.

8
Things Are Different This Year

Olive Poliks

Things are different at my school this year. The classes are still over-loaded, it's a bleak forecast for salary negotiations, there's still crime and violence in our community, and fine young people are still being lost to the pressures of their peers.

But things are different. We are different. Teachers are more mellow and far less stressed. I'm the school counselor and I find myself laughing more and being more comfortable with my mistakes. My husband tells me I've been sweeter these last few months and that sometimes he wakes up in the night to find me holding him in a vise-like grip.

Things changed dramatically since graduation day last June. Jerry, our science teacher and eighth-grade team leader, took an extension cord and hung himself in his basement. Jerry's death changed my life and the lives of my colleagues.

At first, rumors flew. Jerry had stomach cancer. Jerry was gay. Jerry was in a gang and couldn't get out. Although the rumors continued, none of them were true.

Jerry suffered from clinical depression for 30 years, but only a few people knew. He had been off medication and symptom free for 17 years. Unknown to us all, his depression came back. Finally, he could no longer stand to be alive. The depression swooped down on him suddenly. He hadn't planned to kill himself. He had my birthday card for the eighth-grade team to sign. He had made plans for a team breakfast for that very morning. He had closed on a new house 10 days earlier. He had plans to live.

I had always thought of Jerry as the cheerleader of our school. He always had a smile and a joke. He was always ready to help. I thought he was one of those rare individuals who are just simply happy to be alive. I remember one meeting when the entire staff spent an hour complaining about everything wrong with the school. Jerry's was the one voice of optimism and hope.

At Jerry's funeral, the pastor said, "No one blames a person who dies of a broken heart. Jerry died of a broken mind."

But why? How? As an educator for nearly 30 years, I have been trained to answer the question "why?" There are formulas, strategies, and lesson plans. We can study the text and clearly find an answer.

There is no answer to Jerry's death. His widow, Judy, continues to struggle with the "why." Jerry was a good man, a good husband, a good father, and a good Christian. How could such a thing happen? Why?

The teachers heard the news of Jerry's death one hour before the final practice for eighth-grade promotion. Jim, the math teacher and promotion sponsor, said "How can they expect us to do this? I can't do this. I can't!" Brenda, Jerry's teammate and an ex-student, couldn't stop crying. Jerry had been her mentor. Calls to the central office were made, but the promotion ceremony could not be canceled.

The ceremony went on for the kids, their families, and friends. There were the normal celebration flowers, flashbulbs, and crying babies. The teachers were professional and stoic. The kids looked to us to hold them together, and indeed, the ceremony came off beautifully. But I could see the pain just beneath the surface.

The day after Jerry's death, Fernando, a 14-year-old student, came storming into my office yelling about what had happened. "I'm pissed and I ain't going to class," he said. "He had signs all over his room, 'Don't quit! Only quitters quit.' Well he was a quitter. He told us not to quit and he went and quit."

Fernando is in high school this year. Does he understand now? Is his life somehow better, as mine is?

I'm a good counselor. I know how to handle crisis. I simply shut my own feelings off. The day after Jerry's death, I went to every one of his classes. I explained about clinical depression. I answered questions. We talked about it. I was helpful and kind. I was numb.

The wake was the largest the funeral home had ever seen. People of all ages streamed through. Jerry was on his second generation of students. Many parents and their children came together.

The funeral was harder. Jerry's students were there. Fernando was there. I was there for the kids. I was kind and supportive and helpful. I was numb. It wasn't real. It wasn't Jerry in that casket. It wasn't his wife, Judy, beside herself with grief. It wasn't really happening.

At the funeral, I sat next to Tom, Jerry's friend and colleague for more than 20 years. He's a big, happy guy. Tom always has a joke and a smile for everyone. He's always laughing and talking about fishing. At the funeral, Tom was crying. His shoulders shook and tears streamed down his face.

I had dinner with Judy last week. She still struggles with the "why." We all do. I am no longer numb. Jim smiles more this year. Tom is far more patient with the students. Brenda is the team leader now. She does an excellent job. Jerry trained her well. Somehow in the midst of our personal struggles, there is a "better" for us. Life feels so precious. It is so short. Did we ever tell Jerry how much we appreciated him? Did we ever thank him for all he did for our school? How could he die like that? Why did it happen?

Why are things somehow better for us? I don't know.

Finding my way has not been easy. Being a counselor has somehow become simpler. It's so much easier to not know the answers than to try to figure them out. It's so much easier just to be present than to try to be perfect. Finding my way is harder than I thought. I'm glad I never have to do it alone.

9

The Dysfunctional Workplace

Beth Soucar

There is nothing like a workplace that actively promotes healthy inter-actions among staff. My master's program and fieldwork placement were wonderful. Ongoing supervisory and peer support helped us work through difficult times toward creative solutions and renewed energies. When a functional system is in place, it is a pleasure to come to work.

Unfortunately, in my first job I made the mistake of staying in a deteri-orating situation that moved beyond lacking support to actively promot-ing dysfunction. Therefore, today, I have my own emotional recovery to work through. I had mistakenly thought, "Well, if I just hang in there, as-sert myself, and try harder, then things will improve."

How does a counselor find her way through workplace chaos?

Increasingly, I find articles addressing counselor burnout or compas-sion fatigue. These articles focus on the trauma of listening to client sto-ries of abuse. We often look to peer support, vacation time, and leisure activities to cope. We may also attend workshops on new techniques or switch to working with a different clientele.

But what do we do if our trauma is brought on by dysfunctional col-leagues, supervisors, directors, and workplace dynamics? Whether brought on by clients or colleagues, the symptoms are the same: fatigue, forgetfulness, cynicism, depression, and decreased productivity. The story of my last job illustrates my point.

For my first year of employment, my job environment was very good and my adolescent drug treatment program gradually grew to a nice size. My troubles started with the arrival of a new clinical supervisor with no background in teen addiction. She made it clear that she did not want to share experiences, collaborate, or compromise. She strove to use her adult treatment models with adolescent clients.

As my supervisor and I reviewed complex adolescent cases, I tried to be assertive. She did not listen to my approaches and insisted she knew better in most cases. When I stood my ground, there were often heated and painful arguments. I had never before experienced being professionally ripped apart! I soon learned that my supervisor enjoyed arguments.

I tried a more passive approach. I sought feedback from trusted colleagues and from a private consultant I paid for out of my own pocket. This worked for a while, but I still had to attend weekly case reviews with the dreaded supervisor.

Over the months, most of my supportive colleagues left for greener pastures. Soon, I had few on-site resources to help me keep my chin up. Most of the staff were new and not yet keen to the situation. I received no support from the executive director despite his genuine good intentions. There was no one with any power who could help me.

I tried to work collaboratively with my supervisor. Again and again, she made it known that her case suggestions were orders that I needed to carry out, regardless of my own views. I suggested we talk about ways we could work better together. After spending too much time trying to make things work, it was time to leave.

I would like to think this experience was an aberration. However, chances are that many others in the field will in some way come to know what I am saying. What follows is some advice drawn from my experiences. Perhaps it will help you to prevent or recognize a bad situation and, if necessary, to plan a solution. Meanwhile, the therapeutic process of writing this down is for me a step in the right direction as I try to process and move forward with my confidence intact.

Know the Warning Signs of an Unhealthy Supervisor–Supervisee Relationship

The reality is that no work situation will be as wonderfully supportive as you would prefer. Beware of the supervisor who shows no compassion. Beware of the supervisor who accuses you of being fatally flawed with some undefinable lack of something necessary to perform your job. If she or he cannot define it, how are you supposed to learn? Also, beware of the supervisor who verbally attacks you when you challenge her on a professional point, such as, "Could you show me the literature that supports that clinical intervention? For my own development, I'd be very interested in seeing it first-hand."

Know the Warning Signs of an Unhealthy Organization

Unhealthy supervisors exist because their superiors let them continue their destructive behavior. Beware of the school or agency where the top managers largely ignore staff input and where there is a high staff turn-over rate.

Network

I frequently peruse the classifieds and talk with colleagues at other agencies and schools. Five months before I resigned, I started attending job interviews. Then, as November approached, I started filling out doctoral program applications. Certain that I'd someday return to school, I figured this was a good time to make the shift. Unfortunately, the jobs paid too little or were too far away, and the application process is a long one. In the end, I resigned with a small savings to get me through to my next position.

As a profession, we need to explore the dynamics of our employers. We need to look at the ways counselors attain supervisory and management roles and what type of formal training occurs. As individuals, we need to remain ever vigilant of moral and ethical issues in our interactions with others. Our agencies and schools are metaphors for the family, and we cannot teach clients how to live better if we ourselves are lost in dysfunction.

As for me, there is no way to go back and recoup lost time and energy. I am finding my way by letting go of the past and moving forward. In loss, there is a new beginning.

10
Living With Our Disabilities

Jewel Dhuru

Following the convoluted path of my life has been one adventure after another. By the time I began my counseling program, I already had a master's degree, had been teaching English as a Second Language for several years, was the mother of two teens, and had been a spouse for 19 years. So I'd had a bit of experience in living. Part of that experience involved having chronic back and hip problems and muscular weakness from an accident many years ago.

I recognized my helpful and insightful nature and felt that I could do more for myself and the community. It took 5 years and a continuous struggle to get the physical accommodations I needed to complete my coursework and practicum, but I learned to ask for the help I needed and to adapt my environment to suit my limitations. Everything took me longer than usual and there were many things I couldn't do, but I enjoyed the opportunity to be challenged, to grow, to develop new helping skills, and to apply my newfound knowledge to my own life.

As I went through the program, I became more and more aware of how my physical challenges both impeded and helped me to find my way. I noticed patterns that began long ago and would persist unless I took some action. My tendency was to immobilize myself when I had pain or faced fear. I rarely recognized it when I was feeling anger. I was afraid of looking foolish, falling down literally and figuratively, and not being able to keep up with others.

I had to limit walking, and even sitting too long became difficult. I went from one doctor to another, looking for answers. One doctor even suggested a test to rule out multiple sclerosis. Internists, neurologists, orthopedists, and physical therapists all said the same thing: They didn't know what to do for me.

I decided that just because certain parts of my body were weak, that didn't mean I was helpless. Other faculties could compensate. Perhaps this was the only way I would have made the effort to develop other strengths. I decided that my strongest parts were my heart and my voice, and both of them worked just fine. I adapted my environment to suit my needs, including chairs with lumbar supports, using handouts instead of writing on the board in class, and generally simplifying so as to work with lighter weights, less walking, and fewer extraneous complications. I taught myself to do many things with my left side to take the strain off my weaker right side. I was getting used to the shock and pity from others. At the same time, I was learning more about myself through my own individual counseling.

The more comfortable I got with myself, the easier it was for others to be comfortable with me. I found that since I had to learn to do things differently, it helped others to understand me if I occasionally disclosed appropriate details about my condition and explained what I was doing. But it was a constant struggle to pace myself. I teetered on the ridge between giving in to my enthusiasm and pushing myself too hard and giving in to frustration and not getting anything done. I enjoy more comfort with taking calculated risks and trusting whatever the results would be.

Learning more about mind–body connections led me to realize that there were reasons my body felt like it did. I dealt with issues involving my parents, fear of abandonment, lack of abundance, and lack of freedom of expression. In the thick of this self-analysis, sometimes my physical symptoms were exacerbated, but eventually greater integration was the result. Instead of feeling inadequate, I gave myself credit for all that I did already, contributing to the aliveness of a marital relationship, mentoring two college students, being a token member of various cultural groups, teaching part-time, creating original paintings and ceramic pieces, and listening actively to friends and numerous voluntary community involvements. As my insight and skills grew, I could listen more deeply and empathize, especially with myself. I recognized how sensitive an instrument my body really was. I could pick up tension from the air and anger and fear from others as though they were my own. And often it was the emotion of childhood that I carried into adulthood with me. Anger and fear had to be held in the body for years, but by this time, I had become aware of it and had learned to express it. Gradually I grew in confidence and competence and focused on my goals. I may be disabled, but I'm not unable to function in some creative way.

And, if I really think about it, we are all disabled in some way or other. Whether it is having a quick temper, reluctance to change, being orphaned at an early age, unsupportive relatives, financial constraints, or something else, we all have some issues. Sometimes our greatest bane can become our greatest strength. Wasn't it Winston Churchill who became an orator because of his determination to overcome the disappointment he felt because he fainted from anxiety the first time he was to speak in public? Our impediments can defeat us and erode our self-confidence, or they can give birth to a determination and perseverance that are unbeatable. Some people are loaded with talent but through lack of focus or lack of opportunity don't develop very much of it, whereas others have only one notable talent, like being able to draw or sing, and develop it to the hilt.

However, getting comfortable with my limitations was no guarantee that others would accommodate them. In my case, librarians agreed to make copies for me so I didn't have to tote about heavy books, and professors permitted me to bring a chair into the classroom that I could tolerate. In my teaching job, my supervisor arranged for an office and a classroom near the elevator, that is, until the university's downsizing made me redundant. Not everyone was understanding. A supervisor at a practicum site gave the break time I needed to rest but no place to do it. She told me that I just needed to take care of myself. I knew that if I couldn't do the job, regardless of what the Americans With Disabilities Act, said, there would be someone else waiting who could.

It wasn't until I graduated that I realized how difficult it was going to be to find a position where I could obtain the necessary supervision, given my physical limitations. I had found in the past that it was more prudent and productive to accentuate my abilities than my disabilities so I didn't want to say more than necessary in my cover letter. But I had to give enough information about my special needs in order to find a place that I could fit. From the experience I got during my practicum and from going for various tours and interviews, I formed the impression that employers would rather deal with able-bodied employees who can jump up and handle an emergency at a moment's notice. After 21 years of parenting, being a homeowner and teacher, and intervals of living in other countries, I've seen a few small emergencies. Besides being able to jump up, I've found that keeping a cool head and making the best use of the resources you have are also valuable assets. From many years of teaching I've learned how to work efficiently and to organize myself so as to use time and energy wisely while accommodating the sometimes urgent needs of students.

The thought occurred to me more than once when I was still a student that perhaps I will never really work as a professional counselor. Maybe all my courses and my own counseling were just meant to enrich my personal life.

Other times I think that maybe the powers that be know I have more serious work to do on my own issues before I turn myself loose on unsuspecting clients. Sometimes I think it would be so nice to have a glimpse of just what the universe has planned for me anyway. But I guess that would rather defeat the purpose of my struggling through it myself, of accepting each day as it comes, of learning to enjoy the present no matter what, of giving up trying to control people and events.

Accepting my disabilities means making the best of what is in the present moment. It means keeping in daily touch with my personal needs, wants, and rhythms and supporting myself, particularly when there's a danger of mental, physical, or emotional overload. Reframing setbacks and relapses so as to keep them in a healthy perspective is also important. It means recognizing and appreciating opportunities and being thankful for blessings as they come. It means taking care of myself in all the same ways that I might suggest to clients.

Part III

Transitions and Transformations

11
The Cost of Clarity

Robert W. Brown

I am dying. We're all dying, I know, but in my case the time I have left is measured in months, or even weeks. The diagnosis of cancer came down very recently. I had little time to reflect on my situation. The shock has been surprisingly easy to get over, easier than you might think. You have to start making your list, checking it twice, because there are some things that have to be done.

Dying is something that we spend our whole lives getting ready to do. Now that the time has come for me, I have to confront a reality that always seemed so abstract, so distant in the future.

I've been a counselor and counselor educator most of my adult life and, in some ways, that has helped me to die with the kind of dignity and serenity with which I have tried to live my life. Being a counselor is about dying because as you work with your clients, you are really helping them to use the days and moments of their remaining life to the utmost. Counseling is about helping people to find their way by making choices. We are making selections about direction. We are making choices about relationships. We choose who to see and who not to see. Each of these choices, whether made by our clients or ourselves, creates a paradigm for dying just as it does for living.

As I look back on my life, what has meant most to me have been those choices closer to my heart than my head. It has taken impending death to give me the courage to risk getting closer to those I love, to be more honest and authentic, to let someone know me a little bit more, maybe a lot more. Part of me needs to find a way to let my own honesty touch myself.

Each of us has within us a reservoir of honesty and clarity that we rarely share with others. Now that I have so little time left I want to tell people at a deeper level how they have helped me. I want to get in touch with a piece of myself that has allowed me to take my next step. In finding my way as a counselor, and as a human being, I wish that I had reached out to people more. I wish I had extended myself to be more honest.

I spent too much time being focused on the past and the future. I have been so task-oriented throughout my life, accomplishing things, getting things done. I thought that was so important. And, unfortunately, I was very good at completing tasks. Yet they were just ways to pass time. I ended up with a false sense of accomplishment.

I've told students and clients my whole life that if you want to be clear, you have to pay for it. I never realized how prophetic that statement would become for me. At this very moment, the price I pay for being clear-headed and cogent is dealing with unbelievable pain. If I take morphine to kill the pain, I can relax, even float to my death without a care in the world. Yet in controlling the pain that is now my constant companion, I also dull my thinking and my consciousness. I can't even cry.

What I am now experiencing at dramatic levels holds true for everyone else. To feel your life, you have to experience your pain. There is such great temptation to get away from feeling things too intensely. As counselors we have so many tricks to insulate ourselves, to keep pain at a distance. I don't mean we should shave every morning with a dull razor but there is nothing wrong with taking the time to feel the edge of pain.

I think about who is reading this and wonder what I have to say before I leave this earth. The whole idea terrifies me. This all has such finality to it. I can't take anything back. I can't withdraw with a smile or a joke. I wonder if what I have to say is original or new. I don't know what to say to people and that really scares me.

Some of the things that have mattered to me have been living my life as deeply as I can in all the moments as I can, living it deeply with friends, being able to live it deeply with the things I do, especially teaching, counseling, flying, and skiing. Each of these things means living on the edge for me, being fully engaged in the now.

Just as I have tried to help students and clients find or create meaning in their lives, I have struggled to do so in my own life as well. Did I succeed at this process of creating meaning for myself? I honestly don't know. I really don't know. Do I feel a sense of contentment? Yes, I do. And what do I have to say to counselors in the field who are trying to find their way, to create meaning in their own lives? Don't take yourself too seriously, but take yourself measurably. Don't take yourself in a manner that is cavalier, but take yourself in a manner that has sincerity and thoughtfulness about it.

Dying is not that big of a deal. Dying is fairly easy to do. But being able to die in a way that allows you to be integrated with your emotion, spirituality, and personhood is the exciting part.

I know how to die. Now I want to die with a sense of enjoyment and laughter and happiness and contentment. I want to be filled with the excitement of every precious moment I have left.

As I look outside, as I see the pictures on the wall of my wife and I skiing last fall, the beauty of the flowers, the rush of the snow through my eyes and through the air, to me that is why it's worth living, why it is worth living through pain to reach perfect clarity.

Dying makes living worthwhile. If you can't die with a sense of excitement and a sense of vitality, you probably didn't live very well.

These words were dictated to Jeffrey A. Kottler just a few weeks before Bob died on September 7, 1995.

12
Nature Nurtures the Heart, Soul, and Mind

Ford Brooks

Throughout most of my adult life I have found solace and wisdom in nature. For me, as a counselor, nature continues to provide me with the necessary insights, faith, and tools to walk along the path of the heart.

In my youth I was fascinated with the shapes and colors of mountains yet oblivious to the lessons they contained. The deep blue peaks and purple shadows sprinkled with fir trees were my first memories of the outdoors and my introduction to the natural world. My woodland hikes and travels have spanned areas from Baxter State Park in Maine to the Shenandoah National Park. Each time I enter the woods I become increasingly aware of the greater meanings in life at a level most difficult to find in the hustle and bustle of everyday routine and managed care phone calls.

As a young man, I did not realize how nature and the creatures in it could give me the insight and guidance I so sorely needed. When I became a fishing guide in my late teens, I observed how nature could both provide and take away. In addition to my guiding experiences were the conversations with my father on nature. He worshiped the outdoors and found particular pleasure observing birds in flight. He was so moved by nature that it slowly became a passion and source of refuge in my own life, providing me with faith and strength as I matured.

As a guide, I felt the wind and power of the northeastern storms crossing the majestic lakes and the smell of fir trees on lazy summer days, yet something was missing. That missing piece of understanding came about through two experiences with nature.

The Boathouse

We walked down the dirt road very slowly and deliberately toward the boathouse, with me holding the tin lovingly in my arms. A misty and overcast day set the mood for the events to come. Per the directions of my father, we proceeded to the end of the old weather-beaten dock and began emptying his ashes into the lake. I looked across this lake, a lake where our friendship as father and son had budded and grown, yet paradoxically was now the place where his remaining ashes would be placed.

We had fished on this lake for years in the dawning hours of crisp new mornings as well as torrential rainstorms that poured ice-cold rivers down our backs as we trolled patiently for trout. It was the lake where I saw my first meteor flash across the sky in fiery brilliance, burn out in an instant, and disappear forever. And now, as I stood on the old dock adjacent to our boathouse with my stepmother and wife, I was about to empty into the lake the remains of that special person who facilitated our growth as father and son.

Deep in my heart, I knew the contents of the $10 tin were not the essence of my father; rather, the spirit of his pained soul was now free in nature to live forever among the trees and water that he so dearly loved. My stepmother and I took turns pouring the sand-like material into the shallows of the cove, watching as the rolls of mist and sediment washed below the surface of the water. In a very reassuring way, I understood that this rolling wave of my father's ashes would somehow reach the distant shores, to be lovingly embraced on his arrival.

During this slow process, not more than 10 yards away, a small fish jumped directly out of the water and spun in the morning mist; simultaneously, the faint sound of a hooting owl could be heard. At the time, I thought this coincidence was quite extraordinary and in some way it comforted me because I did not know the synchronistic, symbolic significance. On returning home, I discussed the experience with my wife only and did not explore it further. Then one weekend 4 months later, I was reading a book on nature, which discussed many aspects of the Native American philosophy and our connection to the environment.

I was beginning to understand how my experience on the dock held significance for my life and that it was now up to me to investigate its meaning. I began reading everything I could on symbols, synchronicity, and nature's ability to teach humanity. Then one day, I found a description of the symbols of both the fish and the owl. My understanding of life, death, faith, and the circular nature of life was beginning to unfold.

The fish, I have come to understand, represents life and the spirit of being alive. The water from which it exploded represents birth and the primary composition of our human body. The owl represents both death and wisdom; this synchronistic and spiritual event on the dock was now quite profound. The symbol of life and spiritual growth jumped as the wave of immortality flowed beneath it.

Simultaneously, the voice of death and wisdom set background music to the scene of my existence and the passing of a loved one. The jumping fish and the hooting owl was the outer experience in nature, as Jung described. The inner experience was the symbolic meaning I have come to understand. The synchronicity occurred when both the fish and the owl and my inner experience met in understanding.

For years, I have seen this phenomenon with clients. As I watch their struggles I also see parallel events occurring in their lives that give me faith in a process much greater than the therapeutic relationship. By being aware of my surroundings and listening to the client, I have discovered I am connected with a process so humbling that it goes beyond words and can at times only be described by symbol or metaphor. To be part of that therapeutic exploration with clients, to see their awareness blossom and connect with their truth, is energizing as well as inspiring to me as a counselor.

The Woods

A similar experience happened in the woods of West Virginia not more than 6 months after my father's death. What occurred that day supported and provided, yet again, more information to help me see the cycle of life through the eyes of nature.

A friend of mine and I had taken six counselors to the woods of West Virginia for a retreat we called "The Hike for Healers Weekend." During this weekend, she and I developed a loosely structured format to help participants use nature as a means to learn about feelings and their direction in life. The exercise we suggested to our participants involved their going into the woods and looking for an area to sit in for at least an hour. During this time, they were asked to clear their minds, to observe sights, sounds, and smells around them, and to come back at a later time in the day to discuss their experience.

As leaders of this group, we also went on our own journey for those few hours. I walked for an hour on a crooked path that cut through a shaded and cool slice of the forest. Even though I was walking, I was getting chilly and was looking for warmth and a place to sit and relax. Out of the corner of my eye, I spotted a beam of light puncturing the forest ceiling and outlining a tree stump on the hillside. A voice inside of me said to go and sit down by the stump and relax in the inviting sunshine, which I did.

I found my mind filled with many thoughts and questions of the past 6 months; however, over the next 30 minutes the overall chatter began to diminish, and finally I began to relax and immerse myself in the life that was happening all around me. After taking a sip of cool water, I leaned back on the tree stump and looked up at the hole in the forest ceiling from where the reassuring beam of light was flowing.

It was not long before I closed my eyes and fell into a dreamlike state. I could hear the birds chirping and the wind blowing against my face, yet I was warm and comforted in the circle of light. After some time, I opened my eyes and began looking around the vegetation, so lush and green from the summer rains, and again lay back against the stump, thinking about very little. And then in a flash of insight, similar to the experience on the dock, I knew nature again was about to teach me something profound. I looked up to the sky and began to understand the significance of where I chose to sit.

In order for me to sit in the warm, bathing light that brought life and rejuvenation to my fatigued and cold body, a tree—a living entity—needed to perish. I was leaning up against the fallen tree stump that had provided a hole in the sky through which the sun could beam down. Nature was once again teaching me about the circularity of life and my existence in it. The tree provided life by giving light, warmth, and age-old wisdom to other vegetation and this tired soul.

The Connection

As a result of these two stories—my father's passing and the death of the beautiful tree—my outlook on life has dramatically changed. That "something missing" I realize was what the Native Americans have always known, that we are all related and connected in some spiritual and profound way.

Nature has allowed me to see and feel that connection. Before these experiences, I allowed control, predictability, and routine to order my life. These events in the woods have given me the ability to let go of control and live life day by day, living each day to its fullest. Nature continues to provide me with an understanding of my life and the lives of my clients. Helping others find their own way and having faith in a greater process has taught me about my own mortality and limitations.

13
I'll Find Out When I Get There

Felicity Monk

I am 21 years old and have just one dimple. I am the daughter of two counselors and can be more neurotic than Woody Allen on a bad day. I have a university degree in psychology. I have been in love twice. I have jumped out of a plane. And I have learned how to be alone. Nine months ago I left my home in New Zealand and went traveling alone. I arrived in London with 200 pounds in my pocket, an incredibly naive understanding of exactly how far this money would go, and a whole lot of misplaced faith invested in the universe. "The Universe will take care of me" I said to myself, "It's Meant to Be," "Everything will fall into place as it should," and a whole other assortment of profound clichés.

Unfortunately, things didn't quite go as planned. Instead of lovingly gathering me up in her arms and hugging me to her bosom, the universe (that had manifested itself in the form of London), swallowed me up, spat me out and then went back and chewed on me some more for good measure. But what London spat out was a new me, a somewhat bedraggled but more worldly, a pasty but more feisty, me. A me I never knew I could be. This is my journey.

I am one of those people who always knew who she was, where she was going, what her favorite color was, and what she was going to be when she grew up (Felicity the cheeky extrovert, to the top, blue, and lawyer, in that order). I was never one of those "can't-make-up-my-mind sorts." There simply wasn't the time. I had too many agendas, I had to write lists about lists, I had to study for my spelling test and save the world. I had never in my life experienced real uncertainty or confusion as to who I was and what it was I was meant to be doing. That was until I left all that I knew and went traveling on my own.

Life before London had been a relatively smooth ride, except for the period when my parents, the perfect counselors, ended their relationship and I was caught in the middle. I thought I had things pretty much figured out in my not so subtle, unassuming way. Life for me was not a mystery, things were not that complicated, I did not need to go and find myself, and anyway, I had drawn a flow diagram of my determined path right through to the next life for future reference purposes.

Friends were never in shortage. I've been popular pretty much my whole life. I've always had people around me or at least I've made sure people were around me. See, I was one of those people who hate to be by themselves. I hated to be alone and would have to fill the silences with television or radio noise, or go down to my local coffee shop where everybody knew my name. Being alone with myself was uncomfortable, it was like the awkward silence between old friends who find they have nothing left to say to one another. And just as the old friends long to escape the awkwardness, so did I.

I have lived with love, expectations, support, and demands all my life. The product of two very loving, highly intelligent and intensely communicative parents, both counselors, only the very best was expected from their loving, intelligent, and equally communicative daughter. To many, I may have seemed like the perfect child of two perfect parents, and for quite sometime I believed this myself. But the older I grew, the more I discovered how stifling and restrictive this role was becoming. There were times when it would feel like such a burden just being the daughter of my parents. I remember being a little girl and feeling so much more mature and worldly than all my friends. I knew what racism was and understood its damaging effects; I knew that talking was a far more effective form of communication then throwing tantrums; and I knew how to spell *psychology*. Though at the time I sometimes felt a little superior and privileged that my parents had taught me these things, it was also frustrating because I felt like sometimes I couldn't just be a kid. I was rarely ever rebellious or immature, even when experiencing my parent's painful divorce, because I always knew that I should know better, that I was mature enough to handle it like an adult.

Knowing that I was the daughter of two intelligent and respected counselors, and growing up believing they had the answers to pretty much everything, I felt as though I wasn't entitled to screw up or make mistakes. I wasn't supposed to be confused or scared or not have the answers. Maybe other people could bumble along in life, making mistakes and learning along the way, but I felt I had no excuse. I had had a wonderful upbringing by two people whose job it was to help fix other people's lives and so I thought that I had been equipped with the necessary knowledge and maturity to run my own life smoothly. I had to know what I was doing and I had to be good at it. Though my parents placed high expectations on me, I learned from a very early age the art of "should-ing," and in the end the expectations that I put upon myself were far greater and consequently far more damaging, and to an extent, still are. Yet sometimes I struggle with the expectations, both mine and theirs, and I have to remind myself that I am 21, I am allowed to feel my feelings and own them, even if they don't seem very grown up at the time.

People have defined me, labeled me, and explained me to myself, and I have let them. And as a result I have defined myself through them, through their perceptions of me. With their well-meaning definitions and labels, "Oh Felicity! You are such an extrovert, you are so bubbly and cheerful all the time, you are so mature," they helped to create a Felicity that perhaps never was or at least *used* to be. Thus, I have never needed to search for, or ask the all-time fundamental identity question "Who am I?" And if I were ever momentarily lost or perhaps a little confused, there would always be someone on hand to remind me of who I am—who Felicity is supposed to be.

I have ridden the train and gotten off at all the right stops, at the right times, and never strayed from the tracks. My journey has always been clearly mapped out from the beginning. Each stop clearly marked, each distance carefully considered, each destination previously identified. That was until I arrived in London. That was when the train derailed.

For the first time in my life I was truly alone. There was nobody to answer to, nobody to understand me, nobody to define me. I arrived at the airport with more bags than I could carry and fewer navigational skills than a monkey with a map. I was terrified. With no job, nowhere to live, no friends, and very poor adaptation skills for the wild, I was in trouble. I rapidly began to lose my certainty about All Things, and I began to question who I was. Could I do this on my own? Had I been pushed to my absolute limit? Where did I begin to forage for friends? The first 3 months in London were among the worst 3 months of my life. I had never felt so lost and alone, and I had no idea how to be on my own. My journal entries reflected this, this one summing up my feelings rather succinctly:

6 November 2000.
London sucks.

Adapting to London lifestyle was harder than I had anticipated, much harder. Finding a job, somewhere to live, and a friendly face appeared all too much to ask for. I was to quickly discover that my university degree in psychology was about as much use to me finding a job in London as a hairdryer is to a fish. I didn't have the relevant or necessary experience. I needed to have a master's degree. I wasn't old enough. I rapidly realized that getting a job in my chosen career path was not really an option.

Now, however, the range of employment opportunities open to me was vast and hideous. And I certainly did my fair share of them.

My initiation into the London rat race began as a "tea lady" (for lack of a better term). This job involved my sitting, waiting, and festering in a little dungeon at the bottom of a big building until arrogant business people ordered tea, coffee, and annoying little cookies that I was to promptly serve, with a smile no less.

I have met the job credentials of being a "bubbly, cheerful, go-getter" (dare I say, superseded them) and answered the advertisement, only to later discover my reward for having such a charming personality entitled me to be knocking on doors on the outskirts of London selling charity in the pouring rain.

I have been the "Project Manager of Austria" I will have you know. For a week. This job required me to call up hotels in Austria and attempt to sell them a page of advertising. The fact that most of them did not speak English, and I, no German proved rather an obstacle to the exercise. The perk of this job, however, was that in the event of my death (which seemed rather likely at the time), my loved ones would get three times my annual salary, probably enough to go out to tea with.

And then there was the job serving chocolate beer.

Oh! And lest I forget, the hours spent perched upon an absurd little stool in an absurd little shop, selling candy, chocolate, and cigarettes to people in suits who clearly did not need these things. And there I would sit and wait. Feeling as though I should be doing so much more, that surely my contribution to the world would amount to more than this. Me, perching and waiting, contemplating my moral destruction, working through some unresolved issues that I'm not sure I ever had in the first place, and wondering how I can consume a Snickers Bar without anybody noticing. Knowing that I was going to be fatally ill the very next day.

But it wasn't just the undesirable job opportunities that I had to negotiate; there was also the small matter of The People. Everyone in London is in a great big rush. The people can be so grouchy, and if you don't watch out for yourself, you can be squished on the street in the blink of an eye. Then there's the dodgy perverts that you have to look out for who frequent the subways and prey on young lasses.

Of course there was the weather . . . dark when I got up in the morning, dark when I got home at night, and well, to be honest, not altogether delightful in the few meager hours in between. And then there was the air, or lack thereof . . . . After spending a day on the London tubes, one's nasal mucus takes on a not so attractive black quality. The cyclists ride around with little darthvader gas masks on so that they can actually breathe amongst the traffic.

But time passed, as it has a tendency of doing, and things started to feel not so strange and alien. I settled into a job that I didn't have to drag myself kicking and screaming to (the chocolate beer job). I learned how to navigate my way around the London underground system like a pro. And I began to meet other people who remembered how to smile. I felt that I had passed the infamous 3-month initiation period of surviving in

London that the older, wiser, and considerably more seasoned travelers talked of. My emails to friends and family were happier and lighter, with a renewed promise of survival.

And so the trains continued to crash, people continued to rush, and one's nasal mucus continued to be tainted with a blackish-gray hue courtesy of the London air. And me, well, I continued to soldier on in this dark, mysterious city making the best sense of it that I could while smiling randomly at grouchy people just to annoy them that little bit more.

Experiencing London taught me the value of being on one's own, of spending time with oneself, of facing challenges and tests while standing alone. This is not to say that having friends, family, and a support system behind you is less admirable or less courageous than being on your own, but it was very much something that I needed to do.

Traveling to a different country, looking for a job, finding somewhere to live, negotiating my way through a big, unfriendly city, and accustoming myself to a different culture, alone, was one of the hardest things I have ever done in my life. It revealed parts of me to myself that I wasn't aware existed, resilience I didn't know I had, strength and a sense of humor that emerged when I was least expecting.

I wouldn't have liked to call myself a pessimist, though I have always been an avid supporter of the Cup is Half Empty team, cheering them on and wondering who drank the other half. But in recent times I have committed the ultimate sin, I have crossed the picket line and joined the other side, those of the Cup is Half Full persuasion. Now, I wouldn't go as far to say that I am a full-blown optimist, but since having been faced with some of the more challenging obstacles in my journey, some of which I didn't even think I could get a leg over, I have come to the realization that positivity and a sense of humor are much more useful then negativity and a scowly face.

It wasn't until I had some distance from the first few months of my time in London that I realized that I actually liked my own company, without the noise, I liked my company in the quiet times. On my journey alone I learned that it was time to let go of the definitions, the labels, and the expectations, it was time to leave room for just being. Being whoever I am at the time.

And so my train continues, hurtling down the track. Destination? Who knows? Next stop? Doesn't matter. I'll guess I'll find out when I get there.

14
Letting Go

Kathy Potter

During much of our time as developing counselors, we are learning and applying therapeutic techniques, clarifying what works for us with our clients, and wondering if we will ever have enough knowledge to feel competent and helpful.

But then, somewhere around mid-life or later, depending on when we started the journey of being counselors, we begin to sense the need for something more than "book learning" and techniques. As a 55-year-old career counselor who has been practicing for approximately 15 years, I am now aware of my growing need to trust my intuition and the "Universe" or "God," or whatever name we choose to give to the "something" that calls and directs us, if we allow ourselves to listen. I still continue to learn traditional ways to improve my counseling skills, and I have certainly not arrived at the end of my learning cycle. Rather, my way of learning has expanded.

In making public some of the following thoughts, I worry that I may be seen as some kind of New Age flake or, perhaps more kindly, a childish, misguided, and silly person. However, I have become more convinced that Western culture in general, and counseling in particular, puts too much emphasis on—and trust in—the rational, logical, science-making left side of the brain and not enough importance on the intuitive, less rational, right-brain thinking.

Most of my own growth as a counselor to this point has been based on education, training, actual experience, ongoing reading, supervision, and other typical approaches. What I am now becoming aware of is how much insight I have always received from other sources and how little I acknowledged that learning. So, it is with some trepidation that I share this particular journey, and I hope that my current ruminations will not be dismissed.

Not having been a person of religious conviction and still not much of a believer in organized religion, I find myself reading more books about how we develop and maintain faith, hope, and a belief in something that helps us to navigate this life. I guess I'm one of those who rather flippantly uses the term "spiritual" to refer to that part of me that is seeking an understanding beyond my five senses. However, I cannot explain in any scientific way some of the events that have occurred to me and seem to be guiding me in a direction I am still trying to understand. The guidance is definitely not coming from typical ways of learning.

I have a story about this push—or pull—from the universe, and I tell it in the hope that it might affirm the reader's sense that perhaps the events that most affect us are not completely knowable. I had been on a vacation of sorts, both enjoying the break from work and investigating an area in my native state that I am thinking of moving to. On a hike with my best friend from 8th grade, we encountered a deer on the trail. Nothing unusual here, I thought; one might expect to see a deer on a mountain trail.

A day later, as I was slowly driving along a meandering road between two small towns, a deer crossed the road, necessitating a quick application of the brakes. The next day, as I was exploring a residential area and driving up a street simply to see where it went, a deer once again crossed my path. Although seeing three deer in as many days would not be considered too unusual, I was aware that I had certainly seen more deer in a short period than would be typical in my travels.

Then, on the plane trip home, I started reading a book, an early passage of which describes a dream the author has where someone gives her a pair of antlers. The antlers are used to "butt out" a dream symbol that represents the traditional approach of organized religion to explaining life's mysteries. As I read the passage, I felt chills cover my body; the hair on my neck and arms stood on end; and tears came to my eyes. I could not believe that of all the books and passages I might have been reading at that time, I opened the pages to a description of a spiritual experience with a deer. When I later explored some of the mythology around deer, I discovered that deer often represent growth and change. I was emotionally overcome.

I knew I was being given a message about my need for growth and, I believe, a need to move back to my native state. Of course, I may have made of this syncronicity what I wanted, but that still speaks to my desire to move in a new direction. In addition, a month or so after my trip, I awoke in the middle of the night, startled from sleep by a realization that had not been anywhere in my waking mind. The realization was that the name of a woman with whom I had done some visualization work around the move to my home state had the last name of Deerwoman. Could all of these coincidences be just that? At this new stage in my life, I have decided that these are messages of great importance and that they are not random.

In addition to these events and realizations, some minor barriers to a geographical move began to drop away. A distance-learning doctorate program I had started turned out to be more expensive and time-consuming than originally indicated, and the distance learning itself proved to be much less to my liking than I had anticipated—so I withdrew, leaving me energy, time, and money to consider a job change and relocation. Also, some activities I had always enjoyed were no longer available, and several of the people who make life stable and enjoyable (my massage therapist, nutritionist, and hairdresser) were moving or retiring. So many endings at the same time.

Most recently, during a time of feeling disconnected and alone, I happened to rent the movie *Simon Birch,* not knowing much about it except that it would probably be a feel-good movie and take my mind off my own not-so-good feelings. Even in my self-absorbed state, I couldn't help but realize that not only is the movie about a young person pondering the purpose of life and his own belief in God, but the pivotal moment in the film is brought about by a deer.

My belief that I am being pulled to do something more in my counseling career and in my life is supported by what I have been reading and experiencing, but lest someone think that I know what that is, I do not. I am learning that finding my way is as much about listening to the messages that I can't explain as it is about doing the rational activities that career counselors and other therapists recommend to clients.

Now, as I sit with clients, I listen as much to what is not being said and what falls between the lines as I listen to the spoken messages. I pay more attention to the feelings and thoughts that are triggered in me as I take in the client's experiences, and I am not as hesitant to check out my responses with the client as I might have been as a beginning—and younger—counselor. I still do my best to differentiate my own projections and perceptions created by my life experiences from those of my client, but after mentally sorting through those differences, I propose interpretations generated somewhere in that intuitive part of me.

The change in the interaction between my clients and myself has been remarkable and clarifying, for the clients and me. I'm not always on the mark with what I pick up with my nonlinear, abstract interpretation, but even the willingness to risk sharing an interpretation with the client seems to move me to a new level of involvement. Is this the growth and change the deer points to?

My search is as much about belief and hope as it is about learning and practicing new counseling techniques and seeking new career opportunities by sending resumes and making networking contacts. And I am learning to trust the universe to provide me with the information I need in order to give to others whatever my unique gifts are.

felt like I was going to fail in school. I was forced to write with my right hand (even though I was left-handed), my teacher called me "Cinderella" instead of my own name and insisted it was a compliment, and she told me to stop asking questions and just memorize the math instead of trying to understand it! After one dreadful day at school where every issue became a problem, I curled up like a little kitten on my Dad's lap when he got in from the field that night and sobbed through my painful story. I remember him saying, "you're so bright, honey girl. I know that you will be good in school and that this problem is about your teacher. She taught school when I was in high school, and I think that she has taught so long that she has forgotten some of her patience with little children. You'll be all right. You'll be all right, honey girl."

His rough farmer's hands stroked my hair, and his voice was low, earnest, and reassuring. That voice stayed with me, and when I was in doubt I could conjure it up as he said, "You'll be all right. You'll be all right, honey girl," and I would feel brave enough to go on.

The fall that I finished my master's degree, we had a Christmas gathering at my brother's house. I was in the process of separating from my husband and almost didn't go to the family celebration because, even though my parents said they supported me, at a very deep level I feared I would never be acceptable again. The occasion brought to the surface a sense of incessant striving to be loved, knowing that you are and yet somehow not knowing it at the same time. I remember arriving at my brother's home as large snowflakes swirled through the darkening sky. The celebration was well underway, and it was a happy reunion. When I walked through the door, my father proposed a toast to his first daughter to getting her master's degree. I was stunned, embarrassed by the attention, and profoundly honored. I had not even gone to the graduation ceremony because I had assumed that no one would want to come! "I'm so proud of you," he said. My tears came instantly as we hugged. These unexpected, authentic, healing words and the accompanying tears immediately washed away all my worry that I was not OK.

If you had asked me if my father had a nickname for me, or for any of us in our large family, I would have told you that we couldn't afford them. It was hard enough for my parents to call out the right name when they needed us, and it would have been impossible if we had nicknames too. So I grew up independent, thrifty, practical, and not needing much because then I wouldn't be disappointed. I didn't even need a nickname.

When I heard my father's voice today, I didn't hear the strong, ever challenging, intellectual voice that I remembered from my adolescence. Instead, I heard a lyrical, gentle voice feathered slightly with age and tempered with the compassion of living. Before he hung up the phone, he said, "I love you, honey girl." I felt as if I was hearing those words for the first time. Could it be that in my search for acceptance, it had been there all along and I had not been hearing it?

Today I finally realized that I had always been accepted in my father's heart, that those deep feelings were about my own conditional acceptance of my self. In my father's heart, I was "honey girl," a name so much richer and dearer than a nickname that it can only be spoken at moments of great connection. My heart and spirit had to grow forgiving and loving enough to finally hear it. "I love you too, Dad," I said in a way that was unconditional and gentle. I felt like both a 5-year old and an equal, both loved and loving, reassured and reassuring, accepted and accepting.

As I hung up the phone and looked at my garden, I realized that the flowers had spread. My heart, too, was filled with wild bouquets of color, dancing like children in the wind.

16
The House That the Seasons Built

Ford Brooks

I stood before the tattered and worn bungalow that in past years had been my refuge. It protected me from the cold early mornings in May, warded off the black flies in June, and sheltered me from the deluge of rain in July and August. Now, almost 20 years later, this hovel was surrounded by 4-foot weeds covering the door and had a weathered look similar to an unshaven seaman. It was here, at this very spot, where I began to understand my own mortality, my freedom, and my life's work as a counselor. As I looked back over the past 20 years I could see nothing but change, metaphorically embodied in this small but special dwelling.

At the age of 20 I became a Registered Maine Fishing Guide, an honor and a privilege that few merit and to which few aspire. After spending most of my young life hiking or fishing with my father, I felt ready to guide and up for the challenge. I was gainfully employed by a family-owned fishing camp not more than 25 yards from the house. This was a great summer job, a transition between college and graduate school, where I could save some money and have fun. For most folks, however, guiding was a way of life, not some transitional summer job. The Registered Maine Guides were a special breed, and at the age of 20, I entered their world of traditions, honor, and culture.

The first summer proved to be one continual crisis, as I was not from Maine and was dubbed the "out-a-stater" by local guides. Having the ability to chat with the best of them, I was able to misdirect my ineptness and, at the same time, have fun and learn about the craft of guiding. Fortunately, the owner of the fishing camp linked me with many of the senior guides so as to help with my skills and confidence. As the first summer came to a conclusion, I felt more assured of my abilities, was able to make a shore lunch for my clients under 3 hours (usual time was 1 hour 15 minutes) and managed to help sports (clients) catch their fair share of fish.

This mentoring process paralleled my development as a counselor and significantly contributed to increasing my confidence. Without this mentoring process, I can see how my path would have restricted me in finding my way and ultimately effecting the clients' movement in counseling.

It wasn't until the second summer that I began to get the hang of cutting wood, tying knots, sharpening tools, and spitting tobacco without getting it on my shirt. I found new fishing holes and discovered undetected rocks (the hard way). At the same time I was growing and developing a sense of who I was and where I wanted to go (I thought) in life. After listening to folks in the canoe day in and day out, I saw how important it would be in my life to connect with nature as much as I could. Most of all, I saw in the eyes of many fathers sadness for not spending more time with their children, more specifically, their sons. Since I was the youngest guide, I typically was charged with guiding the father and son teams. The sons were usually 12–13 years old and, more times than not, uninterested in fishing unless a fish was on the line every minute or two. I could feel the awkwardness, like that of two strangers in an elevator, where the silence between father and son spoke volumes about their life together. I learned to break the silence and eventually generate conversation between them, an invaluable experience to me as I began my career as a counselor. I realized how my ability to facilitate and reflect emotions of clients in the canoe would be essential in my work as a counselor. Although they were there to fish, I understood how that was a distraction from the unspoken stress in their lives.

As I continue to stare at the weathered hovel, I can see, feel, and smell those two special summers. I can still picture my roommate Andy, a significant person in my life then and today. He was a Mainer, a man's man that almost cut off his finger with an axe, and then put a Band-Aid on it. He could lift an 18-foot wooden canoe and move it onto a trailer without wincing, and smoke at least a carton of cigarettes a week. Our adventures of living off of noodles, doing eight to nine loads of laundry 60 miles away at the closest laundromat, not bathing for 2 weeks because the lakes were too cold, or looking stupid after a few too many beers, were the young adult experiences that are still so special to me today. We lived in the cold, one-room shanty with his dog Sam, one lightbulb, and a propane grill from which we cooked our succulent meals. The two beds were stuffed into a closet-like annex attached to the hovel where piles of fish-smelling clothes permeated the room.

And although we smelled, lacked a bathroom, and had only cold running water, it was one of the richest times in my life. To be a Registered Maine Guide meant to listen, to learn, to be humble, to go without (a lot), to be humorous, and as a result, to become more of who I wanted to become. Being a guide helped me find my way as a fledgling counselor and showed me the deeper meanings of day-to-day living. Guiding was more than fishing; it was the gestalt of nature, my roommate, other guides, the sports, and my interaction with them all.

Counseling for me is more than techniques, theory, or education. It's all of these plus the interaction between me and the client. A simple, wonderful, and indescribable connection that is so essential in the healing process. The connection is also about my awareness of all that is around me in the session. The client's breathing, eye contact, and body posture all give signs of what the client may be struggling with internally. When I was out on the lake early in the morning, I was tuned into wind direction, the smells of approaching storms, the clients in my canoe, and the type of fishing they wanted to do. Listening to the environment and where my sports were in relation to the context was so important in helping them relax and ultimately catch fish. We are all guides in some way who first need to find direction in our own lives before we attempt to help others find theirs.

I stood at the small, weed-covered shanty for 15 minutes, reliving a special time in my life, and although it was 19 years ago, it was like yesterday. Yet, the shanty before me showed its age. I am not that 20-year-old anymore, nor is the shanty. Underneath it all, however, we are both sturdy, and with some trimming and a few coats of paint, our spirit is intact, albeit different.

As I was about to leave, I took a picture, as I had done 19 years before. When I got home and looked at my photo album, I could see how the building had changed. Beside the hovel was a picture of me with my favorite flannel shirt and my trusty fishing hat. It was at that time I looked into the bedroom mirror to examine my reflection and how I had changed. A little wiser perhaps, a few more lines on my face, some gray hair, yet in many ways I was still the young man in the picture. Just like the small house that I called home for two summers, I had weathered many storms and stand waiting for that next season, that next storm, that next adventure.

Part IV

Learning
From
Failure

17

To Fail in Order to Succeed

Shannon Hodges

Last summer my wife, our German shepherd, and I piled into our old, ridiculously overpacked van and traversed the vast regions and pockets of the United States. During the months of June and July, our trio logged some 13,000 miles, looping through the Midwest, the South, then the West Coast, and finally back home to Minnesota.

What I treasure about a long drive is the time it affords for introspection. Having spent a good deal of the past 14 years crisscrossing the continent, I have found that the best ideas often come during the idle moments the open road offers. Experience has taught me to keep a tablet handy should some noteworthy idea emerge in my conscience, as I find such peak thoughts have a brief half-life in my short-term memory.

After we had been on the road for a month, traveling through the barren, open country of West Texas, it dawned on me just how far I had come since my undergraduate days. In no way could I have fathomed earning a doctorate degree, running a university counseling center, and teaching college students. John Lennon once said, "Life is what happens when you're busy making other plans." When I began college, I had no real sense of the range of my talents, skills, and interests. Coming from a small Ozark town of 1,500 souls (where everyone was White, Christian, Protestant, and spoke English), with little exposure to outside cultures, ill prepared me to face a diverse university environment. In no time at all, I was overwhelmed and floundering in a social and academic milieu as alien to me as the great plains of Texas.

My once clearly defined path suddenly merged into a confusing shade of gray, where my sense of direction and purpose was obstructed. Psychologically, I had left the safety of my own youthful captivity to venture out into a vast desert, where natural landmarks and geographical signs were vacant. Freedom is a difficult responsibility. Freed from family and small-town umbrage and left to rely on my own resources, I soon began to have serious doubts about my personal and academic abilities. What had appeared as unlimited vocational opportunity suddenly and unexpectedly narrowed.

What was formerly a clear purpose had been replaced by uncertainty, doubt, and fear. In desperation, I tried several avenues, only to discover they took me further from personal fulfillment. While doing graduate work in a program I eventually abandoned, I recall one long afternoon spent aimlessly wandering through the hills above the city, covering miles and yet going nowhere in particular. Naturally, such was a mirror of my life. I could discern no clear direction that made any sense to me, and like many youthful idealists, I had lost my way.

Life is like this at times. Even our well-constructed foundations can crumble like sawdust. Carefully cultivated paths sometimes leave us unexpectedly aimless and wandering. At times one can feel so hopelessly lost and alone. Yet paradoxically, lost may be exactly what a person needs to experience to understand the nature of their life journey. During this tumultuous time, the inner message of John Newton's transforming hymn, "Amazing Grace," resonated with me. That is, we must all leave our place of comfort to journey out into the unknown, facing all the risks, where we must come to rely on and listen to our own soul voice. Part of this "nomadic" experience involves setting aside parental, teachers', and others' expectations of us.

Parker Palmer, a mystic-teacher, illustrates this beautifully in his book, *Let Your Life Speak*. A truism from Palmer's background is "A way will open." While we can learn from teachers, counselors, and parents, we cannot force our lives to unfold and develop in a particular fashion. It is our lives that unfold to us when we are ready to be taught. While I could not necessarily have foreseen a career in counseling, my genetic code, interests, and early experiences were forces transcending my own control. Certainly, at points along the way I realized there were choices inherent in the life process.

A person may well know which of the divergent paths to take yet choose the one that is socially acceptable, offers financial success, or is what someone else wants. Such abdication, while alluring in its certainty, is destructive to our psyche. The lesson herein is the same we all face as counselors, educators, and people. The journey to ourselves is an often frightening, uncertain, lonely one, as difficult as it is necessary to self-hood. Yet in working through the process, there is emancipation through the realization that one does not need to be Carl Rogers, Victor Frankl, Virginia Satir, or any other notable figure to be an effective counselor.

Still, I have found the role of counselor to be a rough and uncertain one. I am overwhelmed occasionally that someone would actually trust me with the intricacies of their life. Clients are in a vulnerable situation when they come to see me, and often I struggle to find a way to be helpful. Sometimes issues emerge that are close enough to my own experience that I actually do feel some of their pain. Sometimes I feel overwhelmed by the nature of the therapeutic encounter, and I question whether I am capable of being a helpful counselor. I get even more nervous when supervisees, faculty members, administrators, friends, and parents seek me out for advice. Such solicitations are a reminder of my own limitations.

As a child, I recall the feeling of safety and security when, late in the night, I would wake to the sounds of highway department trucks out clearing the road of ice and snow. During our youth, we want to believe that someone responsible is out there watching out for our best interests and clearing a path for our own security. When I began the master's in counseling program, I was just as naive. Surely the esteemed faculty in our program, by virtue of their education and experience, always knew what to do in any given situation. I longed to be one of those people in the know.

Two advanced degrees and 15 years of experience later, it is perhaps an irony to feel more humble than when I began. Students, faculty, and counselors I supervise seek me out for guidance. Frequently, no clear answer emerges when I am called on for consultation. Often, the best service I offer is serving as a sounding board—hearing the message, asking for clarification, and putting the issue back on the individual seeking help, tapping their creative resources (most know the solutions, but need help in implementation).

In the vast majority of situations, a junior counselor, a student resident advisor, a biology professor, and even a building custodian can serve as a helpful resource. Wise "counsel" is helpful in walking clients and others through their situation so that they can arrive at their own workable solution. The reality is that we are all finding our way along the uncertain path of life. Therapeutically, strength lies in letting go of the expert role and embracing our humanness in whatever helping relationship we provide.

The supreme irony I draw from my journey is that I am succeeding now only because I failed earlier. It is odd to reflect that I had to fail in order to succeed. Yet, failure is not something we are taught to embrace. Society often holds up an unhealthy ideal. Yet, few if any are ideal: most of us are not bursting through the ceiling on the SAT or the GRE, nor dazzling faculty with our brilliance. We're a little lost. We struggle and challenge the patience of our teachers and professors and often disappoint our parents. Finding our way, paradoxically, may have far more to do with understanding and learning from our disappointments and heartbreaks than basking in our success and glory.

I have come to understand that, paradoxically, "finding my way" sometimes means that I must first lose it. Community is very important, but the needs of the many must be balanced by the needs of the self. Along with taking copious notes at national conferences and from esteemed professors, we must heed our own voice. Discerning our own path—vocationally and spiritually—does not mean scrambling toward some prize just beyond our grasp or heeding a call from a voice "out there." As Rabbi Zusya once said, "In the coming world they will not ask me, 'Rabbi, why were you not Moses?' They will ask me, "Rabbi, why were you not Zusya?'" If we are to live our lives fully and creatively, we must learn to honor our limitations in ways that do not distort our nature. We must take the way that closes and find the lesson it offers, just as we joyfully embrace the ways that open.

On that long, hot, dry, winding, empty ribbon of West Texas highway, some 1,200 miles from my beginning, I had never felt more at home.

18

Growing Pains

Brenda K. Garboos

It was June 1979 and I was elated about obtaining my first position only weeks after graduation. I was offered a vocational rehabilitation position at a sheltered workshop for mentally retarded persons in New York City. My assignment was to work with the more mentally challenged clients to help them improve their work skills so that they could function successfully in a sheltered workshop.

I must confess that, as a rookie in this field trying to find my way, I was glad to "get my feet wet" with counseling a population I had viewed as receptive to counseling. I had assumed that my clients would be cooperative and compliant, eagerly willing to participate in treatment plans set up for them. The greatest challenges I thought I faced would be to simplify and customize prevocational evaluations, modify counseling interventions, and shorten the duration of the sessions. My caseload size appeared to be manageable—a mere 20 cases. This put me at ease, as I did not feel prepared to deal with people in crisis.

One of my first assignments was to inform a female client of her termination from the program because of highly inappropriate acting out behavior. On my first afternoon on the job, this client had struck a fellow client in the face. She had committed a similar infraction on two other occasions and now had violated a condition in a behavioral contract that was established by my predecessor. Although I had perceived this as a "no-win" situation for me in counseling this client, I felt a great deal of anxiety and fear during this counseling episode since this client had acted out physically toward me. I was concerned that either I said the wrong thing or spoke too much to the agitated client, which may have set her off. Initially, I was reluctant in sharing my feelings of failure with my supervisor and other relevant staff. My concern was that I would be harshly criticized for making an avoidable error. However, I took the risk and raised my concerns, delighted to discover that I was given positive feedback for my efforts in dealing with such a difficult case. In fact, I was given unconditional support from my supervisor and other staff. Gradually, I began to feel less self-conscious and self-doubting about my abilities and felt more effective in dealing with client crises. I realized I had to exercise my assertiveness skills in order for me to function more confidently as a professional.

In reflecting back to my graduate training experience, although I was told by my professors that I had the potential to be an effective counselor, I also knew I had my limitations. A main concern was my personality—I was both quiet and shy in nature and avoided potentially confrontational situations in which I had to be assertive. Even my internship professor had expressed her reservations about my performing effectively because of my apparent unwillingness to provide critical feedback to my fellow students during case presentations. I now realize that I was experiencing "growing pains" as both a counselor and as a young adult. Each time I encountered a client-related crisis, I was forced to test my inner resources. In most instances I was able to resolve the crisis and consequently build my level of self-confidence. Having this awareness enabled me to remain in the counseling field despite the uncertainties I have and will experience as a professional. As I began to be more willing to take risks by asking for input or feedback of client related issues from my peers, I began to grow and develop a more positive outlook of my abilities both professionally and personally.

We may feel the need to be perfect counselors because we feel it is expected of us by other staff, or even by ourselves, to fix the client's problem or to eliminate his or her negative behaviors. In graduate training, we have a good grounding in counseling theories and techniques. Some of us may have been able to implement some of these approaches on a limited basis during our fieldwork training. However, those experiences can be limiting in that we have built in safety nets, that is, our field supervisor or academic advisor. We may have been instructed to "Know Thyself," but it is quite different to actually put this maxim into practice.

I now believe that feeling effective as a counselor is a process that begins before you become a practitioner. Theory provides a framework for the counseling process, but for one to feel effective and dynamic, to be successful as a neophyte counselor, one must be both open and flexible when communicating with other staff members about client-related crises or issues. Furthermore, you have to accept your fallibility and the fact that there will be circumstances beyond your control that will result in failed interventions, but support is there—even if you have to work hard at seeking out your supervisor or a sympathetic colleague. Through the years, I grew to realize that my achievement was not based solely on how many clients I had successfully rehabilitated but on my willingness to acknowledge my shortcomings and strengths.

Now, as a seasoned professional, I believe it is my obligation to provide that guidance and support to my newer colleagues. Several years later at the same sheltered workshop, I had the opportunity to assist a new colleague with developing strategies for effective client crisis intervention and to streamline the counseling process for less debilitated clients. When I spoke with this colleague many years later, she expressed her appreciation for my availability to her at a vulnerable time in her life. She told me that as a new counselor, she had the desire to achieve success with her clients, yet she felt insecure about her ability to deal with crises.

My encouraging feedback and frank discussions about counseling success had enabled her to evaluate her goals as a counselor—both personally and professionally. She was able to begin the growing process and to sustain herself during the ensuing "growth spurts" in which effectiveness as a professional is not always readily apparent.

I must admit that crisis intervention is not a major job responsibility at this time. However, the awareness that I gained from my earlier experiences has enabled me to deal more effectively with the stress that comes along with new challenges I face both on the job and in my life.

19

Out on a Ledge

Sherrill Wiseman

When I told a friend that that I was writing about finding my way as a counselor, she practically spit coffee in my face, guffawing out loud. And I quote, "Oh my god Sherrill, you didn't have to find your way! You were on an eight-lane express highway leading directly there!"

I beg to differ. From my perspective, it was not as easy or clear or straightforward as being on a road to anywhere. Finding my way into counseling felt more like rock climbing, having to search for every hand-hold and toe grip. It didn't seem to matter that I always knew I was physically safe because there were so many times I felt that I was in psychological jeopardy. Often it felt as though I was climbing out on a really narrow ledge trying to balance my self with my self-esteem and my sense of competence. It was hard and embarrassing and even at times downright humiliating to go back to school after achieving competence in another field. I always knew, in the back of my mind, that counseling was the profession I wanted, but it took successive approximations and a number of personal struggles to get me there. I expect my friend meant that I was " the counseling type" and I expect that she was right. She knew that I liked people, that I found their stories fascinating, and that I found great personal meaning in trying to be helpful. It was a good start but it wasn't enough.

Growing up in a middle-class, traditional, "Father-Knows-Best" type of family, I accepted early on that I was probably headed for one or another of the "pink ghettos." Since I have never felt particularly comfortable around small children, other than my own, it wasn't going to be teaching. That pretty much left nursing. Not a bad choice I thought; I could become a psychiatric nurse. I had read *I Never Promised You a Rose Garden,* and I was in love with the idea that I could reach someone or help someone in a way other people couldn't. Possibly a touch of megalomania. Unfortunately, psychiatric nursing didn't turn out to be quite the niche I had been looking for, since 30 years ago, in the hospital where I trained, nurse–therapist was an idea not yet coined. I found myself, for the most part, handing out pills, playing cribbage, and leading exercise classes when I could round up some of the more tractable and docile patients. Good experience though. Through it I learned that the world of the emotionally ill could be a scary place, and not just for the patients. I learned never to discount the perceptions and intuitions of even the most seemingly disturbed, and I learned that I could affect the patients I worked with in ways I never imagined or wanted.

My first nursing intake interview was with a woman who had been diagnosed as being paranoid, psychotic, and "uncooperative" and had been brought into the hospital by the police. I knew this because even though we had been expressly told not to preview the patient's chart so as to be better able to form our own opinions, I had read that chart cover to cover. No way was I going in unprepared! Being possessed of a vivid (read overly active) imagination, I walked to her room flashing back to the movie *A Nun's Story*, where Audrey Hepburn is attacked by a scissor-wielding psychotic patient who calls herself the Archangel. My patient looked equally sinister, gaunt, wild-eyed, and totally unpredictable. Although, truthfully, given the frame of mind I was in at this point, the Easter Bunny would have looked menacing.

I perched on the end of her bed, as close as possible to the door, prepared to bolt at the first sign of violence on her part. Hyperventilation was probably the least of the signs of my anxiety. Not surprisingly, I was not great at establishing rapport; blending was nonexistent. After a few nonproductive minutes, I suggested that possibly this might not be a good time for her (note . . . for her!) and offered to come back later. She immediately agreed and I hit the ground running.

The following week I was to visit with her again. In the interim she'd had shock therapy, which I was gratified to hear would probably have wiped out her short-term memory. I hoped she would not remember our first session. I met with her in the lounge and began with "You probably won't remember me . . . ," at which point she looked directly at me and cut me off by saying, very gently actually, "Oh yes, I remember you. You're the student nurse who came to talk to me last week. You sat on the end of my bed. You were so white and you were breathing so strangely, I was afraid you were going to faint. I didn't know what I was going to do with you if you did!" I remember looking back at her feeling quite disoriented, as in, "Tell me again? Which one of us is the patient?"

Essentially, it was about fear. Fear that I might get hurt. Fear that something I did, or did not do, might adversely affect my patient. Fear that she might have presented me with behavior or symptoms I couldn't handle.

Fear that someone might have witnessed me goofing up. Fear that, ultimately, I wasn't going to be any good at doing what I had decided I really wanted to do. And, as it turned out, that episode was merely the flagship of an entire armada of worries and anxieties that seemed determined to set sail with me wherever I went professionally. I think the anxiety, largely internally generated, was mostly around the awesome responsibility of ministering to another human being, whether it was in my capacity as a nurse, or later on, as a counselor and teacher. Any time I felt unsure of myself, or didn't know exactly how I was going to proceed, the responsibility could, and often did, feel overwhelming. Feeling overwhelmed was, more often than not, accompanied by a pervasive sense of shame at being less than "perfectly" competent. Those were the times when doing a balancing act on that " ledge" became exceedingly precarious.

Finding my way has had much to do with learning how to survive and subdue the anxiety around my own competency issues. It was, no doubt, a double-edged sword. Perversely, the very anxiety that could absolutely torment me was probably also the driving force behind my ultimately becoming competent and effective wherever I chose to work. It's just that, so often, it felt like such a painful struggle to get there.

A huge part of finding a way past my fear was accessing mentors and colleagues who, with infinite patience and inexhaustible humanity and compassion, both guided and supported me as I "climbed."

Part of subduing the anxiety came from understanding, finally, that although obviously important, it wasn't the content or the techniques I brought to either nursing or counseling that would matter the most or necessarily even be the most healing factor for any particular patient or client. It was the process between us, and I was responsible for my part of the process. I could almost always be in charge of doing that well, as long as I was able and willing to be open, honest, respectful, and congruent. As one of my mentors once remarked, "Your clients will forgive you any number of errors in content; what they won't forgive are errors in process." I found that hugely comforting as well as being largely true.

Part of surviving the anxiety has been realizing that, while I am capable of worrying to an absurd extreme at times, I am really not alone on that ledge. I can't think of a single colleague who hasn't experienced acute episodes of anxiety when second-guessing their handling of a case or wondering how they ultimately stacked up as a professional.

Finding my way was also about learning to let go. Realizing that acknowledging and talking about the mistakes I have made, or the times when I could have "done it better" actually helps take the sting out of accepting that I'm not always going to "do it right." I went for years feeling that any missteps on my part had to be kept a deep dark secret lest I be judged and condemned as a total incompetent. The relief of being able to talk openly about the times I feel I've goofed or blown it has been incredibly liberating. Not to mention that talking about it then creates an opportunity to get helpful feedback and brainstorm around finding a better way.

Finally, it's about balance and coming to know that the balance can and will shift over time. I suspect the learning curve will always be agony for me. I think that comes from a basic desire to always "do it perfectly" complicated by large doses of the Impostor Syndrome having been thrown into the mix. Somewhere along the line, though, I have learned that even if I start off feeling mostly incompetent and only occasionally competent, in time, with experience, support, and guidance, I can reverse that. I know now that I will end up feeling very competent most of the time. Finding my way is accepting that, regrettably, since I am never going to be perfect, most of the time will have to be good enough!

20
Reflections of a Journey in the Life of a Physician

Rafat Hussain

Prologue

It would be a rarity to find a physician writing a piece for a book like this; in fact many of you may be nonplussed or even annoyed at finding an interloper. Yet while the discipline-specific approaches may markedly differ, the underlying goal for all health practitioners remains the same—to alleviate suffering. I know it sounds terribly clichéd, but what fascinates me is the process, the personal journey that care providers make (or refuse to make) in accepting the limits of their power and their response to failure.

Scene 1

8:00 a.m. Grand rounds are under way in a medical ward of a large teaching hospital. The interns anxiously follow the Head Resident from bed to bed and present their respective cases. Time is short and information needs to be presented concisely and factually. The group moves to bed number 36. It is my case, and the bed is empty—for its 24-year-old occupant died the night before. I begin to describe what happened but find myself mumbling incoherently. More shocking is the realization that there are tears rolling down my face and I am all choked up with emotion. My supervisor looks appalled, and another colleague steps in to provide a quick clinical summary. My supervisor's gaze is firmly fixed on me. His dismay is not related to the death of the patient, for that was expected. No, it was the shockingly unprofessional behavior of one of his interns who seemed inca-

pable of handling a somewhat routine clinical issue—death. A stiff repri-
mand was in order. I feel humiliated and listen with my head down

Later that day, I had a long hard talk with myself. I was both angry and
disappointed by my own reactions. I had always been terrified by death as
a child and the sight of a funeral procession would send a shiver down my
spine. Yet 6 years of medical training should have taken care of that fear.
After all, not only had I spent long hours dissecting human bodies in the
anatomy lab, but I had also seen the process of dying and death of other
patients in the hospital. Therefore, there ought to have been little, if any,
reason for me to get so emotional about the death of one of my patients
even though he died at a young age and was the only child of his parents.
Their emotional devastation at seeing him die should have had nothing
to do with me. I know I had done all I could for the child.

I had lied to the child and his family about the true nature of his dire
condition. I genuinely thought I was sparing them some pain; in actual
fact, I did have a responsibility for preparing them for the worst. I kept
brooding about what I could have done differently.

My peers all seemed so professional in striving to provide the best of
care but without any emotional outbursts. I promised myself that I would
try to emulate them by creating some emotional distance between my patients and myself. It never occurred to me that perhaps what I needed was
someone to talk to, someone who could help me understand my emotions better. But the medical model did not allow for any of this "woolly-
headed" training. One learned the facts, the "science and art" of reaching
a diagnosis and instituting treatment regimens, the "etiquette" of bedside
behavior and the "protocols" to follow in the last stages of the patient's
life. Little wonder, then, that I agreed with my supervisor's assessment
that showing undue emotion was unacceptable behavior in my chosen
field. So I embarked on a new resolve—no more emotions, just highly
regimented behavior incorporating the best of clinical care possible. It
was not easy to be so impersonal, but after months of persistence, I think
I slowly got the hang of it. And, yes, I did feel proud of my achievement.

Years rolled on and I moved away from a purely clinical practice into
the public health arena. I continued to provide clinical care but mainly
at the primary care level. I functioned at a comparatively "safer" level—
lots of acute and chronic illnesses, but I no longer had to deal with critically ill patients except occasionally when an emergency was brought to
one of the outreach satellite clinics. But even then there was little danger of finding myself in an emotionally distressing situation. I acted
"professionally" and made the necessary arrangements to ensure that
the patient was quickly "dispatched" to the nearest hospital emergency
room. Yes, I felt sorry whenever I came to know that the patient had
later died. But then I had learned to expect and accept death as part of
my profession.

My principal interest at this time was teaching public health and helping medical and nursing undergraduates understand the interface between clinical and community health. I had also developed an interest in research and was thrilled when my first grant as a principal investigator was funded. I felt I could now truly claim to be part of the academic world.

Scene 2

I am sitting in a small room listening to Aashi explain how her 7-month-old daughter died of pneumonia a couple of days ago. I have managed to bring up all the right expressions of a sympathetic listener—for Aashi's daughter was one of my research "subjects." While I make the right noises, I also keep glancing sideways to make sure that the little red light on the tape recorder is flickering and recording this part of the story. I feel sorry for Aashi, I truly do, but it is sympathy and not empathy that drives my reactions now. I also have to admit that deep down I am excited by Aashi's story for I have a great case history to present.

The story has all the ingredients of a powerful narrative—a vignette that tells far more than numbers can. Like a consummate professional, I presented it at conferences and seminars, with a steady and well-pitched voice, with the face bearing an appropriate expression of dismay at the needless death of an infant. Most importantly, my eyes were always tear-free. The years of self-training for creating a space between the professional and the personal self had held me in good stead. How I wished that some day, by chance, I could end up meeting that old supervisor again and show him that I was not so unworthy a pupil as he once thought.

After the initial euphoric phase, a sense of unease started to creep in. I was disturbed at the ease with which I could now handle death. The initial reaction was, as expected, that of denial and then a resolve to crush any sentimentality. After all, a great deal of effort has been expended in the transformation process and after all these years, there simply was no place for emotionalism. The questions to myself over time, however, became tougher and more frequent: Is this what I really wanted to be? Was I to become a semi-robotic professional incapable of feeling the pain of others? As my research career progressed, I found myself increasingly dealing with morbidity and mortality assessments. Questions on death became an integral part of my research. I was regularly confronted with the anguish and sorrow that come from losing a loved one—expressions of deep grief and distress. I had learned over time how to behave as a clinician when faced with the death of a patient. But being a researcher was a different ballgame; now it was I who needed my subjects rather than they needing me. I had a drawer full of ethical guidelines and so forth, but they were of little help in easing my confusion. There was still a small part of me that wanted to reach out and console the bereaved, but I didn't know how.

I felt that I should perhaps offer assistance to defray some of the medical costs, but I was not sure whether it would be misconstrued as a backdoor mechanism to ease my way back to fill in some of the blanks for my research subjects. I was not sure whether altruism had anything to do with my feelings, for I was also acutely aware that I could not afford the luxury of too much "missing data." So I kept asking myself: Is it even ethical to contact the people again? I knew that my return visits were potentially distressful. As families recounted events, they often talked about the medical system failing them. They saw me as part of the system but were too polite to ask me to leave. Deep down, I too felt angry and frustrated at the narrow confines in which orthodox medicine works and angrier still at my own helplessness and confusion. But as a researcher I was required to keep my distance in order to maintain "objectivity." I had few answers, and I was too embarrassed to share my anguish with others. Would an admission of emotion be likely to be viewed as an admission of failure? Would I be making myself a sitting target for jeers, this time perhaps more subtle ones? I guess the confusion and turmoil that I thought I had left behind me had never really left. All I had achieved was an illusion of self-control, as I tried to hide behind a totally false image—an image that I never really managed to ingrain as part of myself.

Scene 3

Fast forward to year 2001. My mind keeps drifting back over many images of the past 20-odd years. Perhaps there is a tale to be told of my own journey—of all the lost opportunities to become a better person and physician. I finally had to accept, with considerable ambivalence, that for the past few years I have been driving in reverse gear. The space between the professional and personal self is vastly reduced, for I can feel pain and I can cry not only at my own sorrow but at the sorrows of others as well. Even media images of death and destruction in far-flung places, some that I don't even have a clear idea of where they actually are, can move me to tears.

So how did this happen? Is it just part of life's journey as I age and become more and more conscious of my own vulnerability to disease and death? Or is it because for the past few years I have stopped working as a clinician and as a researcher, moving away from face-to-face encounters to working on large-scale data sets where participants are coded with an ID number. In my work now there are no names or faces.

Despite having never had any training or even a tangential brush with counseling skills, I seem to have become my own therapist. I have learned not to suppress questions but to mull over them. I arrive at different conclusions at different times, but gradually I have gathered enough courage to admit that I did not want to be the person the system was forcing me to become. I am glad that I opted out while there was some chance of salvaging myself from a life of ongoing conflict and much self-inflicted misery.

I let images of different encounters and experiences fill my head and then I try to deconstruct them. I find it amazing that every story, despite being thought and re-thought time and again, still provides new insights: about myself, about people, about how things could have been dealt with differently. Some of the most poignant lessons have come from encounters with some of the poorest people in the world: the stoicism with which they accepted their fate; the dignity with which they handled adversity; and the generosity of spirit they demonstrated even when materially they had very little to share. They have all enriched my life in so many ways, but this realization is a much belated one.

As I write these words I have on my desk the latest and perhaps the last piece of writing by the ailing Gabriel Garcia Marquez "if for an instant God were to gift me with a piece of life, possibly I wouldn't say all I think, but rather I would think of all that I say . . ." For some unknown reason my thoughts go back to that old supervisor and my fellow interns of yesteryears, who are all by now well-placed experts in their own right. My erstwhile colleagues shake their heads in dismay at the "wrong" choices I have made in life . . . and I often wonder, how well did they preserve their spiritual and emotional self in the process of becoming the ultimate professionals?

I also need to acknowledge that the issues underlying my struggle are in no way unique. Many other clinicians have struggled with these dilemmas as well—but all wait for someone else to tell their story before they are ready to share their own. And for many, the years of withholding emotions have taken their toll. It is no small coincidence that despite devoting their best years to clinical medicine, they have now decided to move away from it. They all feel that the system failed them, but for those within the system, we were a bunch of failures anyway.

21
Personal Integrity and the High Road

Fred Bemak

I was in disbelief and at first couldn't put all the pieces together. An important meeting with the superintendent of schools of a large urban district that had been scheduled for 3:00 p.m. had been held at 10:00 a.m. What had happened that the meeting actually took place five hours earlier? As I stood in the foyer outside the superintendent's office speaking with the executive administrator, I heard the story unfold. "We had heard that you just couldn't make it," he told me. "Sorry you were busy and had that conflict." I was shocked. Probing further, he shared that my colleague had changed the meeting time 3 weeks earlier. I had never been informed.

As I drove back to my office, I was in disbelief. It was such an outrageous act on the part of my colleague that it was hardly believable. Even after hearing this from the executive administrator, I was still doubtful. "Maybe it was my oversight after all," I thought. "Let me double check, just to make sure." Rechecking my appointment book, it was clearly written, "3:00—superintendent of schools." Still not wanting to take the leap prematurely, I went back to emails with my colleague, the superintendent, and other key participants in the meeting.

Once again, the 3:00 time checked out. Finally, as a last check, I called a close colleague from the public school system who had planned to attend the meeting. "Yes, we had the meeting at 10:00. I was surprised you weren't there. I heard about the time change a few weeks ago from your colleague, and it was clear that you were requesting the change and would be attending the meeting." He went on to say, "Your colleague indicated that you were busy and wouldn't be able to attend. In fact, I got the impression that you were going to step back from this project given other commitments. I was surprised since you really got this thing off the ground."

Hanging up, I was speechless and angry. It was not only certain that my colleague had changed the original appointment time of the meetings but had also spoken about my lack of future involvement or interest. Sure, my colleague and I had strong disagreements, didn't like each other very much, and had completely different worldviews, but still . . . to change the time of an important meeting that I was to run and not inform me, I just couldn't believe *anyone* would do this. I'd heard rumors about this person doing things like this to others in the past to gain power and status and promote their own career but had discounted them as "stories" that were farfetched. I found myself faced with a profound dilemma about what to do with my anger, strong resentment, and growing lack of respect toward this colleague.

My career, like those of many of you who are reading this, has presented numerous personal and professional tests like the one described above. Although many of these "tests" are with clients or students, deadlines, institutional obstacles, policies that make no sense, or unsupportive and unreasonable supervisors, one of the problems that seems to cause the most difficulty is that of working with impaired colleagues. Much to my surprise, numerous colleagues have shared with me their stories of pain and anguish related to their own trials and tribulations of working with impaired colleagues. The stories abound—using clients or students for sexual liaisons, outright lies, falsifying information, attacks on one's job performance or tenure, character assignations, spreading rumors, and the abuse of one's position of power to harm others in less powerful positions.

Impaired colleagues present unique problems. For me, and the large numbers of colleagues I have spoken with, the challenge has been how to take the "high road" and stay true to one's personal integrity and core values of decency, openness, nonjudgemental stance, and respectfulness. I am reminded of two stories related to this struggle. A very close friend of mine who was quite high up in federal government has been known for her evenness, objectivity, and excellence as a professional. When faced with the highest levels of administration negatively targeting her, her demeanor and outlook slowly changed, causing great internal conflict. "I know this is wrong, but I want to get them back. I've never felt like this before, but they are trying to ruin my career, and they have the power to do it. It is just mean and vicious." She continued, saying, "I never believed I would think this, given who I am, but it is real. I'm just not sure which way to go, with my pride and honor about who I am and have been, or their way, which is down and dirty."

The second story is similar and told by a well-known counselor educator who quietly confessed to me one day that early on in her career she was so distraught and upset by a colleague's continual meanness, derision, and sexism, that after another harangue in a faculty meeting she finally threw something at this person in a meeting. "I was shocked at myself, but he was just so mean and awful." These two individuals, like so many of us, struggled with their own value systems, selfimages, beliefs, and sense of personal integrity while living in harmful and malicious professional environments.

I would suggest that tests of this sort present themselves to us throughout our entire careers and set the tone for our professional, and to a large extent, personal lives. I remember my own first professional hurdle I faced as an undergraduate student that dramatically changed my perception of the professional world. This situation posed a great dilemma and much consternation, yet in retrospect, set the course for facing future similar difficulties. I was directing a university-based student volunteer program that sent out volunteers to work in a psychiatric hospital in the Boston area. The program had over 120 student volunteers and 15 paid psychology graduate students who provided weekly consultation to small groups of 8 volunteers. It was a highly successful program with tremendous opportunities for growth and expansion. In the position of director, I was in an admirable position of playing with new and exciting ideas to enrich this program and provide more service to the community. As a young and eager undergraduate student, I approached the hospital and mental health administrators to propose an extension of this program—a community-based component that would follow up with clients in the community as well as work with youths exhibiting drug and alcohol problems in an innovative prevention model. I was somewhat awed meeting with administrators who all had joint appointments at a revered university, worked at the prestigious university-based hospital, and seemed so knowledgeable.

The administrators were very interested in my proposal and asked me to return the next week to discuss details. Excitedly, I returned the following week to finalize the proposal. Yet, there was a turn of events. Their support was unanimous until, much to my surprise, these "distinguished and accomplished" professionals candidly told me that they wanted to ingratiate the police and wanted my student volunteer program to work in the community and report the names of youths using drugs as we would have easier access to the community. I can still remember my shock and confusion at being asked to assist and support a project that was contrary to my beliefs and values. Shaken and bewildered, I told them "No," despite their persistence and promise for more access, support, and resources for other programs. In retrospect, this laid a foundation for my career, to not get sidetracked, seduced, or professionally bullied by others. I believe now that if I had agreed to the offers of money and additional programs (which I never requested), in return for this "small" favor, my professional life would have been quite different, and future stories would have very different endings.

It has been very interesting and sometimes painful as I have continued on my journey. I have professionally experienced colleagues who were jealous, vindictive, competitive, and hostile, similar to professionals that my friends in government and counselor education faced. It is a story I hear repeatedly from colleagues that generates a deep-rooted conflict—who I am versus what I feel toward mean, angry, and unethical people. This presents us with an added dilemma being in the counseling field, one that ideally produces insightful, aware, and collegial professionals. As one of my former doctoral students who was experiencing vindictive peers naively asked me, "How can people in counseling do this and be this way? It just doesn't fit." With difficulty, I had to explain that in my experience simply being a counselor didn't automatically translate into goodness, kindness, caring, integrity, and honesty.

I have thought about that student's statement many times over the years and do wonder about the personal and emotional cost as well as the potential to drift from our sense of integrity and values. It is clear to me on the basis of my own experiences and stories of others that all counselors are not nice, honest, or decent people, a realization that is difficult to accept. One place where I worked had a small cluster of individuals who routinely did things such as change the departmental minutes to support their positions, rearrange meeting times without informing others in order to maintain control over decisions and votes, make racist or sexist comments in private and then deny them, abuse their power by bullying students, and even write numerous private memos to administration attacking junior faculty's behavior and tenure, making up stories that had no basis in truth. To work in a world like this for me, and for most of us, is intolerable and against everything we believe. And yet, we are always left with the ultimate choice of what to do with our own strong reactions to such negativity and destructiveness.

Although it is sad to be presented with these challenges from other professionals, I don't think it is a "bad" thing as the truth is that people and professionals come in all forms and types. It is simply life. What is more important here is what we do when confronted with these issues. How do we maintain a sense of balance and integrity when others aren't "playing fair" or by the rules? It is my firm belief that we must stay true to ourselves and our own values. At the end of the day, we are living with our own thoughts, feelings, and actions. Taking the high road and maintaining personal integrity, even in the face of the highest forms of negativity, is a virtue that can only be rewarded deep inside oneself. From my own experience I would simply say that it's worth it. Stay the course—take the high road.

Part V

Cultural Clashes

22
Growing Up Biracial

Leah Brew

So many factors have contributed to bringing me to the profession of counseling, and as I have been confronted with different challenges, my counseling interests have changed with them. However, my first and most difficult life challenge forged a path to counseling for which I am eternally grateful. I survived ignorance and racism in elementary school.

In order to understand some of my path, I need to start with some background information. I was born as an only child in Japan, to a Japanese mother and a Caucasian-American father. We moved to Texas when I was nearly a year old. My mother was excited about becoming an American and had no interest in passing down her Japanese heritage to me. She wanted me to be 100% American. Of course, her culture affected me in many ways in spite of her efforts.

I had no idea that I looked different until we moved from a medium-sized town to a very small one. To my knowledge, we were the only minorities in the area, and I came to this conclusion because I was the only non-White person in my small, elementary school of about 75 children. I remember being impressed that when people met my mother, they knew she was *my* mother. I wondered how they knew; of course, it was because she was Japanese, but at the time I was absolutely unaware of ethnic differences. Everyone in my world had been Caucasian until middle school. I did not know my mother had an accent or looked different from other people . . . she was just my Mom.

I did not realize that I looked different until I changed schools in the middle of the third grade. Many children made fun of me for being different, for having small eyes. I was also quite tall, so I couldn't hide from anyone. They called me Chinese in the cruel way that 8-year-olds do so well. I heard over and over again, "Chinese, Japanese, dirty knees, look at these!" I specifically remember going home and asking my mother if I was Chinese. When she told me I was Japanese, I was so relieved. I thought that everything would be fine, but it wasn't. They continued to make fun of me for what felt like years.

I felt defective by being different. I was ashamed of my heritage, and I felt ugly. For three years, I only played with kids in the neighborhood who were told to play with me, and we played infrequently together. Mostly, I spent time alone in my room at home. I barely passed school. I had daily headaches and almost weekly migraines. I was miserable, depressed, and suicidal. I would try to starve myself to death to punish everyone for hurting me, but then I would get hungry and eat. Thank goodness!

You might expect that my parents should have noticed something was wrong, but I later learned that they did not understand the extent of my depression. They just thought I had difficulty adjusting to a new school. Furthermore, they were involved in their own struggles. My father had been in a car accident and had sustained a serious head injury. In retrospect, he was fighting his own depression and suicidal ideation. My mother had never wanted to be a mother and because of her upbringing was more focused on teaching me to be independent rather than providing me with empathy. Neither of them had experienced racism or discrimination in any way, so this never crossed their minds. When I tried to talk with them about how I was treated at school, they minimized my feelings by telling me I was overreacting. Furthermore, my mother was struggling with her marriage because of my Dad's depression and his way of coping by becoming a workaholic.

Then something changed. In the sixth grade, a new student moved from the Northeast where there was more ethnic diversity. She and I became great friends. She didn't seem to notice that I was defective. At the same time, I had an extraordinary teacher who would accept nothing but my best and did this with great empathy. He required that we all read a self-help book as a homeroom project. I hated reading, but I wanted to please this teacher. So I chose a popular self-help book from a transactional analysis orientation. I actually understood it, and for the first time I experienced real empathy. The author seemed to understand my pain. I realized I was not alone. As a result, I became a voracious reader of self-help books. Over the next several years I probably read 10 or 15 books on cognitive therapy, transactional analysis, psychoanalysis, gestalt theory, and existential theory. It was at that point that I decided to become a psychologist. . . . I didn't know about counseling yet. I was going to help teenagers like me. I was going to let them know that they were not alone, and I was going to give them the support that they may not be receiving at home. However, I still assumed that I was defective in some way by being biracial.

By high school, I had assimilated, had made some friends, and seemed to be functioning as a normal teenager involved in many extracurricular activities. However, my parents were going through a divorce, so outside of school I kept myself isolated. In college, I majored in psychology. I had to pay for my own school, so I worked full-time, and with a busy schedule, I stayed mostly isolated. It was terribly difficult, and I didn't particularly like what I was learning in psychology. I know now that it was because the professors were primarily from a behavioral orientation, and that didn't fit with what I wanted to do. Furthermore, the information I was learning did not seem to address the struggles I had experienced. I was discouraged about my future.

After college, I got married to a man from Thailand, and this was where I had to face racism once again. The people in my life and in the area were still primarily Caucasian-Americans at the time. So occasionally we had difficulty when shopping at upscale stores, buying cars, and so forth. My husband was an avid golfer, and we had joined a country club. He would frequently be unable to get onto the golf course. We could get seated at the country club restaurant, but we received poor service. At first, we thought we were experiencing ageism because the other members, who were mostly older, would come in and leave before we would get a menu, but at last we realized that it was, in fact, racism we were experiencing. These struggles amplified my feelings of being defective, of looking ugly. We did not know how to deal with it, so we quit our membership at the country club and only frequented places that would give us good service.

While married, I started working for a major company in a large city where the staff was ethnically diverse. After several months, I began to feel a sense of belonging to the group with whom I worked. However, in spite of building some relationships, I hated the work. In addition, my marriage was failing because my husband was addicted to cocaine. After several years with this company, I decided to go back to school. I sought career counseling and found that I still wanted to become a therapist. The career counselor introduced me to counselor education, and so I applied and was accepted to a nearby university.

Being in a counselor education program forced me to work on so many issues from childhood, some that I didn't even know existed. It was in my graduate studies that I learned about diversity issues and was relieved that it wasn't just me; it was a cultural phenomenon, which I needed to learn how to manage. I was able to finally build my self-esteem and not see myself as defective, but rather as different.

I divorced, and I fulfilled my wish to become a therapist. I loved the work. I was so impressed with the beauty of every person without his or her masks. I wondered what prevented people from becoming authentic. Why did we wear masks or focus on the outward appearances of others? I was impressed with watching people survive great difficulties and bloom into beautiful flowers in spite of challenges. The potential for self-actualizing tendencies was being proven to me over and over. However, I also found while working on my internship, that I missed school. I became acutely aware of my limitations as a therapist.

At the invitation of two professors, I chose to obtain a doctoral degree. During this program, I continued to build my skills as a therapist and to work on my personal development as well. I joined a gestalt-training group where I further worked on my issues while learning to be a gestalt therapist. The combination of this extracurricular group and my formal education has given me confidence as a person and as a therapist that I do not take for granted. Between my master's and my doctorate, I have taken more than 20 hours of extra courses. I am still hungry. I want more. As a result, I decided to use this degree to teach in a university so that I will have the freedom and motivation to continue learning. I will also have the opportunity to learn more about and advocate for diversity awareness.

So here I am; I am finishing my doctorate this summer, I hope, and I am going to a start a new position as a full-time lecturer. I will be moving to an area that is full of ethnic diversity, and I think that I am as excited about the diversity as I am about the position. I did not think it was possible, but I am so happy, happy to embark on my new career, and happy to fully enjoy my life. I only wish I could put these feelings in a pill that I give to my friends, family, and clients so they know their own potential for happiness. Perhaps I'll find a way . . . .

23

Combating Racism: Speaking Up and Speaking Out

Rita Chi-Ying Chung

My connecting flight was already delayed 4 hours because of weather. I was tired and hungry at this late hour, sitting alone in a restaurant in the airport in Houston. Tiredly eating my sandwich, I overheard someone at the next table say, "Chinese?" Then I heard the all too familiar comments and laughter, "Ching, chong, Chinamen." I looked up at a group of adolescents making the comments and taking sideways glances at me. As I turned my head toward them they looked away, still giggling and laughing. As I gritted my teeth, the emotions of degradation took over, the anger, the annoyance, and the disappointment of once again being faced with ignorance, intolerance, and bigotry.

I knew that even though I was tired and hungry, I had to deal with this. I quickly pondered about the most effective and positive way of handling this. I realized looking at the t-shirts of the adolescents that they belonged to a group. I noticed the adult supervisors wearing the same shirts, wearily sitting on the floor near the restaurant's opening. Standing up, I walked over to the supervisors, who were sitting on the floor holding onto a large, 3-foot trophy and explained what had happened. They were horrified and embarrassed, explaining to me that their group had just won the "good character" award at a national Christian youth weekend and shouldn't be acting that way. They hastily expressed their profound apologies and stood up to go over to the table of adolescents, promising to confront their behavior. I walked away, back to my gate to wait for the weather to clear.

It is these regularly occurring incidents of racism, which can happen at any time and in any place, that prompted me to write this article. Sharing this personal story and journey is difficult for me, being Chinese, as "loss of face" makes it difficult for me to "put my story out there in public." However, I have decided to take the step and share my story with the hope that it will assist others in finding their way.

Although racism has been discussed and addressed in the counseling field with great frequency, I am still struck by the numerous comments that I hear when I talk about the experiences of racism toward Asians and Asian Americans. Typical comments I hear are, "Really, Asians experience racism? I find that hard to believe . . . I thought everything was fine with Asians." Because my daily experience and the experience of my Asian-American colleagues, friends, and acquaintances is not always fine, and because racism and intolerance affect all people of color, I decided to share my personal story.

After taking the first step of agreeing to write my story about the type and degree of racism I encounter and how it has affected my journey, I felt undecided about which story to talk about. There are so many stories in my life's journey, with each being intertwined and impacting the others, that have contributed to finding my way. Then, when I think I've found some direction, clarity, or understanding, yet another situation occurs that causes me to reevaluate the context and meaning of the other stories, and subsequently my life, yet once again. So, as I thought about what stories to share, it dawned on me that I am choosing small poignant moments in an everlasting process. Situations will always occur that force me to self-examine, self-analyze, and self-reflect, all of which are part of finding one's way.

Although many stories come to mind that are powerful in contributing to my personal and professional growth, I have decided to share a few incidents that I hope will assist others in similar situations. The story is about the racism that comes along with being an Asian woman in the profession of a counselor educator and focuses on the intersection of ethnicity and gender. Being an Asian woman, I am often stereotyped as passive, obedient, quiet, and living up to the myth of the china doll syndrome. Often men who are seeking this type of woman will be attracted to me or other Asian women, assuming that because I am Asian I must possess such characteristics. Examples of this manifest frequently. In one university, the Chair of my department upon entering a faculty meeting told me that he can "speak for me" during the meeting. I was puzzled by this and asked why. He was insulted that I did not passively and gratefully accept his offer and questioned his generosity.

Similar situations appear in other venues. When I speak at meetings I am sometimes asked to repeat myself because I am either, according to the other faculty, inarticulate, soft-spoken, and hard to hear, or my accent is difficult to understand (having grown up in New Zealand, Hong Kong, and the United Kingdom, I have a British accent). Interestingly, a prominent counselor educator recently articulated his dissonance, hearing me give a keynote speech at a national conference. He said, "I couldn't look at you. Your accent and tone of voice didn't match with your physical appearance. It just didn't fit." This discordance is not unusual, given stereotypes and perceptions of Asian women. The striking difference is that when I am with my peers, U.S. Asian-American psychologists, they tell and applaud me for my differences from other Asian women in that I break stereotypical images, especially that of being quiet and passive, as well as speaking with a British accent!

Time and time again, I have been told that Asians do not experience racism and discrimination because they are the "model citizen or immigrants," or the "model student." This type of labeling does not praise Asians but contributes to the stereotypes and the continued racism encountered by Asians, making it more difficult to be oneself and break out of stereotypes. One Asian stereotype is that we are hard workers and exemplary mathematicians, but because of the lack of communication skills, we do not have good leadership skills. It has been interesting for me to observe how these stereotypes have affected me in the tenure process. For example, articles with coauthors are questioned. I am asked, "how much work did you 'really' do on this?" "Are you being 'carried' by the coauthor?" Other comments are contradictory but fall along the same themes. "By co-authoring, it is difficult for us to assess whether you display independent thinking." My experience tells me that this is not only related to being Asian but also a gender issue. Similarly there are issues that surface regarding my teaching. Although I have obtained high teaching evaluations that are regularly in the top 5th to 10th percentile, the question arises on my effectiveness in communicating with students. Yes, the language and accent issue again. All of these types of issues present additional challenges to the already demanding process of tenure, advancement, recognition, and professional success.

Other situations also contribute to challenges as well. In another situation, a group of faculty colleagues attempted to institute racist policies regarding the Asian international graduate students who were admitted to a highly competitive program. They constantly argued that because of these students' poor English language and written abilities (all of them had excelled on the Test of English as a Foreign Language [TOEL] tests), the Asian international students should all plan for a 3-year master's program instead of the usual 2 years. Faculty felt sure that they could impose this on the Asian students because they were confident that the Asian students would not "make any trouble" and would passively and obediently accept the situation. It also became apparent to me that the attacks on the Asian students were indirectly aimed at me. Thus, I find myself fighting not only for my own rights and fair treatment but for equity and justice for others as well.

There are many stories similar to the ones above. But instead of telling countless stories the question is what one does with these situations and what one learns. Racism is debilitating and has the potential to silence you or me. It eats away slowly and painfully at self-worth, self-confidence, and self-esteem. In a video I show to my multicultural counseling class is a clip of a Chinese woman talking about how she deals with racism. She states "I can be invisible. . . . I have it down to a science, I am invisible to the extent that people who don't want to see me don't have to—yes, it's a response to racism." The Chinese woman describes her cultural response to racism, to be invisible and therefore to be silenced. I am tired of being invisible and will no longer be silenced. A response to the Chinese woman's comment was by an African American woman in the video, who stated "Your preference to be invisible hurts my heart, because there have been people who have shed their blood so we can be seen not as faceless people, not as people of color, but people who we are, because people have died so we can be who we are."

The African American woman's comment is the reason why I will speak out for myself and for others. A major lesson that I have learned from racism is that being invisible and being silenced are exactly the dehumanizing outcomes of racism. I cannot, in good conscience, play the game, even passively. I will maintain my integrity by not allowing racist comments, behaviors, and attitudes to make me invisible and I will not be silenced. Being silenced hurts not only me but everyone around me.

Lessons I have learned are to have courage, to work through my issues, and not to let racism transform myself and others into quiet, obedient, and passive objects. Stand strong, fight for my beliefs. Racism may affect self-confidence and damage self-esteem, but it cannot take away personal dreams, hopes, beliefs, integrity, or spirit. Through racism and intolerance I have grown stronger personally and professionally. In finding my way through all that I have endured and will (unfortunately) continue to encounter, I am reinforced to excel even more. Ironically, racism has provided a philosophy for the type of work I do, that is, teach tolerance, social justice, and advocacy through my research and classroom teaching. If early in my life someone told me that I could benefit from racism I would never have believed that person. Yet racism has given me the opportunity for extensive soul-searching and has assisted me in my own growth and development. Although this experience has been a painful one, it nevertheless continues to make me a stronger person. Yes, there are days that I get tired of racism and don't want to deal with it. However, I'm even more tired of being invisible and silenced. Instead of letting racism win, like a master of kung fu, I will turn racism against itself and continue to speak up and speak out.

24

Sometimes I Can't Tell
My Arm From My Leg

R. Terry Sack

he view from my hotel window out across the Cochabamba valley is
truly magnificent. In every direction rise the distant peaks of the surrounding Andean mountains. On a nearer hilltop stands a huge
white statue of Christ. Brightly illuminated by night, it overlooks the city
of Cochabamba and its roughly 500,000 inhabitants. Proud Bolivians repeatedly inform us that the statue is taller and bigger than its older coun-
terpart that looks down on Rio de Janeiro in Brazil.

Undoubtedly, most American-born counselors would expect to have
an interesting cultural experience if they were to find themselves plunked
down here in the middle of South America. Indeed, they would be correct. Quechua- and Aymara-speaking Bolivian natives, many still wearing
traditional multicolored clothing, are a regular part of the street scene.
Their dress, languages, and lifestyles provide vivid contrasts to other
Bolivians who dress in modern day clothes, who use automated teller ma-
chines and cellular phones, and who cruise the city's narrow streets in the
latest model sport utility vehicles.

This is also an environment that, unless you speak one of the two in-
digenous Indian languages, is unrelentingly Spanish. The problem of
finding one's way down unfamiliar streets pales in comparison to the
stress of constantly communicating in a foreign language. Only a few
Bolivians have some limited knowledge of English. For the rest—this includes customs officials, baggage handlers, taxi drivers, hotel staff, wait-
ers, shopkeepers, teachers, and university professors—it is Spanish,
Spanish, and more Spanish. I would like to share a little of what this kind
of an "immersion" experience feels like. I think there are lessons here for
all monolingual American counselors who work in environments with

non-English speaking or limited-English speaking students or clients. It also speaks to the great national educational debate over bilingual education in our schools.

A colleague and I have been here in Cochabamba for nearly 6 weeks now. Rotary International is sponsoring our trip. We are giving a series of talks on modern day counseling theories and techniques to psychology majors at one of the local universities. In addition, we have also spoken to staff from several group homes who work with "street kids" to try to help them put their lives back together. All of these presentations are done in Spanish and without a translator. Our Spanish is pretty good but far from perfect. For example, one night, after lecturing to the students for nearly an hour in Spanish about sexual abuse, I pointed directly to my arm and said in very clear Spanish, "No vean aqui mi pierna?" ("See my leg here?") Their quizzical looks only strengthened my efforts to communicate. "You know, this LEG here," I practically shouted as I continued to point emphatically at my arm. Several more awkward moments passed before I was finally able to realize just how publicly I was embarrassing myself. This is not the only example I could give of what I call "language overload." At these moments, one's mind works about as well as an engine without oil. Fortunately, on this occasion, the students and I ultimately had a good laugh over my goof of not knowing my arm from my leg.

Other "Spanish-only" situations, from this and previous visits, have generated far more anxiety and stress. We have dealt with lost luggage; airplane flights that are delayed to the next day; passports that get stamped with the wrong date and year of entry into the country; items confiscated by overzealous customs agents; calls home that won't go through; and unexpected street demonstrations. It's pretty clear that the more that is weighing on the situation, the more anxious we become about our ability to understand and to be understood. Of a more intermediate nature are activities like verifying luncheon dates and meeting times, getting directions, and so forth. In any case, it is hard to get over those nagging doubts: "Did I really hear what I thought I heard?" and "Did I really tell them what I was trying to say?" Chances are the same interactions in English would bring forth a lot less stress. Unfortunately, a little drop of doubt becomes an excellent lubricant for anxiety to flow in and really impair one's ability to communicate.

So we struggle with these difficult situations and have our occasional language lapses. At the same time, it should also be clear that we have a degree of language fluency and an educational background far exceeding that of most newly arrived immigrants to the United States. If Spanish, at times, feels unrelenting to us, what must it be like for elementary students in our classrooms as they struggle all day to understand their monolingual American teachers and counselors? Like the non-American children in the lunchroom who want to sit and converse with their "own kind," my colleague and I have most of our meals together and can relax and converse in English. At least here in Bolivia we aren't hassled by someone saying, "this is a Spanish-speaking country, so speak Spanish."

I learned Spanish the hard way, as an adult. Few Americans seem to realize that it takes thousands of hours of contact with a second language in order to become fluent. Advertisements for language materials that purport to teach another language in "Six Easy Lessons" only serve to perpetuate this myth. Sadly, American schools still don't seem to be particularly good places to learn languages, either. Only a few American students of foreign languages actually master them while they are in school. The results of all this are fairly predictable. When we don't learn as fast as we think we "should," we become disappointed and disillusioned and blame ourselves for our failure. Because our failure is a personal one, it means that we can still hold to the idea that others, for example, non-English speaking immigrants, can and should learn English in a short period of time.

Unfortunately, more often than not, these same concerns apply to those well-meaning language "short courses" that are offered for mental health professionals, police officers, firefighters, hospital workers, and other emergency personnel. After all, it is not a lot of help to be able to ask a person in their native language, "How are you feeling?" and then not be able to understand even the gist of their response. However, to the extent that the focus of this type of training is "cross-cultural" rather than purely language lessons, it may be of some limited value.

As our time in Bolivia draws to a close, I can see that I'm going to miss this picturesque view from my window. In spite of the stress, immersion has been good for my Spanish. It's also been good to have some "language breaks," so I'm thankful for CNN International on the television and relaxing conversation in English with my good traveling buddy. I'll probably still confuse one part of my anatomy with another during my next trip here. But, in the meantime, I'm also going to have a lot more empathy and patience for everyone who is trying to learn to speak my native language. These 6 weeks of living and working with Bolivians have also helped me find my way to a deeper understanding and appreciation of their language and their culture, and I'm delighted to be taking that home with me.

25

Honoring Moments and Processes

John McCarthy

Same world, different planet. Or so I initially thought in the midst of my 5-week sojourn to rural, southeastern India nearly 5 years ago. As a beginner to the field of counseling psychology, the world of relationships in this country fascinated me. "Welcome to India and the World of Arranged Marriage," I said to myself a week or so into the adventure.

Oh, sure, I had lived and traveled overseas before. I had experienced various customs and witnessed what were, to me, unusual and strange rituals. I had slept on the floors of huts while trekking in the mountains of northern Thailand. I had sold lottery tickets door-to-door in Dublin. I had witnessed parades worshipping local gods in my neighborhood in Taipei. And on top of these, I had taken a multicultural counseling course. I considered myself "culturally aware."

How wrong I was.

And I had some pretty strong reactions, surprising ones at that, around the concepts of dating and marriage. Sure, I thought to myself, the idea of "partnering" was common in most every culture. The process in India, though, was a world apart from what I had seen or heard. In this patriarchal society where, I was told, 90 percent of marriages were arranged, a premium was built around "compatibility."

"You Americans have it wrong," a man married for 25 years told me. "In your country, it's love-live-marry. First you fall in love, then maybe live together, and finally get married. In our culture, it's marry-live-love. We get married because we're compatible and then, through living together, the love develops."

My instantaneous ethnocentric reaction was one of alarm and defensiveness. "Wait a second," I yelled inside. "We *Americans* have it wrong? What about a person's freedom to choose? How different would this country be if it were more like American society?" Unlike the commercial that espouses "Be Like Mike," I was finding the American system of "pick your own partner" to be correct and was internally urging them to adopt our system.

I found people who were adamant about the concept of arranged marriage, despite my protests. The stories offering anecdotal support for arranged marriages continued. One middle-aged Indian business person related the story of his arranged marriage.

"Only one thing was important to me: She had to be able to speak good English," he explained. The man eventually married a distant cousin and has been happily married for 21 years.

"I really didn't even have to meet her before agreeing to marry her," he said. "Obviously, I knew all about her family, her upbringing, and her education. I just wanted to know that she was fluent in English."

"Besides why should I get together to talk with her? I knew I'd have to listen to her for a lifetime anyway," he offered with a hearty laugh.

Finally, one similarity to the American system, I thought to myself: Men joking about the stereotype of their female partners talking more than they do. Yet another difference was around the corner, leading me to question the "legitimacy" of cultural differences further. Premarital dating was frowned upon.

"You see, dating is not accepted here," one professor of psychology told me. "To be involved in a love affair with a girl takes a lot of mental attention away from the student, and he won't be able to concentrate on his studies."

He maintained that attraction to a student in a different caste only compounded the problem. Even if the two students belong to the same caste, the situation was far from perfect. Financial conflicts often arose, especially from the parents of the male involved in the nonarranged relationship.

"Boys get a lot of dowry here," he went on. "In the love [nonarranged] marriage, you don't get a dowry." He added that "love affairs" were present in about half of the cases in which the presenting problem was a lack of concentration on studies.

I could only shake my head and chuckle to myself as I left my meeting with him. The word "dowry" conjured images of colonial America in my mind. The concept of dating taking much "mental attention" was similarly amusing in that it sounded like a nine-to-five job, not the enjoyment with which I perceived it. And, finally, "love affairs" bringing down college students' grades was laughable to me in that moment.

After all, dating was an integral part of college, wasn't it? Or does it have to be? According to some Indians, the premarital dating of "love marriages" leads to boredom.

"Most of [the excitement] is over," one husband explained. "She's told everything about herself. He's told everything about himself. After a while you have nothing else to say. Everything is finished by the time you marry. There's nothing new to find out about your spouse. Here [in arranged marriages] everything is new. Every step is new."

My mind darted back to the clients with whom I had counseled in practicum, particularly those who worked on relationship issues. Would they not have even struggled with such things in India? I thought of married friends in America. Perhaps they were serious when they jokingly talked about their marriages being boring. This concept in India became more and more intriguing.

One Indian man took the issue back to the foundation of compatibility. "In arranged marriage there is a saying: 'You marry and then you start loving.' That is why it works," he said.

Slowly my cultural blinders were melting in the warm February sun. Perhaps my individualistic mindset needed some rearranging, as I rethought the value of autonomy in my freedom in choosing a partner and the contrasting importance of family and community in collectivist societies. Arranged marriages began to make some sense. If, as some research indicated, people married people similar to themselves, then maybe the Indian system provided a nice shortcut in the partnering process. Perhaps, too, when it comes to partnering, Father and Mother do in fact know best.

Five years later I find myself continuing to digest this experience and its meaning to me as a counselor struggling to find my way. The Indian lesson has spurred me to become even more sensitive to the cultural portion of my counselor and educator development. I've come to honor moments and processes to much greater extents. The word *namaste*—in part honoring the place in the universe where one resides—makes much clearer sense to me now. I more deeply understand that more than one way, and oftentimes many more ways, to do one thing exists and that various cultures have various creative solutions in developing answers to social issues. Whether "arranged marriage" or "love marriage," they both work in respective cultural ways.

In my attempt to become a multiculturally competent counselor, I continue to learn lessons about myself as I look back at a lifetime of experiences. From growing up in small town America to having rich experiences internationally, a vast amount can—and will continue—to be gained about my own cultures, biases, and values.

Finally, the whole theme of arranged marriages opened my eyes to a broader perspective, for I now see the words *arranged* and *arrangement* in a different light. I previously disliked them. My connotation of the words was one that involved rigidity and a total lack of personal control. I've come to realize, however, that we each live in our own personal, familiar "arrangements" in life. In India I discovered myself comparing my arrangement with those in that country. I reacted, processed, and eventually grew to understand and appreciate. My own cognitive arrangements of cultural beliefs, relationships, marriage, and life began to crumble and to be rebuilt in a more accepting way. I can only believe that this will help as I find my way as a counselor and educator.

Maybe, just maybe, "arrangements" may not be so bad after all.

26
Unlearning Racism: A White Counselor's Journey

Stuart F. Chen-Hayes

I remember after graduating from my master's program in counseling feeling that I had learned well the traditional theories and techniques of counseling and had something to share with clients. My first job, as a residence hall director, however, proved that I knew little about issues of race, ethnicity, and culture. I had graduated from a master's of education counseling program in 1987 in which multicultural issues were rarely discussed and no multicultural coursework was available (although at the time I'm not sure I would have taken it as an elective). My first job became my classroom, and I became the student as my clients, supervisees, and colleagues challenged me in finding my way to unlearn racism.

Actually, I learned not to question the racial status quo in my graduate program, where my classes were taught exclusively by White faculty and where all but two or three students were White. I learned to accept my many privileges as a White person in the United States. Although I knew racism was wrong, I had only experienced racism from a distance—intellectually. I had little experience with the emotional side of racism and how it hurts both the target of oppression (in the United States, people of color) and the oppressor (White persons).

When I arrived at my first job, I remembered feeling that I adequately answered questions in the interview about how I handled issues of racism. What I hadn't expected was to find that so many of my supervisees and colleagues were persons of color. Although I was excited about learning more about persons different from me, I didn't expect to be confronted so strongly about my own racism.

There were many incidents as I attempted to find my way. One day in a meeting with other residence hall directors, the meeting was particularly tense. One colleague, an African-American man who directed the residence hall, specializing in programming and cultural events for persons of color, was especially angry during the meeting. I was tired of his outbursts and said I was tired of his "wearing his race on his sleeve" all the time. The silence in the room was deafening. He responded it was all he could do to keep from coming across the room and punching me out at that moment. I was in shock, frightened, and unable to figure out what I had said or done to cause such rage.

A year later I had employed a staff of resident assistants who were all students of color, including persons of African American and Asian American ethnic and racial identities, along with one Jewish resident assistant. During the year, a White resident attempted to sexually and racially assault one of the women of color on my staff. I was able to be supportive of her and the ordeal that the student, the university, and the police put her through, and we were able to get that student out of university housing. What I wasn't prepared for, however, was to see a pattern of institutionally racist and sexist events occur in the ways the university and the police department handled the situation. I felt very stuck and had grave difficulty doing much more than validating her fears and anger. She needed a stronger systemic response to the secondary victimizations that she felt from the university's slowness and the police department's callousness and insensitivity. I didn't know how to fight the system on her behalf. I felt ashamed that I couldn't be more helpful.

That same year, I hired a woman of color to replace a White woman who I had fired for smoking marijuana with her residents. I immediately felt that the woman I had hired and I were at odds and I couldn't figure out why. I was baffled by her aloofness and coldness toward me. At the time, she seemed angry at all White people. I tried hard to win her over and failed miserably. I found myself in power struggles with her, and I was shocked and disappointed at my inability to connect with her. I wish that I had known about models of racial identity development at that time. She was in a cultural immersion period where she was proud of her own culture and deeply devaluing of anything and anyone White, particularly a White man in a position of power over her.

Through these incidents, I began to shift my thinking about racism and my own journey. I began to see that I was responsible for being racist and that I had to deal with my own emotions and racial identity. I moved on in my career to a new job as a family counselor with primarily Portuguese immigrant families in southeastern Massachusetts. I was amazed at the variety of racial, ethnic, and cultural identities that I found in working with Portuguese immigrant families in that agency—persons of African racial identity from Cape Verde, Brazilians, persons from the

Azores, and persons from the Portuguese mainland in Europe. Yet, each family also related stories of the pain and hatred they experienced from persons of English and French ethnicities (White persons) in the United States who looked down on persons of Portuguese ethnicity or Portuguese-influenced cultures. Although I was empathic, I realized I needed much more training in how to be culturally competent in validating the varieties of ethnic identities and ongoing struggles against racism.

When I returned to graduate school, I sought a PhD program where I could be challenged about my racism and study multicultural counseling. I was thrilled to learn the concepts of ethnic identity development, world view, and oppression. These terms are central for understanding how well inculcated in dominant culture I have been as a White person. Janet Helms's work on racial identity models of White people and People of Color has especially helped me find my way as a White counselor. As a counselor, initially I was clearly in what Helms refers to as the pseudo-independent White racial status. I was the "good White liberal" of racial identity. I had intellectualized myself in a way that led me to rescind responsibility for my participation in racist acts as a White person. When I was confronted with racism, I didn't know what to do and I didn't take responsibility for my role in it. I felt alone, scared, angry, unprepared, and clueless.

Over time, however, I had the chance to reflect on what occurred. I learned that I have to be vigilant daily toward my own racist inclinations. For example, after moving to Chicago to teach counseling, one day I was walking down a city street and a man of color approached me asking for what I thought was "currency." I replied, "I'm not carrying any money." He said, "No, I'm not asking you for money, I'm asking directions for the currency exchange." I had said to myself, "Here comes this Black guy asking for change." I felt embarrassed and angry at my misinterpretation.

Racism runs deep. Although I actively work to fight racism in myself and in other White people, it is a constant struggle. I get angry when I hear White counselors say, "Oh I'm so tired of that multicultural stuff. I don't need it anyway, I'm not multicultural." Yet, we are all multicultural. For those of us with White privilege, we will never end racism in our profession and our communities until we become experts on "Whiteness," including our own racial and ethnic identities, our European worldview, the positive parts of our racial/ethnic identities, and our deficits based on racism.

I now live in a multiethnic and multiracial community in Chicago composed mostly of people of color and I teach in an almost exclusively White suburb. As a White person, I am safer living in a neighborhood composed primarily of people of color than my neighbors of color are. Also, I am safer as a White person traveling in White suburbs than are my students or colleagues of color, who are more likely to be stopped for a traffic violation or followed in a store on suspicion of stealing solely because of having dark skin. These are examples of White privilege.

Similarly, when I teach multicultural counseling and require students to attend an event as the only person of their racial identity present, the fear is palpable amongst many White students about going into a community of color for a few hours. However, after students have completed the experience—entailing a direct, personal confrontation of inner fears and White racism—they often emerge with a conviction that they can fight racism. It takes action, understanding the history of resistance to racism, acknowledging White privilege, and crossing social borders to begin the journey.

To paraphrase one economist, racism in counseling will end when White counselors, counselor trainees, and counselor educators get as angry about it as people of color have always been. When each White counselor confronts his or her own racism, lists White privileges, and uses White privilege to interrupt racism in the lives of students, clients, and colleagues of color, our profession will be anti-racist.

27

A Road to Cultural Sensitivity

Marva Larrabee

Since my teenage years I've done a lot of introspection about the meaning of events that I experience. Lately, I have used my personal introspection skills to learn from people I've met, taught, and counseled. I have been reflecting on many of the taped counseling sessions I've listened to while supervising practicum and internship students. When I've heard culturally biased remarks that students make, I've worked to help them realize they are communicating their own culturally established attitudes and behaviors to their clients. As I remember making similar remarks unintentionally, my introspection has focused on how I became aware of the potential negative client interpretations that are implied in specific verbal interactions. Knowing the importance of becoming more culturally sensitive led me to look back on my own road of learning the subtleties of interaction that convey varying levels of cultural sensitivity. I'm grateful to an African American colleague who helped shed light on that process. The conversations we shared focused me on interpreting my specific cultural background to better understand others and to keep myself growing in self-awareness. Three specific events were the first ones that came to mind as milestones on my road toward cultural awareness.

Years ago I was teaching mathematics to 7th- and 8th-grade inner-city students. I came to grips with the fact that I didn't know what it was like to be poor or to be African American. I had been fascinated with cultural diversity since the summer before my senior year in a racially segregated high school. That fascination grew into an appreciation for the great diversity within and between various groups of people. I looked back in time to identify my first verbal interactions with an African American, which took place during my teenage years.

The summer before I was a high school senior, I went to summer school at the only high school in the district offering typing courses at that time. The first day of class I became aware of the unique experience this venture into an unfamiliar school would be for me. I arrived early and noticed a large group of White students standing outside the typing classroom. I saw nobody I recognized; therefore, I entered the room to obtain a front row seat. Only one other student was seated, but several students were sitting in the back of the room. My naive mentality quickly turned rational when I realized the student by the window in the front row was African American. I walked straight down the center aisle and chose to sit at the desk beside her. It became obvious that comments were being made by other students as I introduced myself to her and asked her why she was taking the class. Deep inside I was outraged at the absurdity of students focusing on us and not choosing their seats until the teacher entered the room. Because the room was not full, I was also pretty amazed that desks behind us were left empty. It was clear that we would be sitting alone.

My conservative religious background and family traditions were strongly entrenched in the belief that all people are created equal and that things that are unjust should be rectified. My personal steps that day opened many discussions between me and my classmate from Booker T. Washington High School. We discovered many similar preferences and activities and were able to compare notes about how different we felt from our respective classmates.

Every day I am grateful for the openness I experienced those few weeks during that summer. The experience led me to a level of awareness that began with curiosity and evolved over time into a deep commitment to taking action to bridge the gap of misunderstanding that exists between people in general and especially between people of different colors and races. Over many years I've reflected on a multitude of similar encounters where my desire to learn about the culture of individuals who differed from me was paramount in my development of greater sensitivity. I focused on finding similarities and differences between myself and others through listening to another person's perspective and suspending my opinions. I became aware of the fact that if I had been born and raised as that specific individual, I would quite likely be thinking and behaving as that person does. My task was always to understand cultural backgrounds and appreciate new aspects of the life experiences of those that I met.

Through my history of dealing with change and learning from as many life experiences as I can process, I've learned that examining my initial awareness in new situations is a critical component of being a life-long learner. I'm still fascinated by similarities and differences between people and their culture. New experiences are learning adventures for me, and I've grown from being open to learning from people I encounter who are from diverse cultural backgrounds.

When I took my first counseling course and became aware of the process we label as developing empathy, I was at ease with the concept when it seemed foreign to many of my classmates. I realized that on the basis of previous experiences, I could operationalize unique aspects of my Caucasian culture. I appreciated the fact that any other person who I encounter has evolved over many years into the person with whom I'm interacting. I can't second-guess, read the mind, or give advice to any person in initial encounters. My first goal must be to listen and learn. That's what I did as a high school senior, and I'm still deriving great joy from the learning that occurs when I encounter each new person in any context. Certainly this is the perspective and self-awareness that was salient in finding my first African American friend.

I was raised in Oklahoma and have spent several months there in the last year. Going home to the culture in which I was raised has helped me to reflect on the most important aspects of my career. Living in a state where Native American tribal business still makes front page news, I place great emphasis on the process of doing everything I can to "walk at least a mile in another person's moccasins." Early on I concluded that this is the best way to begin relationships, and it is essential to counseling and supervision relationships. I know meaningful learning begins with self-awareness of my potential cultural biases and the ability to suspend judgment, to step into another person's shoes. I am confident that this step of understanding one's own culture is the beginning of culturally sensitive behavior. Over time, the capacity for intimacy results in my best lessons.

One example is a teaching experience in which I used my personal vulnerability as a classroom learning exercise. Just prior to entering an afternoon class I taught on basic counseling skills, I called the veterinarian to check on my 17-year-old cat. I was shocked to find that my precious companion who had seen me through divorce and career changes was dead. The grief that swept over me was undeniable. At first I thought I couldn't teach, but for many years I had valued dealing with emotions straight on. This awareness led me to decide to make that class a realistic learning opportunity for students. With tears in my eyes, I faced the students and said, "It is probably obvious to you that I'm quite emotional at this moment. Therefore, I'd like for you to be my counselor. I'll be your client because I truly need some help right now. Your job is to help me."

As the class asked questions and demonstrated other counseling skills, I revealed my loss and grief. The peak moment of the experience occurred after about 15 minutes when I stated that I had just learned of the death of my cat. When several members of the class started to laugh, I couldn't hide the hurt that penetrated the existing emotional wound. I stopped the session and struggled to be the teacher to assist students in processing the effects of that laughter on me as their client. The power of the learning took place in the class discussion in which the students identified presumptions underlying the laughter and the cultural roots that were unique to them as individuals. Because I could be "real" with them, I provided an unusual learning experience regarding unintentional biases and the need to develop self-awareness of reactions to others. Several White students talked to me later to thank me for helping them to see that as Caucasians they were unaware of how their cultural background impacted their work.

It is rewarding to discover that I am becoming more culturally sensitive as I process my life events on a continuing basis. When I've left my comfort zone and examined my behavior in light of my unique cultural background, I'm motivated to thank all those people who helped me learn to value diversity. It all began with one friend in summer typing class.

Part VI

From
Around
the
World

28
The Face of Chaos

David Leary

I could sense a quiet almost unspeakable doubt and anxiety within me before the Olympics. Living in Sydney was like riding a roller coaster or teetering on a knife-edge. Could we do it? What would happen if it flopped? How would we deal with violence if it occurred? Does this massive country in the middle of nowhere with an almost minuscule population have the capacity to pull off such an event involving people from all over the globe?

Well it happened, almost flawlessly. We all saw the best side of Sydney, Australia: sun and sand, vistas and spectacular sunsets on the harbor, a casual lifestyle, friendship, and of course, *joie de vivre*, a joy of living in a clean, well-to-do, safe, and peaceful country. Enormous capacity on the one hand, doubt and anxiety on the other. Paradoxically, all are key features of the Australian psyche.

Ian Thorpe, the lanky Sydney-sider with the mammoth feet that propelled him into swimming history, continued to break world swimming records in the pool after the Olympics. Eighteen years of age and the world at his size 17 feet. I feel a great sense of relief and joy when I hear such stories. It somehow energizes my faith in youth as full of potential that *can* be realized.

After the Olympics, other realities began to assume their rightful place in the daily rhythm of my life. I am a counselor finding my way in the daily grind of helping homeless young people. This is an all too familiar part of the Sydney landscape.

It's a little after 10 A.M. and I'm wandering around the counseling center located in the inner city. All hours during the day, teenagers drop in for some food, a shower, a place to sleep, or a chance to talk to someone who won't beat or abuse them. I am speaking to some other staff members, but all I can hear are screams coming from the parking lot outside the center. I can hear two adolescents shouting abuse at each other. This is hardly an unusual event, but today's chaos is somehow different. For one thing, the voices are unusually loud and violent. Secondly, the argument goes on and on, moving from one end of the grounds to the other. To make matters worse, all of this occurs within earshot of a police station, a primary school, a church complex, several other kids in trouble, and a professor who just happens to be on my doctoral committee.

Verbal abuse turns to violence. The girl involved in the fight seizes a backpack from her combatant, a boy I know and recognize as her boyfriend. She slashes him repeatedly across the face until blood starts to run in streamlets. Rather than fighting back, he just stands there mute, cowering from her rage. All the rest of us are paralyzed, frozen, unable yet to respond to this spectacle.

Eventually the steam runs out of the argument when the guy retreats and runs away, muttering that he is going to kill himself. When he returns a few minutes later, he is seen to be a member of the staff. Bruised within and without, he appears shocked and confused. The girl is still screaming outside, but we are eventually able to calm her down. At this stage, it's hard to know what the fight was about. It's even harder to know where to direct restorative or any other energy.

We all continue to function but feel stunned and wounded. A number of us have tried to intervene, to stop the fracas, to keep the peace, to protect other young people, and to separate the warring parties. It's crisis mode, and all we do is restore order and prevent the resurgence of further violence. Eventually the antagonists leave. Business resumes. Other young people return to the Center to deal with their own crises. Some are HIV-positive. Some are addicted to drugs. The majority earn a living on the streets selling their bodies.

The young people seem unaffected by the events of the past 30 minutes. Could that be true? Have they become numb and blasé to the negativity in the lifestyle they lead? Or is their apparent ease really a shutdown of emotions, just another way of dealing with the external chaos and pain? Whatever their reality, I'm not okay myself, and neither are members of the team.

I can somehow understand their shutdown. I think that's what I began to do as the incident unfolded. We had a scheduled meeting of the team that afternoon and the event dominated discussion. There is no bypassing the reality that such events produce doubt and struggle in each of us at the Center. But how do we deal with this stuff? How do *I* deal with the violence, the pressure to protect, resolve conflict, and keep a team together? At the end of this particular event, I was more than anxious. I simply wanted to disappear, forget the whole thing, including my responsibilities, and gain some measure of peace.

Within this fair city there is both tragedy and the efforts of some to impact on what appears as a never-ending cycle of violence and despair. We are a small group of youth workers and counselors. For us, violence and suicide are core experiences with which we work, a daily part of our lives. What is just as difficult is the burgeoning awareness and fear on the part of many young adults that this project, their lives, may well be beyond their capacity to manage.

When I remember and ponder the day dominated by Danny and Samantha, I'm filled with uncertainty and fear. I remember a sense of panic, embarrassment, and helplessness in the face of their uncontainable rage and fury. Despite the pain it produces, I must focus on these experiences, as they contain the kernel of growth for which I constantly search.

The helplessness is perhaps the easiest to understand. I'm standing there in the open parking lot in the presence of an emotional tornado. What else could I expect to experience but helplessness? However, this is not nature at its most natural but human nature at its most tumultuous. It has agency, intention, desire, and vindictiveness. It is not of us, but we are caught up in the web created by their chaos, and we have little or no control. That sort of helplessness—being at the mercy of another's nastiness—is hard to fathom and impossible to manage, except in retrospect. Strong emotions arise, not the least of which is the desire to be nasty in return.

I have no desire to cheapen the reality normally associated with such words, but working with marginalized adolescents is like being in a war zone. The unpredictability of the people and the environment elicits a sense of helplessness that should never be downplayed. There is a secondary traumatization that comes with this territory. Not to acknowledge this is to flirt with an emotional time bomb.

During the afternoon staff meeting, the chaos of those 30 minutes filled the entire meeting, leaving all of us with a question, a thoughtful thread that reverberates still within the team. What does this experience do to *me* and to *us*? Can I forget about the clients long enough to remain with the experience and think through the consequences of exposure to such violence? Can I dare to be the person within the counselor? Can I dare to remain with the loss of control? Can I dare to see and experience the very human mess within me that is triggered by the public chaos of others? Can I dare to admit my own humanity and stay with the fact that such experiences strip away the role, any power and position, leaving only the person and my very human experience?

I began the process of becoming a counselor with a highly charged sense of wishing to be heroic, to relieve people of their misery. This was a playground for the development of denial, avoidance, and defensiveness as I increasingly discovered a flawed heroism. It was very much about *doing* and very little, at least initially, about *being*.

There is a tendency within me to ignore the personal and the ugly within me, to simply perform the task at hand. I believe I project that tendency to split off my *broken bits* into my team, and that was evident as we began to debrief from the incident. It is said that truth is found in the meeting of opposites. The truth of me is found in the blending or clashing of what feels like disparate opposites. It is this holding of opposites I struggle to nurture, but to avoid such an experience is to relinquish responsibility for my own project. So it is with my team. So it is with Danny and Samantha. But the place to begin is with me.

I will remember that team meeting for some time to come. It was feisty, challenging, but mostly a moment where, as individuals and as a group, we were called to account, to face the reality of our own humanity and to explore the feelings that generate fear and passion. What has stayed with me? That it is easier to focus on the other, the clients, than on our own experience as individuals and as a group. So what have I learned as a counselor and director in a busy inner city service? That time is of the essence. I know that change cannot be hurried. Externals can, but inner change can never be rushed. What I struggle to hold onto with alacrity is that counselors need time, even though such a commodity is always in scarce supply.

Sydney is a wonderful place to be. It is indeed made up of the images captured by the Olympics. But it is also much more. Like any individual or group, it is full of opposites, and any true vision of this fair city or its people must grapple with the opposites that are its soul. I am a counselor, but I am first and foremost David. The truth of me lies not in a black-and-white image but in my complexity, a cluster of opposites. The truth about me is gained by touching the opposites at once and attempting to occupy all the space in between. Quite a challenging journey!

29
A Kiwi Immigrant

Gerald Monk

I am a new immigrant to the United States of America and have resided here for just over a year, teaching school counseling. I am a New Zealander, otherwise known as a Kiwi, not because I identify with a brown whiskery fruit but because I am named after our national symbol, a brown, blind, pathologically shy, flightless bird. I have wanted to live in the United States ever since I was 12. For years I've been seduced by the media images of Hollywood and popular culture presented in American movies and television programs.

It is no surprise to me that I would leave a tiny, isolated, unpopulated country and move to Southern California to live amongst an exciting and fast-paced culture. After all, I moved to a country that possesses extraordinary human, material, and spiritual resources that surpass anything that has been seen before. I have joined a nation of people who are known to New Zealanders as a bit ethnocentric but passionate, intellectually curious, purposeful, and courageous risk takers.

To be honest, I am not doing a very good job finding my way right now. I don't feel on top of things at work and I have lost that initial euphoria of finally attaining my heart's desire to live in this country. While some people call it culture shock it feels to me more like a dose of unanticipated anxiety and depression. As I write these words, I am really struggling against the desire to withdraw from everybody and closet myself away. I feel an uncharacteristic anxiousness and tightness in my body. It is a shock to own up to myself that this has been my reality for the past few months. A few people have been commenting recently on how tired I look. I feel tired a lot and feel lethargic even when I am walking regularly and going to the gym twice a week. My body is healthy but my spirit is drained.

I now live in one of the most beautiful cities in the world with a temperate climate where the sun shines virtually every day. It is tough admitting to being anxious and down when from nearly every standpoint I have the perfect life. In fact how dare I be depressed! Perhaps I am in the midst of an existential crisis. I have been through many of them over the years. But it is not the kind of crisis that has me questioning the purpose of life exactly. I don't even think it's about my failure to make meaning of suffering. I am not sure of this but I think it is more about my day to day experience of trying to find my way as a professional counselor educator in a culture that I have looked at from afar, briefly visited, but have never lived in.

I have never really thought about what it means to live in a large sophisticated country in a densely populated state. To manage a complex, technologically advanced country requires a huge bureaucracy to keep track of what everybody is doing. I have never felt so regulated as I do living in this country. I often feel like I am struggling to create an identity that is more than my social security number. When I want to communicate on the telephone with any organization, I have to enter in some kind of code before someone will put me on hold while I wait my turn to be attended to amongst thousands of others. While I enjoy the anonymity of living in a large city, I miss recognizing somebody I know in the street. I miss being identified other than by the badge I wear on my jacket when I supervise students in the schools. With so much anonymity people struggle and compete with one another to be recognized, make an impact, and get noticed! Now I understand the eagerness of Southern Californians to make an impact on others with the car they drive, with the place they live. People here quickly make disclosures to total strangers in their lives in order to be seen even momentarily before they pass on by.

I live in a large apartment complex. I have neighbors all around. I get a nod and a friendly "hi" before they scurry indoors. I had this fantasy of meeting my neighbors and playing tennis down at the local court like I used to at home. I have learned that my neighbors don't want to engage in that way. It is different here. This is not home. There is simply not the time. There are too many things to accomplish. Many people I meet work at an unrelenting pace. The children, the teachers, the counselors, the administrators all have goals to fulfill and targets to reach. There are endless tests that must be passed and evaluations to deliver. Everybody must be accountable. I am accountable. I feel the weight of this accountability. Everybody must feel this weight of the performance demanded by this culture. Maybe people are used to it. My breath is shallow. My chest is tense and tight. People are on the move. There is little time to play and rest.

Everybody is working. There are few holidays for most people. How do people work these long hours without rest? Many have two jobs. The parents juggle the kids. The days are long. I am beginning to internalize the demand in this culture to consistently perform. I find myself feeling guilty if I am not delivering at the rate of everybody else around me. I feel I shall be left behind if I am not producing, creating, and writing. I must pick up my tempo even at a time when I want to fade into the background.

Right now I wish I had more answers. I am out of my depth. I am struggling to give myself permission and allow myself to not know how to find my way or to figure what the future holds. What I am grappling with is too immense for me to control or take charge of. I have rarely had the experience that I am not in control. I feel my human frailty and vulnerability in this moment. It is striking me as both a painful and useful lesson. The steps I am taking are small, humble ones. When it becomes too much, I work at noticing my breathing, feeling my steps when I am walking, and seeking to escape the tyranny of thoughts of the anticipated demanding future and the punctuated negative thoughts of failure from the past. Grim as this may sound, I am committed to this journey. In the grip of this anxiety and distress I can still feel the sun on my face, the smell of spring flowers, the sustenance of hot tea, and the taste of a shrimp burrito!

30
Through the Cultural Looking Glass

Smita Nagpal

I came to the United States to further my education. I am from New Delhi, a large metropolitan city in India. I was certainly not prepared for the personal challenges that I experience when confronted with a set of rules in the United States that was different from the ones I grew up with.

During the next 3 years I continued with my studies and started practicing the art of counseling. I struggled with the craziness of knowing that the rules that my culture had taught me were sometimes different from the rules that guided the practice of counseling in the United States. For instance, I battled with issues of time and structure. My natural clock refused to tell clients that their time was up when they were obviously still in the middle of talking about a meaningful issue. My supervisors instructed me that in order to be a good counselor, I would have to learn to end my sessions on time. In fact, my evaluation might depend on it.

I also struggled with the impersonal framework within which I was required to conduct counseling. The message I received was that my work should be conducted in a businesslike setting and that competent counselors do not get personally involved with their clients. I am from a country where the population has recently crossed the 1 billion mark. Personal space tends to be much smaller in a country with this large of a population. Cultural norms also appear to favor closer contact between people. However, my attempts at discussing the possibility of cultural differences in therapeutic boundaries did not meet with much success.

I struggled with the contradiction between my cultural inclination toward more informal relationships and the rules of my training in the United States. For instance, it was clear to me that counselors were to avoid having dual relationships with clients. I was quite uncomfortable with this mandate. It was my feeling that dual relationships might be more of a norm in the Indian cultural context. Counselors practicing in

India might meet with clients in their homes rather than at an office. Clients might be people that are known to them through relatives or friends. This perceived difference between India and the United States in the context of counseling perplexed me.

Perhaps I evolved from being a confused counselor to being more myself in therapy as a result of my interactions with clients. When I first began seeing clients, I would often engage in conversations relating to my national origin. Clients would quiz me with questions about the national language of India, my ability to speak English, why some Indian women wore dots on their foreheads, and whether or not elephants and snakes roamed the streets of India.

These conversations could go on for several minutes, until the client's curiosity was satisfied. I had started seeing myself more clearly through the differences I observed between myself and the other Rome group members and the similarities I observed between myself and the Romans. However, I had not yet fully defined my personal cultural identity. Therefore, these conversations would throw me off balance. Sometimes the power imbalance between me and the client that arose from these interactions would get in the way of a productive therapeutic relationship.

The turning point came one day when I was assigned to a family with five curious children. The issues I was attempting to deal with were serious in nature and could result in out-of-home placement for one or more of the children. Needless to say, I was not inclined to spend our time on idle chatter. The two older boys had already worked with several other counselors and were experts at distracting them from the tasks at hand. Very soon they found a topic that would save them from having to focus on other important areas, namely India.

This time, I was prepared not to let my nationality get in the way. I asked them to hold their questions and told them that if they answered my questions honestly during the therapy hour, I would give them a chance to ask me three questions at the end. Surprisingly, they agreed to my offer, and I had an eager group of children willing to answer even the most difficult questions that I asked. I felt for the first time that I had been able to use my cultural self in my work as a counselor.

From the time of this event, I have become increasingly open to staying in touch with my cultural self when working with clients. Doing so gives me access to parts of myself that I could not reach before. It increases the congruence between who I am and what I am doing with clients. When I stay in touch with myself, I ask questions that I may not have asked before. I am able to access useful ideas and images to represent what the client is saying or doing in therapy. Perhaps most important, I am able to free myself of the cultural rules that an individual client or a family brings with them. I can then present different perspectives on an issue that may open up new channels of healing.

It is a continuous challenge to stay in touch with all the different parts of myself so that I may remain congruent with my clients. I am finding that staying connected with my culture plays a critical part in remaining centered. I may do so by cooking an Indian meal, calling up a relative and talking in my native language of Hindi, sharing memories via e-mail with a childhood friend who now lives in another part of the globe, or reading a book on meditation.

I do believe it was necessary for me enter a new cultural context in order to see myself and my own culture more clearly. My experiences with the cultural differences between India and the United States were—and are—at times confusing and disorienting. The journey is by no means complete. The next step in developing personal–cultural congruence, perhaps, is to meet fellow travelers and share their tales.

31
Building Monuments and Ourselves

Gudbjörg Vilhjálmsdóttir

According to an Icelandic saying, unborn children reside in God's cap. When I used to ask my mother, "Where was I when you were a little girl?" she would answer, "You were still in God's cap." Since then, I have always pictured God with a cap on his head.

Many things happened in my family while I was still in God's cap, things that have all the same affected my life. For example, I got my first name because of a dream my grandfather had many years before I was born. His late mother came to him and asked him not to forget his sister, Gudbjörg, who died in 1906, when she was only a teenager.

When I was born, half a century later, he asked my parents to give me his late sister's name, so she would never be forgotten. As a result, I was given the few earthly possessions my great-aunt had owned; for example, an embroidery of a cat curled up on a cushion. Under it she had stitched her name—now my name. Wherever I have lived, it has always been with me. It hangs on my wall right now and I have only to turn my head to see it.

My brothers and I were always very close to my grandfather, who moved in with my family after my grandmother passed away when I was a teenager and they were little boys. The stories he told about his childhood in the barren northwestern fjords of Iceland were especially close to our hearts, not only because of the poignancy of his sister's death on Christmas Eve so many years ago, but also because of their father's tragic drowning in 1899 when my grandfather was only 8 years old.

My great-grandfather, Jóhannes, was the captain of a small fishing boat, and it so happens he was involved in one of the most important events of Icelandic history at the turn of the 19th century. As it still does today, Iceland relied heavily on fishing 100 years ago. However, the fishermen were poor, and most of them had only small, open boats, while foreign steam trawlers were starting to fish in Icelandic waters, often ruining the traditional fishing grounds with their heavy trawls.

In the first days of October, a British trawler appeared on the fjord and started fishing. The captain and his crew seemed oblivious to the fact that they were infringing on the official fishing limits. The local people couldn't do anything about it. A messenger was sent to alert the authorities, many miles away. When the governor of the region heard the news, he saddled his horse and set forth to try to stop the poachers.

When he arrived, my great-grandfather and his men were at their boat. When they brought their boat alongside the trawler, the governor demanded to be allowed to come aboard. The British sailors refused to comply. They then rammed the boat, sending all six men into the cold sea. No attempt was made to save the men despite their cries for help, until another boat came from ashore. By then, my great-grandfather and two other fishermen had disappeared into the water, never to be found again.

This event was an important one in Icelandic history, because with it began Iceland's struggle to obtain control over its fishing grounds. The final victory was achieved in 1976, three fourths of a century after my great-grandfather met his death. During all those years, this event was invoked each time we had to fight a cod war. After all, these three men were the only Icelanders to die in the whole struggle. Now it has been slowly fading from people's memories, despite the fact that Iceland wouldn't be the prosperous and affluent country it is if this battle hadn't been fought.

Seven years ago, I visited the place and went to see where my great-grandparents' house had been. I wanted to show my children where our family came from. As I stood there, looking over the fjord, thinking about how sad my great-grandmother's life had been—but also what a loving and close-knit family they were and how warmly my grandfather had always spoken of his childhood—it dawned on me that there was nothing there to remind passersby of what had happened. I said to myself, "I am one of only a handful of people that know about this battle fought between poor fishermen and foreign sailors. When I am gone, nobody will know and no one will care." I decided that something must be done to preserve the memory of this event.

Exactly 100 years after the battle, a monument was inaugurated to commemorate this event. I will never forget that day. Before the ceremony, we had a memorial service in the old country church. The story of my great-grandfather and of his family was told and people were deeply moved by the drama in the story.

My husband sometimes says jokingly to me that by telling us the tales of his childhood, my grandfather programmed me and my brothers to keep alive the memory of his father after he departed. I think he is right in a way and that by building the monument, we were doing something important, not only for my great-grandfather's memory, but also for our-selves. After all, my name is also my great-aunt's. Her story is my story too and, by bringing it to life, I am also expressing an important part of me.

The whole process was certainly a very constructive one for me per-sonally, helping me to find my way as a woman and a counselor. I think that the reason for this lies in the example of my great-grandmother. First of all, it reminded me of the value of forgiveness. There was never any ha-tred in my family toward the wrongdoers; instead, they were pitied. Another part of this legacy was the way it has influenced so many of us to go into humanitarian work. Last, but not least, I learned that difficult memories and traumatic experiences from the past can be transformed into something beautiful in which we can take pride. Because of how im-portant my past and that of my family are to me, I have been able to make something new and beautiful of it.

Maybe I am more aware of the importance of the past in constructing identity because I am an Icelander. My country probably would not exist today if it weren't for the ability of its people to find in the past the strength to go on living in our inhospitable land. Indeed, the only reason Icelanders found the courage to fight for their independence from Denmark in the 19th century was because the sagas they had conserved from the Middle Ages told them they had once been independent.

The sagas are narratives composed in the 13th and 14th centuries, when Icelandic society was going through dramatic changes. The sagas express the medieval Icelanders' preoccupation with these changes. How? By reconstructing the past. Indeed, most of the sagas are about peo-ple who lived even earlier, the distant ancestors from pagan Scandinavia, the 9th and 10th century Vikings who settled the country, and the genera-tion that decided to convert to Christianity in 1000, exactly a millennium ago. By exploring their past, the saga authors found the strength to deal with their present. Indeed, the sagas are precious works of literature, monuments to the men's and women's ability to transform human expe-rience into art.

So how did this experience help me find my way? In that fjord 7 years ago, I believe I received some sort of a calling, a very strong message that this past mustn't be forgotten. The main force behind all this was no doubt my grandfather's love for me—and through him, my love for his sister and other family members. It also brought me closer to my parents, brothers, and the culture of this family branch. Through the enthusiasm we felt together for the project, we felt love and care for one another, as we hadn't before.

It has also taught me that maybe we should teach our clients to look at what's in their past in order to build themselves. Perhaps we should en-courage them to explore their own past and that of their families, to find and identify the unfortunate things such as failure, accidents, illness, and death and to come to terms with them, recognizing that they are over, and transform them into something good. We should also point out to them the good things in their past—the treasures of dignity, strength, and love that can be found in the heritage of every family—and teach them how to value this heritage, to make of it a monument with which to construct themselves and their lives.

Part VII

Clients as Teachers

32
Mixed Missions and a Little Kid

Brent Bandhauer

As counselors, we know there will be days when we may be asked to take charge of a group of children. We are, after all, responsible adults. I'm a big man who weighs 180 pounds, confident that I can manage small and large groups of children effectively. Children need to have firm limits set in a caring and respectful manner. School counselors preach these words, so it only seems logical to practice them as well.

Recently I found myself as the only state-licensed, responsible adult on the playground where 350 first- and fifth-graders were playing after eating lunch. The administrators were busy interviewing potential teachers and appointed me to supervise the lunch recess. All went well for a while. I milled about the playground and talked with adoring first-graders about their pets and video games.

Suddenly, several children ran to me to report a fight in progress. "Not again," I thought, "why do I have to spend my precious time dealing with stupid behavior?"

When I found my way to the scene, four first-graders were swinging and swearing like sailors. Two of them stopped when I commanded, while two others continued to punch wildly. A fifth-grader grabbed one child and I put my hands on the shoulders of the other thinking he would be relieved to be stopped and settle down. The other student relaxed, but the one I intervened with escalated the struggle in my direction.

I applied the current restraint technique advocated by the school district and tried to steer him away, but he didn't want to leave. He struggled to continue fighting with the other child. Because he wouldn't walk with me and because he weighed approximately 60 pounds, I decided to carry him as if he were my own child.

When we found our way to the office, he continued to struggle furiously. I sat him in a chair and he immediately got up to run to find the other child. I stopped him and was surprised at how determined he was in his anger. He wouldn't respond to my repeated inquiries about why he wanted to hurt the other child. "Wow," I said, "he must have really done something mean to you. You are so angry." He said nothing. Each time I let him go, he attempted to run out to find the other child.

I felt completely confused. Usually I can find my way through displays of emotion by addressing the underlying issues. But what were the underlying issues? Seemingly, this child was angry at another child because of a playground conflict. Usually children in this situation will eagerly explain how they are being victimized hoping that I might punish the "aggressor."

But this child wasn't going to stop. Perhaps it wasn't the other boy at all. Perhaps it was the excessive way that I, the licensed responsible adult, handled the whole scenario. I physically carried him away when he didn't want to leave and then I kept restraining him in my office when he wanted to go. Firmness with dignity and respect is my battle cry, yet where is the dignity in a large man holding a small child in a physical restraint? Where is the dignity in allowing an angry child to strike another child at school, which is supposed to be a safe, nurturing environment? Where is the dignity in seeing children killed at school by angry students with guns and bombs?

I didn't want to hold onto this child. I told him how much I hated doing it. I pleaded with him to tell me about his anger. I offered to let him draw pictures of what he would like to do about his anger. Yet every time I released him he angrily approached the door to leave. "Where would you go if I let you leave?" No response. Perhaps I was being manipulated. Maybe this child was having the time of his life forcing me to stay inside and neglect the other 1,000 students who attend this school. No response about that theory either.

Finding my way through these situations isn't easy. Some of my colleagues often state that our role as counselors doesn't include disciplining children, for such actions would damage the image that the counselor is a benevolent, trustworthy adult. I like that thought but fundamentally disagree. Whereas I refuse to deliver punishments for other people, I can't turn my head when I witness a wrongdoing.

If I don't set limits at these moments, I'm showing children that certain boundaries are easily crossed. As a well-functioning adult (as all counselors are), I must be a model of healthy behavior. Many of my students come from homes where boundaries are very inconsistently enforced. How will they learn to set important limits if no one models proper limit-setting behavior?

Finally, after 90 minutes of wrestling with this angry kid, the school principal arrived. I gladly turned the situation over to him and left to lead a class guidance activity. By the time I returned to the office, the student's mother had taken him home. The principal brought in the other students to sort out the details and handle the situation administratively. The very next week, this same student's uncle died and he was gone for 2 weeks. I saw him outside one day after he came back. I expected to receive a look of scorn, but much to my surprise, he gave me a genuine smile and said, "Hi, Mr. B." Even now he acts like this traumatic afternoon never occurred. Perhaps it was more traumatic for me than it was for him.

My mission as a counselor seems clear. I want to be able to find my way by helping children become more capable of handling their own lives in a way they are most happy with. I've never thought it necessary to physically restrain a student in a counseling session. Yet restraining this little kid came all too easily while acting as an authority. I let my mission be influenced by the role assigned by my employer. How could I have felt so superior that I could justify the use of physical force? Do I ever use nonphysical force when I want students to do something different? How often have I nonphysically restrained children in developmental counseling sessions? How does my forceful influence help children handle their own lives? I'm learning that perhaps finding my way will require me to frequently turn around and look at where I've been.

33

Sometimes Life Really Does Suck

David S. Shepard

I was doing an internship at a community mental health clinic, and I was given the assignment of working with a 38-year-old woman named Sheila who had told the intake worker she was depressed. Having just completed a doctoral dissertation on depression, my brain was crammed with possible treatment approaches. I knew psychodynamic techniques to help her vent repressed anger. I knew cognitive–behavioral techniques to change her dysfunctional thoughts. I was ready to do Gestalt empty-chair work and ask solution-focused miracle questions. In short, I believed I was ready to help Sheila.

There was a deep sadness in her eyes, but Sheila was a smart and witty woman, with a sarcastic edge that matched my own sense of humor. Those first several weeks of counseling, when I knew my only job was to develop a therapeutic relationship, went extremely well, and I was feeling pretty good about myself as a counselor. I listened carefully as Sheila graphically described all the bad things that had happened to her in her life. Sheila had a formidable list of reasons to feel miserable. She had an MBA and had lost a good job in a marketing firm when depression mysteriously swept over her spirit and destroyed her ability to concentrate. Her boyfriend of 4 years had left her, frustrated by her constant complaining about how depressed she felt. As a child, she had been physically abused by an alcoholic father who had later deserted the family. Her mother died when she was 13, and she was sent to live with her cold and unloving grandmother. Nothing gave her pleasure. She didn't think she would kill herself but couldn't imagine life going on like this. She had tried every antidepressant on the market, and they made only a dent in her suffering. Yet, despite all her disappointments, she held out the hope that I could help her.

After a month of patiently listening to her story, a little voice in me began to whisper as though I were Kevin Costner in *Field of Dreams*, "Alleviate her pain." It would become especially loud about a half hour into the session, when I would feel guilt surge up in me that I hadn't done anything about her depression; that would be when I would turn to one of the treatment approaches I had studied. First, it was psychodynamic, and with 20 minutes left, I would start making interpretations. One time I said, "You're worried that I will abandon you just like your father did." She responded, "No I'm not. You need your internship hours—you won't abandon me." She was right.

The next week, with my guilt increasing, I switched to a cognitive–behavioral approach. "Can you see," I said gently, "how your 'should' thoughts are contributing to your depression?" She replied, "I get the idea, but saying 'should' is the only thing that *does* motivate me. Why would I want to stop doing that? Then, I'll have no motivation at all." I insisted that sticking to this inner work would ultimately pay off, but I knew I sounded more like I was trying to convince myself than her. Sheila and I repeated this pattern for weeks, with Sheila countering every intervention I would try by reminding me of the indomitable facts of the lousiness of her life.

As both of us were plainly becoming increasingly frustrated, she said to me, "I want this psychological stuff to work. I really do. But don't you see, my childhood was a disaster, my marriage was a failure, I'm broke, I feel like I'm living in a black hole. My life really does suck!" I'm sure I muttered something back that sounded like reassurance, but everything Sheila said was true. Her life *did* suck. She had convinced me. I simply could not get around this fact; I had to surrender to the inescapable conclusion that Sheila *should be* depressed. And yet didn't admitting this go against everything I had learned in graduate school? Didn't it violate the cardinal rule that a counselor never buys into a client's negative view of reality?

However, I did not want to tell her that I agreed with her anguished view of herself. The last thing I wanted to do was confirm that I felt as helpless as she did. Yet, clearly, my attempts to alleviate her distress by using the techniques I had learned were not working. What was I doing wrong?

During the time I was in the middle of getting nowhere with Sheila, I developed a painful skin condition, apparently an allergic reaction to some item in my home. No doctor, however, could figure out what that item was, nor find an effective treatment. My wife and I repainted and recarpeted with hypoallergenic materials; we removed all the plants; we cleaned the house of all mold, bacteria, and any other living thing that could conceivably be the source of my woes. Nothing worked.

The condition grew progressively worse, and I felt helpless and scared, with no end to the pain in sight. I am anything but a stoic; I moaned and complained to my wife virtually every night, draining her usually large resources for sympathy. "What was wrong with me? What if this went on forever? What should I do?" One night, as we were lying in bed, I launched into one of my complaining fits, being particularly dramatic as I described in gruesome detail every aspect of my pain. My wife tried to help. First she offered, "Maybe you should check out that alternative doctor my friend Susan knows." I felt my body stiffen defensively, my voice rising. "No! Any doctor Susan knows is a quack. Forget it." "All right," my wife said, "What about a good massage? Maybe you need a lot of touching." "Are you nuts? It's my skin that's killing me" "Well, maybe you should go back to therapy . . . it couldn't hurt." Now I started getting really mad, even though I wasn't sure why. She was only trying to be helpful. " This is in my skin, not in my head! Believe me, I wish it were psychological. But it's not!" My wife started to cry.

"What do you want me to say? What do you want me to do? I want to help you and I can't. *What do you want from me?*" Under the pressure of her demands, the words just came to me: *"I need to you to say, 'Poor sweetie, this must be awful for you!'"* We suddenly became silent as the simplicity of this became clear to both of us. She looked at me, and said those very words, and she meant it. "Poor sweetie. This really must be awful for you." I felt my body relax in a deep, mysterious way. Then, I started to cry.

What had happened here? All of my wife's suggestions were good ones, but I refused to take any of them in; in fact, I fought her, until she validated how really badly I hurt. That was what I most wanted from her. After I received her understanding, I was then able to reflect upon some of her suggestions, ultimately agreeing with her that checking out an alternative physician and seeing a counselor might be helpful.

Reflecting upon what happened to me that evening, I understood why I was failing with Sheila. I had never honestly acknowledged to her that her depression was a terrible thing and that she had every right to feel as awful as she did. Instead, I had tried to take away her emotional pain by applying techniques from all those theories I had learned in graduate school. I also was afraid of acknowledging the depth of her pain. I was using theoretical interventions to avoid opening a door where I could have entered the darkness of her inner world and experienced it with her. By over-relying on the magic of techniques to protect myself, I had failed to hear what Sheila so desperately needed from me.

The next time I saw Sheila, after she finished her recital of complaints about her miserable life, I said to her, "Sheila, you're in such pain. It must be terrible for you. Your life really does suck." She started to cry but also smiled, letting me understand that these were tears of relief. Later, we talked about that moment, and she explained to me that I was the first person to let her know it was OK to feel such pain. Everyone had wanted her to feel better, and their efforts had only made her feel guilty that she was disappointing them when their suggestions didn't work. She needed people to appreciate that this depression was bigger than she was; when people tried to help her without first understanding this, she felt frustrated, even angry, and refused to listen to their help. She wasn't trying to push people's help away—it was an instinctive defensive reaction because people were refusing to validate her right to feel miserable given the harsh realities of her life. She had been pushing *my* help away, because, like everyone else who had tried to take away her pain, I had failed to validate her reality.

As I continued to work with Sheila, I discovered that when I truly acknowledged the depth of her pain and made no effort to relieve it, she would then be open to theoretical interventions. I suspect any theoretical intervention could have been productive at that point. But she could not have worked with any of them until I had first communicated to her, with true compassion, that I too believed that things were as awful as she said they were. I now believe that this acknowledgment is a critical piece of our work as counselors if healing and growth are to occur. It tells clients that it is not their fault that they are unable to escape their pain; it gives clients permission to stop blaming themselves. When they start letting go of self-blame, they can be open to all kinds of counseling help, including theory-based interventions.

As a postscript, I can say that I did find an effective treatment for my skin condition, although the cause was never determined. Sheila gradually emerged from the depths of her depression but continues to have periods of being back in her black hole. I cannot say how much of a role I played in her feeling better. What I do know, is that as I continued to acknowledge how badly she felt, she began to feel more hopeful; the hope gave her more energy. She began to participate in a variety of growth-oriented workshops, and she joined a therapy group for children of alcoholic parents. She did this (and continues to do this) on her own; she is the one taking responsibility for relieving her pain, not me. Although I no longer work with her, when she is going through a particularly bad time, she will give me a call, so she can hear me say, "Sheila, no wonder you feel awful. That really sucks."

34
The Parts of Me

Mary Read

Each time I greet a new student, client, or supervisee, I am never quite sure how to introduce myself. How much information will help create a well-functioning working relationship? Of all the ways I identify myself, which ones will foster a sense of connection and empathy, and which ones would get in the way? Some of my identifications are more obvious than others, yet the kaleidoscopic subtleties of these "parts" of me unfold in relationship over time. At times I notice myself almost "looking out" through myself, as it were, surveying the landscape and the multiple possibilities present at that moment.

I remember feeling a shock of recognition when I saw a client doing something similar, almost peeking out at me. My sense of connection to her unspoken question was both instantaneous and visceral. Watching her decide how to identify herself to me, I waited for what she might share.

Helen had come for an intake session 6 months previously and, after some initial discomfort, had admitted to using methamphetamines half of her life, starting at age 16. She didn't see that as particularly problematic but wanted support to feel less depressed and guidance to "help life feel worth living." We talked about the context of counseling and the need to save her life, which only she could do. She decided she wasn't ready then either to stop using drugs or to start counseling, so I gave her permission to check back in when she thought she might want to look at those options.

It had been hard for Helen to accept my validation of her courage for even considering beginning the change process or any other complimentary remark. Now she was back, half a year later, ready to begin the journey. We began the process of sorting through her life, to identify (and hopefully strengthen) her motivations for making such major changes in her early thirties. In the process, we both were learning more about how to identify ourselves to others, how to move into and past the labels that are shorthand for unique personal experiences.

Helen wore the same big, black sweater-jacket to every session, whatever the outside temperature. It was oversized, with deep pockets and a huge collar behind which her face would regularly disappear. Whenever the therapeutic material became uncomfortable, Helen buried her face. Still, she came back each week to face new possibilities and process more of her pain. After several weeks, intuitively sensing something was missing from the puzzle pieces of her life story disclosed thus far, I asked her if there was anything else she thought I needed to know about her in order to be of more help to her. That's when I saw her peek out from behind her big, black collar, sizing up the kind of response she expected to what she was considering revealing. I related to that look on several levels.

Helen's shame became palpable in the room. I could smell the rank scent of fear in my cozy, comfortable office, and it became almost a foreign place—yet still familiar, hauntingly so. Helen finally squeaked out a self-deprecatory statement, something about being "weird," as I recall. Then, as I asked for clarification, she called herself a pervert and several other things in rapid succession, before identifying herself (in a tiny voice) as a lesbian.

The spell was broken. Helen had approached the "hot topic" of her identification with me, and now we were able to explore her comfort/discomfort with it. With my acceptance and encouragement, we began to speak of the unspoken. After a time, I asked her if that was one of the factors in her choice of me as a counselor, and she admitted it was. I was again grateful that I had made the choice to be "out," so that another option besides living with the internalized shame and guilt, born of prejudice and secrecy, could be exercised. I wish I could say that Helen felt a flood of relief as a reward for her courage but that was actually a long time in coming.

Identity issues feel slippery to me, partly because it's human nature to categorize and partly because I cherish privacy and an individual's right to choose whether or not to disclose information about their own lives. My decision to share information regarding my sexual orientation is couched against this tension and is intended as an act of liberation and celebration.

People make assumptions about other people every day, instantly, constantly, and often unconsciously. Outward appearance does not tell the whole story yet sometimes begins the tale. For instance, my pale skin, pink freckled cheeks, and red hair point to my European bloodlines, but the part of me that is descended from a French Canadian *voyageur,* who married a woman from the same tribe as Sacajawea (who greatly facilitated Lewis and Clark's famous expedition), is less visible. I like to think that my willingness to move "all the way to California" from Wisconsin was born of that same adventurous spirit.

When I identify to clients (or students) regarding my European heritage, I usually speak of the Irish and German parts of me. From the Irish comes my love of words, stories, poems, and the sound of my own voice. Learning to love silence as much as sound has been a journey of growth in my adulthood. The Irish are known for being both merry and maudlin. I have worked to find a balance between using humor as a connecting point without deflecting deeper feelings when they rise and to temper the telling of long, sad tales. Avoiding the polarities of extreme positions allows me to savor the richness of my heritage without feeling bound by it.

This is particularly salient for the German part of me, which loves to follow the rules and becomes very uncomfortable when someone violates them. From this I notice that, in my clinical work, I tend to spell out the boundaries of therapy very clearly, to make the context as safe and predictable as possible, while allowing for variety and spontaneity within the context of those rules.

As an instructor and therapist the feminist part of me wants to share the power inherent in relationships, to co-create and co-construct who I will be in this moment to this client or student. I want to deconstruct the hierarchies (while still maintaining some semblance of control, thank you!) and participate in naming the possibilities for cooperation in our voyage together.

The lesbian part of me wants to be out, to acknowledge the unspoken, breaking the silence to lay the groundwork for accepting others' differences by naming one of my own, and to move the discussion toward nonjudgment in hopes of promoting both an inward and an outward celebration of diversity on our tiny planet. Sometimes I believe that everyone must know my orientation already, that I'm only traversing well-worn ground—no longer breaking it, because I have been vocally, visibly "out" for over a decade. I realize, however, that this identification is largely invisible, and therefore I cannot make assumptions about whether my orientation (or my liberalistic attitude toward it) is accessible information in new relationships.

Sometimes visibility is not enough. For instance, it is easily visible that I am a "woman of size." My attitude toward my size, however, is largely internal, and usually bears in discussion only if I bring it to the table. My very first supervisor (a well-respected clinician and lifelong slender person) asked me, just moments before I went in to meet with my first client "so, how do you think it will be for you seeing clients, seeing as how you're fat and all?" Certainly, it was germane to my clinical work as my body would be "in the room" for every subsequent session, yet the timing of her question felt more related to her fat-phobia than to my development as a therapist.

Helen had many connecting points with me. She, too, was White, a woman of size, and college-educated. Our attitudes toward those identifications varied considerably, for both the visible and invisible similarities. Her reaction to my openness regarding my lesbian identification, information she had before she met with me the first time, became part of the groundwork for our relationship. Inherent in choosing me, out of all the therapists she could have worked with locally, was at least a willingness to see how it might be for her if she chose to become more accepting of the sexual orientation aspect of her life story. That she got there, able to love herself, engage in a loving, intimate partnership with another woman (for 5 years now!), and identify herself as a lesbian when she feels comfortable in a setting, is a testament to Helen's courage and perseverance.

It has helped me in this struggle over the years to remember that people are always making decisions about who I am and that being open and self-disclosing with them assists the process. I don't fit anyone else's "boxes," and they don't fit mine, and that's really okay with me. The various parts of me hope for connection with you, in all your kaleidoscopic splendor.

35
Getting What You Need

Judy Provost

A kind of folklore exists among counselors that goes like this: If you have an issue you haven't worked through or resolved, you can be sure your next client will present to you that very issue. Our struggles often parallel those of our clients. Often we don't wish to recognize within ourselves unfinished parts or unresolved issues—after all, we are the experts on personal development and change! Yet our clients' presenting problems and dynamics frequently confront us with the issues we are most reluctant to face. It's as if some mysterious force provides us with the specific opportunities for growth that we most need.

When I was in my thirties, I was struggling to resolve disappointments and frustrations with my parents. At that time it seemed that almost every client who walked in the door of the counseling center was working on this very same issue. Even if I had tried, I could not avoid my own personal work nor the emerging countertransference I needed to process.

I continue to find this phenomenon both in my own clinical work and in my supervision of students. My experience with Hank, a supervisee, brought me a renewed appreciation of this process. Hank had just begun his practicum in a master's program in community counseling. In our first session together he said, "I picked you because I wanted a supervisor that would give me honest feedback."

I was puzzled by his statement, so I asked him to elaborate. "Can you be more specific about the kind of feedback you're looking for?" For some reason, Hank either could not or would not respond specifically to my question. Instead he reiterated his enthusiasm for beginning practicum and the supervision process.

Exploring Concerns

In our second meeting he brought a practice counseling videotape made with a classmate for us to review. Looking a bit nervous, he warned me that he wasn't altogether happy with his performance. I asked him to tell me more about that. Hank explained that he didn't like his hand movements and mannerisms in the taped session. When I encouraged him to elaborate, he said that he thought his movements looked "effeminate." We explored this concern on several levels: How his preoccupation and self-consciousness got in his way and took the focus off the client; his "self-talk" during the counseling session and its connection to his nervousness; and his worst fears about how he appeared to others. We explored how he could modify his self-talk to be more comfortable during counseling and thus shift the focus back to where it belonged: on the client. Hank was not yet ready to articulate concerns about his sexual orientation, and I didn't force this discussion so early in the supervision relationship.

In our next meeting, Hank wanted to discuss his experience co-leading an adolescent group. He reported being a little shaken by the confrontational style of many of the teenagers. "They ask such direct questions of both of us leaders and expect answers," he said. "One teen asked me if I had a girlfriend. What's appropriate to disclose? I want to keep my personal life separate from my professional image."

We explored the feelings and thoughts he had while leading the group and made connections to our previous discussion about his self-consciousness. We then discussed issues of self-disclosure and its consequences. Then, Hank hesitantly shared that he was gay. I affirmed his honesty and courage in disclosing this to me and my good feeling that he trusted our relationship.

Although he felt reassured by my response to his disclosure, he shared that he was troubled about what to do if his clients asked if he was gay. I could not provide him with a recipe for how to handle questions about his sexual orientation, only support his own reflection about this issue. I did challenge him to think about what he was doing with his energy, how much of him was with a client, or with anyone, and how he would like to be.

Self-Disclosure

Soon it was Hank's turn to be assigned the next client who called for an appointment at the clinic. The client was a man named Jonathan, and he was about Hank's age. Hank walked into our fourth meeting holding out his videotape of the first counseling session with Jonathan and said:

"You're not going to believe this. I can't wait to hear what you think, whether I did the right thing or not." He seemed quite energized.

In the session, Jonathan articulately presented his concerns about career and life decisions. Approximately 5 minutes into the session, Jonathan paused and said there was something he hadn't written down on the intake information sheet and he wanted to be honest with Hank. He disclosed that he was gay and in a long-term relationship. He went on to further discuss his career concerns. Hank displayed competent attending, although his mind was racing with thoughts surrounding possible disclosure of his own gay orientation. After Jonathan talked a few more minutes, Hank shared that he, too, was gay. The focus then returned to Jonathan's pending decisions.

Hank was very concerned about what I thought—should he have disclosed being gay? I turned the question back to Hank. How did he feel disclosing? What did he observe in his client? How did he think the session went? What reactions did he have as we viewed the tape together? How would he be able to tell whether a disclosure was well-timed and appropriate or not? These questions led to productive reflection and discussion.

Together we appreciated the irony that Hank had been concerned that a client would ask him if he is gay, and yet the client was the one who disclosed in an appropriate and congruent way that he is gay. We marveled together that Hank's first client provided exactly the learning experience Hank needed and was ready for.

On one level, I am not surprised by situations such as that experienced by Hank and his client. On another level, I continue to be awed and sometimes delighted by the irony that counselors often face. There are times in supervision when I'm tempted to rescue or prematurely reassure a student counselor. In Hank's case the poignancy of his vulnerability as he struggled to integrate his sexual orientation and his counseling self pulled at me. My belief that Hank's self-discovery and self-support were the most important outcomes deterred me from prematurely intervening. It provided a client who both facilitated Hank's resolution of his concern and reinforced my allowing the process to unfold. Hank's experience with this client reminded me again to trust the process.

I try to remind myself to stay open to lessons clients and supervisees are offering me as the lyrics of a Rolling Stones' song play in my head, "You can't always get what you want, but sometimes you might find, you get what you need."

36
The Middle of Nowhere

Kathy O'Byrne

For several years, I offered to meet with all the prospective students for our graduate counseling program. I would hold individual meetings with anyone who wanted to meet a faculty member and ask questions about the program or the field of counseling. When I took the job, I didn't think I would be too busy. To my surprise, there were people booked in every one of the office hours I would offer.

I began to notice a pattern in these meetings. More than half the time, people would come to see me and start apologizing for all the things they had done that didn't fit with counseling. They were almost all nervous. They didn't think they fit the mold for a master's program like ours. They worried they were too old or had been out of school for too many years. They would tell me they had been working in occupations and careers completely unrelated to counseling but felt unbearably unhappy. They would tell me that (until now) they had no choice but to care for ailing family members or small children. They would tell me that they had pursued a career that a parent had demanded and now wanted to follow their original longstanding dream of becoming a counselor. Or they would tell me they were suddenly single, as a result of death or divorce of a partner and had to find some way to earn a living and make a fresh start.

Now I couldn't tell any of these things by looking at them. In the privacy of my office, they volunteered things about themselves that I wouldn't have known otherwise. They shared their vulnerabilities and perceived liabilities to me, a perfect stranger. And most of the time, I reassured them that I didn't label these life experiences and situations as barriers to becoming a counselor.

I always wondered if somewhere, through media representations of counselors or real-life role models, these potential counselors had gotten a visual image of who our perfect candidate would be. Would it be people who were all alike, who were perfectly prepared for this work, and who fit some institutional or professional definition of "normal"? I didn't know of such a template or a book in which I could look this up. How come my future students were so aware of their oddities or self-conscious about their differences?

I found I could certainly relate to them, so my encouragement came easily. After all, for nearly my entire life, I've been keeping secrets of my own that are not visible to the casual observer but that contribute to an occasional sense of inferiority.

I grew up in the middle of nowhere, in a rural area outside the limits of any city. It was out in the country, with the nearest neighbor about a mile away. There were fields on all sides of the house. Across those fields in one direction you could see the outline of the county fairgrounds and the place where the minor league baseball team played. In another direction, you could just barely see the screen from the one and only drive-in movie; with binoculars you could see pictures on that screen. When you got to the nearest town, there wasn't much there other than a grocery store, gas station, and a library. We lived on a road with no curbs, sidewalks, streetlights or other trappings of urban life.

In the summer, if you were lucky, it *wasn't* the year when they planted corn on all sides. It they did, no summer breezes made it through once the corn got high. That was a hot summer. You'd wish for soybeans on at least one side.

In the winter, we'd wait for the snowplow to come by and make a tunnel for us to get out. Some years, there would be a tunnel of snow on each side at least 6 feet high. We'd look out the car window into sheer whiteness, and we'd be driving through a hallway of snow.

Needless to say, there weren't any kids around to play with. And so vast expanses of space were combined with vast amounts of time, that were oftentimes filled with "chores," like taking care of chickens and collecting eggs, or maybe just pulling weeds and picking up apples. Seasons marked the year, not days and weeks so much.

The farmers' ways shaped a way of life. There was a big emphasis on not wasting anything or ever throwing away food. Growing things or making them yourself was always the way to go. And in my particular situation, because farmers learned how to deal with poverty, rhubarb and weeds could become a side dish and scraps of material became quilts (long before it was popular).

Needless to say, when I finally went away to college and chose to go to the East Coast of the United States, I wasn't eager to share much about the middle of nowhere. It was definitely not "cool" to know about farms, barns, and tractors. I could "pass" pretty well for a person from the city, unless someone noticed I pronounced a word differently. I learned how to hide my membership in this hidden culture and didn't volunteer much. I certainly didn't come across anyone else from "the middle of nowhere." Even persons from far away places and countries were from places with lots of people. How sophisticated! How cosmopolitan! How could I describe an entire summer afternoon spent with my sister counting how many cars came down the road?

When I became a counselor, I think this came in handy. I know what I show and share willingly; I assume others have things about themselves that don't garner the admiration of others or earn any kind of preferential treatment.

The silence and pace of the wide-open spaces seem similar to the "space" I try to create in a counseling session. Apart from the hustle and bustle of everyday life, we create this place that actually reminds me sometimes of "the middle of nowhere." Things go slowly. Things take time. It seems familiar to me.

There were other things from this childhood that served me well. I would check out the maximum number of books allowable at the public library. I read all the biographies first. I wanted to know what people did with their lives, and the early seeds of a counselor were planted as I followed their twists and turns.

It was often lonely. So the intimacy that is created in a session, and the chance to talk and listen to people for a living has never lost its appeal. People are fascinating to me still, perhaps because I was somewhat deprived of contact with them early on.

I still don't meet many people who grew up in an environment like I did. I can't think of anyone with whom I have this in common, other than my siblings. The chances actually go down every year of finding someone who experienced this kind of lifestyle. A few years back, I went to see where I lived all those years. It was gone! In the same exact geographical location, there were neighborhoods, with curbs and sidewalks and streetlights. There was even a traffic light. It's gone; it really is "nowhere."

So I can relate to feeling different. My own children, who have grown up in and around the biggest cities in the world, certainly don't get it. They live in the hustle and bustle of urban life as easily as I could find my way down an unmarked lane alongside the fields. They think these stories of my childhood are weird. They are not bragging about them to their friends.

My colleagues don't get it. Once not too long ago I attended a professional conference where, as an icebreaker in the opening session, we played a bingo game. We all had to find people who fit categories on a game card. There were things like, "speaks two or more languages," or "lived more than one year in another country." And wouldn't you know it? I was the only one in the entire place that every single person had to use for the category "grew up on a farm." I really wasn't looking for that kind of attention and even people I had known for years didn't know that about me, until that moment. There was plenty of awkward stammering and no sense of being special in a "good" way. Exposed in public! What things do I still NOT know? Are there still deficits in my coping and survival skills? Do others now see me as having come from television sitcoms like "Andy of Mayberry," "Green Acres," or other equally unflattering portrayals of less-than-hip nonprofessionals? The odds are very high that this will not come up again, and people will not want to talk about it.

So, I look for ways in which students *can* feel comfortable talking about anything with me, even though I'm a faculty member. I'm especially interested in and listen for ways in which they feel unprepared or unqualified. I try to encourage students who think they can't be counselors by telling them about ways I also haven't "fit in" during my professional adult life. I raised my three kids while I was going to graduate school, and I was a nontraditional student who came to graduate school the second time at an advanced age.

When I see students walk across the stage every year at graduation, I connect with their struggles and their accomplishments. And we are all "somewhere."

37
Not So Different From Me

Richard Gariolo

During my first field placement in graduate school, I found that each of my four clients were affected in some way by drug or alcohol abuse. This opened my eyes to the reality that in order to be an effective professional counselor, I had better learn as much as possible about substance abuse.

As fortune would have it, I came across an announcement for an internship at a drug rehabilitation agency, and I jumped at the chance. I began this internship with the notion that I was going to learn something about what makes those addicted to drugs and alcohol different from us. This, I felt, was the key to learning about addiction and finding my way as a specialist in this area.

What began to take place was quite to the contrary. I was learning a great deal about the mechanics of addiction, such as attachment, tolerance, and withdrawal symptoms. But there was also this gnawing feeling that these individuals were not so different from me. I say it was a gnawing feeling because it went against my preconceived notion of such individuals. It continued to gnaw at me because I wanted to accept this feeling that addicted individuals are not so different from us. But something was telling me that if I did accept this feeling, I would be missing something important.

Perhaps it was my budding sense of professionalism telling me to be properly objective. In my coursework at graduate school, I was struggling to understand the difference between a counselor using his or her own experiences, perceptions, and feelings productively with the client and the counselor's becoming helplessly enmeshed in the problems of the client. Maybe working with those addicted to drugs and alcohol put me too close to that fine line separating appropriate use of one's experiences and enmeshment. Or maybe it was my fear of learning something uncomfortable about myself. After coming face-to-face with the demands of working with addicted individuals, I was concerned that even after 3 years of having been in therapy myself, I was not far enough along in my own development to be of much help to my clients.

Finally, I gave in and accepted the feeling. I even began verbalizing it to others: "You know, it is amazing that the more I work with addicted individuals, the more strongly I feel there is not much difference between me and them." It was such a relief to admit this that I did not mind the strange looks I would receive. I set about the task of figuring out why I felt the way I did. My experience as a former addicted cigarette smoker had something to do with it, but I knew it went deeper than that, much deeper.

Two strong themes recurred in sessions with addicted individuals: the desire to deal with hurtful emotions and the wish to rise above the problems of everyday living. Things began to fall into place. Is not that also what I have been seeking all my life? I call it transcendence. That is it, I thought. That is the reason why I feel that there is not much difference between myself and my detox patients. I had that delicious feeling of a mystery solved.

My internship evolved into a permanent position counseling residents and outpatients at the same drug rehabilitation agency. I felt that recognizing the similarity of goals that existed between myself and my clients— a desire to deal with negative emotions and the wish to rise above the mundane—made me a more empathic listener. As I worked with my clients, I observed that a major aspect of their struggle was to overcome the tendency to transfer dependent attachment to someone or something in place of their chosen substance.

There was one key difference after all, I thought, between myself and addicted individuals. Those who are addicted look outside themselves for answers, whereas I looked within for growth, or so I believed. I went along with this observation, feeling that I was making headway, but the feeling began to fade. Something was not quite right. It seemed I unraveled the mystery of what made me feel a similarity to addicted individuals only to find that there is a major difference between them and myself.

But the feeling that there is not much difference between myself and my clients just would not go away. I tried to take the easy way out. There is nothing wrong with a fairly well-functioning individual looking outside himself for validation and approval from time to time, I told myself. Don't we all have our little crutches? Is it not human nature to be addicted to something? The solution is to choose an addiction that is socially acceptable and harmless while devoting most of my energy to looking within for growth.

I soon found that this way of looking at it only intensified my ambivalence. The situation became uncomfortable to the point where it forced me to take a closer look at myself. Was I really looking within for growth?

Did I really see my salvation in uncovering my authentic self, which I say I believe is in union with God? Or was I, like those with addictions, seeking my salvation in something outside myself?

It is important to note that I changed careers to actualize my long-standing desire to become a counselor. Becoming a professional counselor has helped me become a happier, more fully functioning individual. But rather than seeing my career as part of the journey, have I instead come to see it as my salvation? Have I distorted the love and regard I feel for my wife and begun to see her as my savior? What about my relationships with family, friends, and colleagues?

The answer I have come to is "yes." When I lose my focus, I look outside of myself for my salvation. Life then becomes chancy. I feel I must then grab what I can because there are not enough of the good things in life to go around. The door is flung open for feelings of envy.

When I am centered on trying to find salvation within, I have that ineffable feeling that everything is all right. I realize then that I am engaged in a process and that the process of finding my way is in part a mystery. I do not have to figure out all the answers. All I need to do is enjoy my sense of wonderment and choose to cooperate with the process. I know then that even if I should relapse and begin to look for my salvation outside of myself, I can read the symptoms of my addictive thinking and work to regain my focus. And I can trust that relapse can be part of recovery and growth.

I find that my rich inner life enables me to derive joy and growth from the world outside of myself through love, companionship, career, and even from the material goods around me. I have learned this power of decision by joining in the struggle of those addicted. I have also learned that accepting my own feelings enriches my ability to be present for others. After all, we are on parallel journeys.

Part VIII

Refining
Our
Thinking

38
Thrown for a Loop

Jeffrey A. Kottler

I f you have ever made the mistake of asking an elated client, rejoicing at the progress he or she has made, what it was that made the most difference, you may not like the answer. All too often we hear about something we supposedly did or said that we can't even remember. Worse yet, clients will mention some incidental thing that happened, completely unrelated to counseling.

I recall one time basking in the pride of a client's excessive exuberance over a breakthrough in counseling. She was absolutely ecstatic about progress she had recently made. All the while she was relating the things that would now be different in her life, I was reviewing in my mind which of many brilliant interventions had made the difference. I was torn between choosing the poignant metaphor I had created the week before and a delayed reaction to the time a few sessions back when I had confronted her vigorously. The big mistake I made was asking her what had helped the most.

"It's your shoes," she told me shyly.

"My what?" What the heck was she talking about? I hadn't created a metaphor about shoes.

"Well, it's just . . . ."

"Go on," I urged her, now genuinely curious about some "shoe technique" that I couldn't even remember trying. No matter, I thought, there were lots of things I did in sessions about which I had little recall but still had a big impact. That, I said smugly to myself, is the value of being a veteran counselor. There are literally hundreds of things I do every session, most of them effortlessly and unconsciously, that produce therapeutic gains. But I still couldn't remember anything about shoes.

"It's your shoe," she said again pointing at my left foot sporting my favorite pair of loafers. I have very flat feet and these were one of the few pair of shoes that actually felt comfortable.

"Yeah?" I said, looking down to where she was pointing, utterly convinced she was losing her mind.

"You've got a hole at the bottom of your shoe," she said, and then looked at me expectantly, as if that explained the dramatic shift in her thinking during the intervening week and all the changes she was now initiating in her life.

"Your point?" I replied, a little more harshly than I intended. I couldn't help it. This was so frustrating and not going at all like I had hoped, especially with a client who had just finished telling me how much she had been helped in counseling.

"Well . . .," she started, then paused, as if embarrassed by what she was going to say. "It's that hole you have on the bottom of your shoe."

I twisted my ankle so that I could see what she was talking about. Sure enough, the leather bottom of my favorite shoes was worn in the center of the sole, showing a rather large hole that I had not really noticed or, if I had, decided to ignore. After all, I'd never find another pair of shoes like this again. "Damn!" I was thinking to myself when the client continued.

"It's just that you always seemed so confident and poised to me, like you can see through me and know things that I'll never understand. That's part of my problem, you know . . . ."

"Yes," I said impatiently, interrupting her so that she would explain what the heck she was talking about. I still had no idea what the hole in my shoe had to do with her stunning progress.

"I figured that even though you look like you've got it all together, there you are walking around with a hole in your shoe. Either you didn't know it was there or didn't care. You probably didn't know that every time you cross your leg—and you do that a lot—your clients have to stare at that hole in your shoe." She looked a little pleased with herself at that point, proud that she knew something that I didn't.

I nodded my head noncommittally, or at least with what I hoped was apparent indifference. Inside, I was feeling utterly bewildered.

"So," she continued at a faster pace. "I thought to myself during the last week that if you could walk around with a hole in your shoe, then surely I could accept the small imperfections that I have to live with. I mean, I'd never . . ."

"Yes?" I said, this time with a touch of anger. She was definitely pushing my button now. Not only was this woman telling me that none of my brilliant techniques had helped her, that it was this stupid hole in my shoe that got her attention, but now she was teasing me for the inattention I gave to my appearance.

I have little recollection about what happened the rest of the session. One thing was for sure: This lady was clearly feeling and acting differently and in a remarkably short period of time. Furthermore, the impetus for this change was a serendipitous moment that was completely unplanned.

In a hundred years of supervision sessions, I would never guess what had helped her. Or what she said helped her, I reassured myself repeatedly.

When I talked about this case to colleagues, they agreed with me that it was obviously threatening for her to admit that something I'd done had been instrumental in her progress. She felt some need to minimize, or even diminish, the power of counseling. "In one sense," a colleague remarked, "she has a need to get some last digs in toward you. She obviously feels some degree of hostility and resentment toward you."

I agreed with this assessment, not because I believed it, but because it let me off the hook. The more I started thinking about the case, though, the more convinced I became that so often incidental, unintentional, and unplanned events become the impetus for change. In spite of our best efforts, most elaborate treatment plans, and well-executed interventions, there really is no way to know for sure what it is that we do that matters most to our clients.

Certainly I created conditions with this client that made it possible for her to have a magic moment of insight. I had worked hard over the preceding weeks to build a solid relationship. She had made small, incremental steps that made her ready for that transformative event. I knew this all to be true. Yet I felt so humbled by this experience. Too often, just when I think I found my way and know what's going on, something like this episode throws me for a loop. I begin to question, all over again, what it is about counseling that is most powerful and influential. My wonder and awe for this wonderful profession we have chosen is reborn all over again. I realize that no matter how long I study this field, no matter how many more decades I practice, I will still never get a handle on what's really going on. Just when I think I've got hold of the thing, I see that I've only grabbed a piece of the tail.

How are we supposed to find our way as counselors when we can't be sure that what we are doing is impactful? One conclusion I came up with is vowing never to ask an exhilarated client what helped most. Sometimes, I'd rather just stick with my illusions.

39
Fitting In

Robin Cook

I suppose I must acknowledge myself as fortunate. With the exception of a longer road than anticipated, achieving the professional status I have cherished for so long has been a relatively smooth transition. I, at long last, found myself at the crossroads of student and full-fledged counselor, trying to decide which path to take.

For the last year of my doctoral program, I worked in a university program serving college students with disabilities. I performed individual and group counseling, determined appropriate classroom accommodations, and conducted faculty and staff workshops. As someone who possessed a strong background in psychology and special education before entering the rehabilitation field, I felt quite at home with these duties. I even considered eventual employment in a similar capacity. I enjoyed most aspects of my job thoroughly, except for possibly dealing with the parents.

Despite having been educated in terms of family issues for students with disabilities, I never expected to see parents in such numbers in the post-secondary field. Fully one half of the messages I received were from parents. They wanted to know details of what was happening with their children, although we were not supposed to discuss this without a signed release.

They called to inform us that our services were not adequate enough. Often the conversation seemed to extend ad nauseam, with discussion of the student's situation from toddlerhood to present day. Only by great persistence were some of these individuals persuaded that much of what we do with and for a student is at the adult student's request, regardless of the parent's preferences or wishes.

Although many times my work with parents and their student left me with a feeling of definite accomplishment and a sense of "having made a difference," I nonetheless became aware of a nagging feeling of discomfort, which I chose to tackle with the time-honored strategy of ignoring the problem in hopes that it would simply go away if I waited long enough.

The clincher came in a series of interactions with various sets of parents with a common theme permeating their otherwise unique situations. I would find myself employing my best attempts at empathy and active listening as the parents delineated the havoc their child's disability had wreaked upon the family. Then, finally, a closing statement such as, "It's just been awful and agonizing for us all. Now my son or daughter is in college and cannot even make the fraternity/sorority pledge cut."

Huh? This was not what I envisioned to be a major concern. What was going on here?

My agitated mind raced with questions. Were these people so beleaguered that they had somehow wandered far afield of the "real" problem: getting through an academic program. Or was there some important meaning in their world that they were trying to express to me? I suddenly heard an adult speaking in my head about "serious" priorities. Bewildered by what was going on, I gradually began to make excuses to put off such calls and meetings.

I was beginning to realize that the passive approach to dealing with all of this was not quite working out the way I had hoped. Some serious introspection was in order here. Was I losing my ability to relate and empathize? Was I becoming disillusioned this early in my career?

I came to realize that indeed I was getting in the way of effective progress. My own parents leveled a heavy premium on academic excellence and had set very clear demarcations about what were "valuable" activities and what were not. Over the past several years in graduate school, I had more so than at any time in my life embraced and lived by those ideals. And for me, sports and Greek activities had always been activities with little relevance to my own life. I now recognized that these personal issues were lurking under my professional facade and waiting for some excuse to present themselves. I knew as a counseling professional that I needed a way to cope if I was to progress as a counselor and be of benefit to these families. But how? And last but not least, shouldn't I be able to "get a handle" on these biases through my counseling training? Or was it possible that I was lacking in skill as well?

I contemplated these concerns as I headed out one glorious late winter morning to do a disability awareness training. The faculty member whose class I would be working with teaches art education and is committed to the idea that all children should be encouraged to use their abilities to the fullest. I thought about how well this teacher seemed to understand that parents so often just want for their child to "fit in." She stressed to her budding art educators that all their creative activities be geared so that children of all abilities can participate. A statement she inevitably offers is, "Remember . . . parents of children with special needs want to be able to hang their child's artwork on the refrigerator, just like all the other kids in class do."

The moment of realization had come. I likened my feelings to those that the cartoon character the Grinch must have had when his heart grew three sizes on Christmas Day. Maybe now I understand. Perhaps it is not that parents do not care about education or understand the limits of our interventions. They may have seen repeated disappointment in the academic sense and could still be searching for a way for their child to "fit in." Had I been missing the point all along that families were anxious too for the normative experiences that others take for granted such as attendance at ballgames and sorority socials?

This understanding provided me with a sense of renewal and fresh perspective. It truly proved to be the missing piece of the puzzle that had troubled me all this time and gave me an important tool with which to begin resolving my dilemma. I was reminded that each individual and his or her family have a multitude of needs, with belonging ranking right up at the top.

40
Speaking the Same Language

Ronald Strahl

How does one choose the counseling theory that will serve as the light source for the dark questions? Just the term *counseling* seems to have nearly as many definitions as there are people to contemplate it. To some, it is the total of all humankind's wisdom condensed into a 50-minute period, with a client metamorphosing quite routinely into an actualized human being. To others, it would appear to be little more than a brief process of one who is stronger, telling one who is weaker what needs to be done.

When I first entered this field nearly 30 years ago, we studied several different theorists but put special emphasis on Rogers, Ellis, and Perls. I learned a great deal about how confusing it was to attempt to reconcile these divergent points of view and very little about how to behave as a counselor. As I would read each theorist, the approach would appear to make sense, and I could feel myself being drawn toward that particular point of view. As we would get into a differing, yet cogent theory, it, too, would seduce me as it wreaked havoc with what I thought I knew about what worked and why. To add to my confusion, some time during the first semester, the question of whether counseling was a science or an art came up. I wasn't quite sure what the differences were but suspected that if counseling was a science, there should be discernible parameters that could be identified and tested. If it was an art, on the other hand, I was back where I started, with the confusion and doubt concerning what really makes it work. To make matters worse, we were required to submit a paper detailing our particular view of the "nature of humankind" and how the process or event of counseling might influence that nature.

In retrospect, it is easy to understand that the assignment was intended to make us think about our own particular theoretical framework, but at the time it served only to send me into a flurry of reading, all of which was intended to somehow help me arrive at a personal point of view about the nature of humankind. As the deadline for the paper approached, I could see that "it" wasn't going to happen, so I chose one of the more prominent approaches and made it my own for the purpose of the paper. As I recall, I became Rogerian. After all, how could you argue with Carl Rogers? If I was truly a Rogerian, I could counter any criticism of the paper with forward posture, a nod, and the all-powerful "uh huh." I got away with it for a while.

The very next semester involved "techniques" with real clients. Actually, I had a client assigned to me from one of the theories classes. My client had to attend at least one counseling session as a requisite for completion of the class. He didn't know that I was only one semester ahead of him and was given the impression that I was the real thing.

So, there we were: me, posing as a counselor, and this student from theories class posing as a client. Both of us were so nervous we could hardly speak. Because I had the job of being the person in charge, I felt the need to keep the session going. That was particularly difficult for me to do, as Rogerians tend to be nondirective. I must have grunted and nodded enough, because at one point, my client interrupted the silence to make the observation that he thought I might be Rogerian. One of his assignments was to discern the theoretical orientation of the counselor when it came his time to be the client. He seemed pleased with his observation and appeared to be hopeful that his theories professor might be watching from behind the one-way mirror. I was hoping that my supervisor was not in the observation room. My client declined to make a second appointment, and our counselor–client relationship expired peacefully.

It was at about this time that one of the major discoveries of my counseling career began to emerge. I began to realize that all these different theories and seemingly divergent ways of approaching life are nothing more than snapshots of what works for the author of that particular theory. Carl Rogers was the only true Rogerian, and Freud was the only true Freudian. All counselors are called upon to deal with clients from the standpoint of one who has a solid vision (or version) of the nature of humankind and counsels consistently from a theoretical standpoint. A theory is like a compass, allowing the practitioner to proceed in an organized fashion, testing hypotheses as the process develops. For the most part, the actual theory of counseling may be less important than the fact that the theory exists and that the counselor is willing to be guided by it. The theory helps the counselor stay focused. When the counselor stays focused, the client benefits from the movement he or she feels. I am not saying that all theories are benevolent or in clients' best interest, only that following a theory will make something happen.

As a practitioner and a counselor–trainer, I hold to the ideal that when the counselor has a cogent and workable theory, there is the chance that some help may occur. The counselor with no opinions or poorly formed opinions concerning the nature of humankind has little chance of success in counseling. Becoming a counselor with a cogent theory is not so much choosing one and sticking to it as it is discovering who you are and what works for you. The confusion begins to fade as we realize that counselors have a right to the same individuality we are so careful to preserve in the client. The theory or approach we choose has to be a personal choice based upon our core system of beliefs.

Another major insight was conceived of on the day that I began to question whether counselors were the only ones who have a working theory about the nature of humankind. I was often curious about why some clients would seem to progress so freely and smoothly, whereas others with similar circumstances and symptoms would struggle to make even the slightest progress. I also noticed that when I would be working with someone who appeared to be struggling, I, too, would feel an extra burden. I would often feel exhausted after these sessions. By contrast, I would usually feel energized after a session with someone who was doing well, regardless of how hard we had been working. Why did so many cases seem to flow so effortlessly while others seemed to be such labor for both counselor and client? One thing began to become more clear with experience and that was the realization that when a client was doing well, I would have the feeling that we were "speaking the same language." When things were not going well, there would be the feeling of needing to interpret carefully every word, to weigh every interpretation, to guard against leading the client into areas where there was no evidence he or she needed to go. In short, it was a struggle to make sure that we were on the same page. Some counselors would likely chalk this experience up to client resistance and proceed from there, willing to accept the fact that "this case will take a lot of time." Client resistance may very well take this form in certain cases, however, it was important to me to be certain that it wasn't something in the counselor.

In an effort to discern my responsibility in these difficult cases, I began to question whether my approach was the problem rather than client resistance. Was something missing in my personal theory about the nature of humankind that could account for a failing in this area? What would I do if I had a counseling trainee who I had to struggle with? Would I regard the struggle as evidence that my student was somehow unworthy of becoming a counselor, or would I regard the struggle as evidence that we had not settled on the language that best reflected his or her personal life view? It is possible that I would recommend that a student discontinue pursuit of a counseling degree, but not before discerning what he or she stood for.

It was at this point that it came to me that clients are going to have a particular life view, too. They may be as different from one another as the theorists are from one another. Is it possible that the cases that seemed to flow so easily were ones where the client's stand on life matched my own well enough that we were able to communicate freely? Is it possible that the cases where there was obvious struggle were cases in which counselor and client were simply not exploring the situation using the same "dictionary"? If this were the case, it would be in my power to do something about it. I could begin looking for my client's theory about the nature of humankind, just as I did with my students. It would require a fair amount of eclecticism on my part, but if that is what it took to become more effective, so be it.

When I began to look for signs of alignment with a particular counseling theory in my clients, the results were amazing. I found that there were Jungians, Adlerians, Szymanskians, Hargravians, Brotherians, and the list goes on. Each client had a particular point of view that was most acceptable to him or her and that he or she understood most readily. I had always made an honest effort to see the world from the client's point of view, but seeing them as fitting a particular counseling theory or another added a new twist that was going to change my approach to counseling. Suddenly, counseling theory became much more than a confusing academic exercise for beginners trying to find their way. It became a counseling tool with implications affecting everything the counselor does.

I began reading everything I could regarding the nature of helping and went back to those old texts of theorists with a new desire to understand what they were saying. I have likely used everything I read at one time or another. I have also learned that when clients feel understood, they tend to do quite well in counseling. I have learned that when I have a client who seems to be moving rather slowly and progress seems to come only with a struggle, I need to consider whether I have failed to properly determine the "language" to which they respond most readily.

There are times when there is a struggle and I can determine that I have done all that I can in terms of communication, but those times are much less frequent than they used to be. My basic theory about the nature of humankind has not changed very much even in light of my insights; however, I have added the observation that everyone has a basic theory about how life works whether they know it or not. There are many times when the client's basic problem is the fact that they have not discerned their own life view.

My responsibility to clients includes helping them find their way through the painful circumstances that inhibit their growth and prevent happiness. My efficacy in this area is strongly dependent upon how well I have studied, not only the theories of my mentors but the theories of my clients as well. If I am to continue to "find my way," I must remain a student, constantly searching out knowledge of yet another point of view so that I can understand yet another "client–theorist." This makes it my responsibility to take every opportunity to learn from my contemporaries as well as from the "masters." This field is dynamic, and the opportunities for growth are endless. I guess that is why I entered it in the first place.

41
Meaning in Context

Mary Lee Swickert

It was very clear to me that the reason I was enrolled in a doctoral program was to do research. I had worked as a counselor for over 20 years, first in an agency setting and then in private practice. My work had included administrative work, supervision, consultation, and counseling. The profession had been very good to me, and I wanted to give something back.

While working on my doctorate, I continued my normal activities: seeing clients every day, consulting with local agencies, reading about astrophysics, and enjoying my home in the woods. I took as many research classes as I could, including three statistics courses. I read journal articles and wrote critiques. I interviewed professors, students, and colleagues about issues in counseling.

Would I find the missing bit of knowledge that would help me get kids off Ritalin and not labeled attention deficit hyperactivity disorder (ADHD)? I was a budding scientist and I was eager to begin my research.

My first attempt at research a decade before was a survey of my high school classmates to ascertain whether their parents had moved away from them: when, why, and how it affected them. It was interesting research, which I enjoyed doing, but when it was quantified, it didn't yield much of significance. Yet, I felt it had told me something. I knew how many of my former classmates felt about their parents. Many of them had written comments on the backs of their surveys and a couple wrote me long letters. They wanted to talk about the questions that I had raised and what their answers meant to them.

Several years later when I stumbled upon a qualitative research class in the education psychology department, I had forgotten my initial research attempt. By then I had become well versed in research designs and design criteria. I knew that research needed to be generalized and what I needed was a random sample. I knew I had to control for all of those extraneous variables and, hopefully, reject the null hypotheses. How else could research be of any value? I needed to be able to use deductive logic and statistical analyses. I understood that research should be built upon earlier efforts and that it was a painstaking process.

On my first day in qualitative research, I heard that Sherlock Holmes did not employ deduction after all, even if that's what the movies say; he used induction. Having been a fan of the pipe smoking detective, I was hooked. What else could I learn in this class? During some periods we listened to The Grateful Dead. Other classes involved poetry readings and slides of artwork. Where was this class going and why was I, a scientist, in it? I read a text that the professor thought contained some pretty terrible research, and I agreed. But, as he explained, qualitative research, though long used in other disciplines, had only recently been brought into education. Again it was interesting and I was enthused by all the talk of medieval ways of knowing through the philosophies of Aquinas, Moore, and others. We talked of constructivism and postmodern thought.

One fine day I was planted in the library courtyard for several hours just looking around. Just observing. I had been instructed to use all my senses as part of the assignment. It was really fun but hardly seemed much like research. I got my usual "A" and thought to myself that this was a really easy class. Yet something was changing, and I found myself looking forward to the readings and discussions.

Although I passed my doctoral exams on research, I was beginning to doubt the usefulness of traditional research methods. I also began doubting myself. Just about this time a book "leapt off the shelf" at me in the bookstore. It was a physics book about myth as a common way of making sense of what is around us. While we once believed the myth of a flat Earth, we now had a myth of space composed of loops and strings. Astrophysicists were using abductive reasoning!

I couldn't get the pieces together quickly enough. I wanted to understand this way of looking at the world. I read and read and read. I read philosophy, astrophysics, and everything I could find on qualitative research. It seemed like such a good fit for a counselor. Qualitative research utilized the researcher's powers of observation, just as counseling did. It used the researcher's abductive thinking skills, just as counseling did. It employed the researcher's ability to synthesize and to create possibilities. It was based in the tendency to feel connected and in relationship. It was meant to determine significance of meaning. It seemed like it was perfect for what I hoped to do.

When defending my research, I sometimes forgot my own years of studying qualitative research and expected people to understand without my having to explain. When an article about my research went back and forth several times to the review committee, I was amazed. Why didn't they understand? To me it all seemed so obvious. Soon I realized that just as there are many different kinds of counselors with different theoretical backgrounds, there are also many different kinds of researchers. Just as counselors have philosophical and procedural differences, so do researchers. And just as we, as counselors, need to communicate, to understand one another, and to support one another, researchers need to do the same.

This was the greatest lesson I learned during my training. The meaning of something can only be understood in context. I understood myself and my counseling practice. Semiotic research became a logical extension of my work, my interests, and my skills. Others will not have exactly the same experience. I know that it is not time to do away with quantitative research, but it is time to understand qualitative research and the knowledge we can gain from it. Semiotic research is theory- or myth-producing and uses the methods of the professional counselor: abducing, theorizing, and predicting. Whether or not we actually help our clients may take time to ascertain. It is the same with this kind of research. It takes time, discussion, and the agreement of others. At this time we need to seek to understand as much as possible through all of the means at our disposal: through observation, experimentation, history, and reflection. The universe is vast, complex, and ever-changing. And we are part of what we are trying to understand.

42
Giving Directions to Those Finding Their Way

Jeffrey A. Kottler

I walked through the lobby of an Australian movie theater with a familiar feeling of anticipation toward the film I was about to see. I hoped it would be good, but I didn't really care: My arms were loaded with a large bucket of popcorn and a Diet Coke. That would get me through the first hour no matter what was happening on the screen.

The lobby narrowed to a corridor where an officious looking young man waited to check tickets. The kid looked bored and stiff in his uniform buttoned tight at his neck. Like anyone else with an official position in Australia—taxi drivers, parking attendants, bellhops—his uniform had epaulets attached to the shoulder boards, giving him a military appearance. I wondered what rank a ticket taker holds in the command hierarchy of a movie theater.

I approached the young man with my popcorn-filled hand extended, the ticket protruding from between my second and third fingers. He looked at me with a bored expression, retrieved the receipt, ripped it in half with a flourish, and then re-inserted the stub between my fingers.

"To the right, Mate," he said.

I dutifully turned to the right heading down the corridor toward my assigned auditorium.

"No, not *that* way," he said with disgust. "To *my* right," shaking his head with irritation and pointing to *his* right, my left.

Feeling censured and stupid that I didn't know my right from my left, or rather my right from his right, I proceeded back the other way. As I passed the young man again, I could hear him muttering to himself about the dumb American.

Was I missing something here? Was this another one of those cultural gaffes in which I was imposing my ethnocentric view of the world, or at least on movie theater navigation? Could it possibly be the tradition in the Southern Hemisphere that just as water circulates counterclockwise when it goes down the drain, so too are directions given according to the perspective of the guide?

I mean, here is a guy who gives directions for a living. He stands in his nice uniform, a corporal in the theater army, and his only function, besides tearing bits of paper that are promptly thrown away, is to tell people whether to go to the left or the right. But, interestingly, he does it according to his view rather than from the perspective of his disoriented clients trying to find their way.

"No Mate!" I could hear the echo in my head over and over again as I tried to concentrate on the movie, the popcorn long gone. "To *my* right."

Incredible, I thought. Give a guy a little power and a cute uniform, and he thinks everyone else is ignorant because they don't follow his directions the way he meant them. He helps people find their way, spectacularly ineffectually, by refusing to see the world through their eyes.

I meant to go back to his station after the movie to watch the show of what he told other patrons (maybe it was only Americans who got the "special" directions). Alas, he wasn't there. Probably on assignment upstairs in the projection room, reversing the image of the screen so *he* could see it better.

OK, I was more than a little irritated by this inconsequential encounter. Something about it was nagging at me, something disturbingly familiar.

As counselors, we give people directions for a living as well, although rarely as explicitly as a ticket taker in a movie theater. Still, we do occasionally tell our clients they would be better off dropping a class, staying in a relationship, talking to their parents, taking a vacation, going to the right, instead of the left. No, MY right, not yours!

Aha. There it was. The nature of disagreement and misunderstanding when clients don't comply with the recommended treatment regimen. We come up with a perfectly good plan, consistent with latest research and theory. We document carefully the desired outcomes and prepare to measure the predicted results. Then we inform our clients—with precision, enthusiasm, and perfect clarity—where they need to go to find their way.

It's amazing, however, the number of times that clients go left when we just told them to go right. Quite clearly. Talk about resistance and reluctance—some people just don't want to get better, we mumble to ourselves, if not complain to our colleagues.

I've been wondering lately about the times I appear to my clients and students like that condescending, know-it-all, officious ticket taker who gives precise, even accurate directions, but fails to take into account the experience and perspective of others. What about you?

Sometimes, we get so used to seeing the world from our station in the theater lobby that we forget what things look like to those who are distracted, disoriented newcomers to our familiar territory, burdened with buckets of popcorn and large Diet Cokes. No, not *your* right, *my* right.

We often fail to connect ideas and translate directions into the language and beliefs of our clients. In part, we are lazy, but even more so, we just plain think that some things are so obvious that we don't bother changing viewpoints. For a job that is supposed to require flexibility above all else, counselors and educators can be extremely rigid, dogmatic know-it-alls. Then we feel misunderstood and unappreciated when clients don't cooperate in the ways we anticipated. They become impatient with us when progress doesn't flow according to their own expectations—they often believe that our job really is to tell them to go right or left. They'd prefer we take care of this business immediately but, if necessary, they will return for another session.

I've often thought how amusing it would be if while we are attending a workshop or conference, to equip ourselves better to deal with obstructive clients, they too were attending their own meeting about how to deal with difficult counselors. Such clients would all get together, complaining and moaning about how unreasonable and rigid we are, how we don't seem to understand them, how we give directions that make little sense or that don't get them where they want to be.

I wonder if, right now, my ticket taker friend is writing his own article for the *Journal of Movie Theater Orienteering* about the problems of difficult patrons who don't follow precise directions.

43

The Demise of Super-Counselor

Joan R. Sherman

My client first told me about her father 10 years ago. He was very powerful back then. I didn't realize how great an impact he would have on my life. Of course, back in 1990 he wasn't dead. Sharon was the victim of incest. She was sexually molested and raped by her father between the ages of 4 and 15. The art of dissociation had saved her sanity. At the age of 20, she discovered why she kept "losing time," why she was terrified of her father, why sex made her feel dirty, and why she hurt herself. Her sister confirmed many of her recovered memories.

Sharon was 40 when she first came to see me. She had been to a number of counselors, psychiatrists, and doctors but had never told them the "whole" story. She was afraid of being called crazy. Sharon was ready to talk when she came to see me, and over time I convinced her that I could be trusted. She was one of those special clients who helped me find my way and helped me clarify my values as a counselor and, yes, as a person. Over the years, we have worked together to find healthier ways to cope with her memories, to alter my beliefs about what counselors do, and to understand my own growth.

I've come to realize that Sharon and I were different in many ways and similar in others. Her experiences challenged me to understand better the place that I came from and the life that I have created for my family and myself. I grew up in a middle-class, suburban family with caring parents. She didn't. I was the youngest of three girls. She wasn't. I was the one who avoided conflict and who watched my parents and my sisters "duke" it out. The similarities do exist! I was the one who agreed with everyone for the sake of peace. I was the one who worked extra hard to impress everyone. More similarities. The good kid, and the good student.

When I first saw Sharon sitting in my waiting room, my eyes saw a scared, guarded, and cowed woman. My head was thinking very uncounselor types of thoughts such as: this person is weird, she is too-far-gone, and I'm never going to infiltrate *this* defense system. As Sharon and I began to talk in my office, my heart kicked in big time. She was too scared to say much. I reacted to her fright and wanted to help her feel safe. At the end of the session, I still didn't know exactly what the presenting problem was and my gut had a very uneasy feeling. It knew what my head had not yet confirmed.

I spent a lot of time thinking about our session. I realized that I was accepting this challenge out of my own stubbornness and pride. I was going to be *the* counselor who succeeded in helping this woman. I would help her find closure and peace where psychologists, psychiatrists, and sex therapists had failed. I would be, in effect, *Super-Counselor*. Super-Counselors are confident. They know how to take charge of the sessions, how to keep their distance, and how to put their own "stuff" aside. This couldn't be too difficult. What a set-up.

I learned quickly that this was an impossible task. The harder I tried to be all of these things, the slower the therapy went, and the more exhausted I felt. I couldn't control a session full of dissociations. I couldn't convince this client that she was not at fault. And I couldn't put aside my own "stuff." Her passivity in life made my passivity stand out. I either had to change my definition of Super-Counselor or admit to failure.

Change was the route. I realized that I wanted Sharon to feel the safety of my childhood and to know that sexual abuse is not the norm. In deciding to "share," I had to rethink the whole concept of boundaries. As I opened the boundaries between my client and myself, I also began to explore the relationships in my own family. I was able to appreciate what my parents had given me as opposed to what they hadn't or couldn't give. I enjoyed the safety and ease of my relationships with my sisters. I learned that I need to and can depend on my family. I learned that I need to teach my children the same thing. I worked hard to make this functional interdependency and mutual respect a large part of my marriage.

Logic has been an important cornerstone of my own life. If something doesn't make sense to me, I have trouble believing in it. As a corollary, it follows that a good counselor can make logic flow in any session. A Super-Counselor always knows what is happening and what is about to happen. My work with Sharon taught me otherwise. I learned that many things don't make sense. This client was immersed in ambiguity (e.g., ambiguity of boundaries), and I had to learn to flow with it. As a counselor, I had to provide the safety for the client to maneuver through these areas. Logic and direction are not all they are cracked up to be. My tolerance for ambiguity has grown since this work.

Then there's the idea that a Super-Counselor is the expert who knows what the client must do to become a functional individual. How presumptuous! Sharon's inability to kick her father out of her life was a point of contention in our therapy. She taught me that I could suggest other possibilities but that I needed to respect her decision to cope with him in her own way. I had to learn to respect another's ability to know what's best for his or her own mental health. I didn't need to know everything. As a Super-Counselor, I certainly felt a need to have all the answers all the time. What a burden! It didn't make sense that I was helping others believe that perfection was overrated while I expected myself to be the perfect person. This realization has freed me up to learn more from those around me—my clients, my peers, my husband, my children, and others.

At any rate, there I was at the man's funeral. I came to the funeral as Sharon's supportive counselor—or so I thought. In the casket, I saw a shell of a man, who was much smaller than I had expected. The perp, the violator, the creep. I felt anger and disgust oozing through my body and mind. I was confused when I looked at my client and saw a woman at peace. No conflicts, no anger, no tears; just peace. As I stood on the receiving line, I realized that I, too, needed closure on the life of this man. I was no longer acting as Super-Counselor; I was being me and it was just the right way to be. I was just a person and a friend at a funeral, not a counselor. The ability to change in and out of these roles is an important one. It has allowed me to be a good counselor as well as a companion to those around me.

The reality of closure that came with this man's death was comforting and invigorating for me. It is clear that as we walk a client through the struggles of coping and understanding, we are not always standing on the sidelines. With some clients we must walk right along and grow with them. When boundaries become fuzzy or too flexible, it is essential that clients and therapists both work to comprehend their own reactions and their own needs.

Super-Counselor is no more. In the process of helping Sharon I was able to help myself discard the unnecessary trappings of perfection. I learned to grow as those around me were growing. Now I am simply a good counselor who is aware of her limits and her limitations as well as her strengths. It feels good to be who I am.

recognize them and gently put them aside for the time I want to help and relate to a certain person at a certain moment.

What follows is a description of five of my favorite and most frequent inner distractions that I cope with daily in the hope of offering absolutely unmixed attention:

My Professional Middle-Class Biases

Because I was raised in a middle-class family, currently live a middle-class life, and have been trained as a professional counselor, I have particular views of the world. These views color what I believe is healthy or unhealthy, suitable or not suitable, functional or dysfunctional, and often create thoughts such as "this person (or family) should. . . ." These views are often a useful and important part of my work and my interactions with people, but I have found that when I want to offer absolute, open attention to a child or an adult, these biases distract me. These views are often critical and judgmental, when what I want to be offering in the moment is acceptance and compassion.

For example, at the school where I counsel children, I was working with a third-grade girl from a family with many children and few resources. The girl was often malnourished, inadequately clothed, and poorly supervised. She came to my office one day in great excitement to tell me of her mother's fifth pregnancy. Although she wanted me to share in her joy, my professional, middle-class biases impaired my ability to offer unmixed attention by whispering, "Oh no, not another child to neglect." At that precious moment when she needed communion, I failed to provide a space of healing and support for that girl. I failed her again 3 weeks later when she returned in tears to tell me her mother had miscarried, and my biased response was relief. My reactions are understandable, but disappointing to me, as I strive to create moments of support as often as possible. What I hope is to accept these biases as a kind of cloak I wear as a professional in the world but that I can hang at the door when I want to create an accepting, attentive environment for someone at a certain time.

My Past and Present Personal Concerns

Like every person, I carry within me a host of concerns and issues, some immediate and some part of the fabric of my past. It is inevitable that as I listen to the concerns of others, I will at times be reminded of my own personal issues, which can cloud my ability to clearly listen to the person I want to help. Being aware of my issues helps me not only attend well but also to maintain clear boundaries. What is always difficult for me is accepting that I am as vulnerable and human as each person I encounter in a day and that some days I need the kind of support I am always striving to give. Those are the times when having a supportive colleague who can offer me unmixed attention enables me to be more effective and attentive in everything I do.

My Mistakes

It is a humbling reality that the process of helping is an art, not just a science, and so is fraught with wrong turns, glitches, and mistakes as well as successes. During any particular day—or in any particular counseling session—I may say or do numerous things that were not an artful choice or may not appear to be helpful. If I hold onto my mistakes by agonizing over them or frantically thinking of something to say or do by way of "repair," I become totally distracted from this moment, with this person. For me, it has been better to note a mistake and allow it to float away like a bubble so that I may stay attentively focused. It is a quick, immediate dose of self-forgiveness for my human limitations.

My Powerlessness to Take Away Pain

As a counselor, a family member, and a friend, I find it both a privilege and a challenge to be witness to the pain and hardships of people. When I am with someone sharing their pain, much of me naturally wishes I could take the hardship away and save the person from suffering. These "rescue" thoughts often encourage me to scour my mind for ways to fix the problem quickly or do something tangible that might help. Unfortunately, these thoughts distract me from being an attentive witness to the person's process, which is often what they need most from me at the moment. By being aware of this powerlessness and not allowing it to distract me, I have discovered that the other side of this powerlessness is a calm acceptance that this unmixed attention I am offering is a powerful gift at a difficult time. Sometimes my human heart cannot accept that such attention is truly enough.

My Thirst to Know

One enjoyable aspect of my work is the challenge of understanding people and finding the best way to help them. Sometimes, however, my need to figure out what is wrong or where to help can cause me to intellectually search my internal professional database while I am with someone I want to help. Although that process will be useful as I reflect on our time together, it often distracts me from the present moment and makes attending difficult. It is better for me to make a quick mental note of something the person said or did and then return attentively to what is happening now, so I do not miss an opportunity to create a healing space. It also keeps me from appearing detached or emotionally uninvolved with this person who is needing warmth and compassion.

This is, of course, only a partial list of the inner distractions I have come to know and cope with as I strive to offer absolutely unmixed attention. Some days, it seems an impossible goal, so out of reach it seems ridiculous to try. But luckily, most days contain one small moment, a gem, when I am able to control my distractions long enough to feel that special communion between the giver and the receiver.

Part IX

Personal
and
Professional
Lives

45
Enjoying the Ride

Jeffrey A. Kottler

Long distance bicycling is all about spin—keeping the wheels and pedals turning at a constant speed. That's easy to plan but much harder to do when climbing the impossibly steep, gutted roads along the spine of the West Maui Mountains in Hawaii. Twelve miles done. Another 48 to go before I had circled the whole Western Peninsula. Already my crotch felt sore, my thighs burned, and my back ached from holding the hunched-over position necessary to keep the bike straight on course.

A friend talked me into this adventure. He thought it would give me a taste for the real Maui landscape if we escaped the tourist-trod spots and instead circled the relatively remote, rural areas along this isolated road of steep ascents and terrifying, uncontrolled runs around blind curves. My wrists ached from holding the brakes so tightly.

The prospect of bicycling 60 miles around the mountains didn't seem so daunting at the time. In fact, this seemed like a wonderful way to visit some of the teachers I was supervising who were working in schools along the way. I had been in Hawaii for a few weeks, teaching a graduate course on applying counseling skills in the classroom. This was an experienced group of professionals, many of whom were specialists in working with at-risk kids often neglected by the traditional system.

I had learned long ago that when working with Hawaiian teachers I had to adapt my classroom style considerably. Family members would often join the class. Food was constantly being circulated around the tables. Lunch breaks provided opportunity to practice hula dances. Each of us took turns cradling the babies who were part of our class family. Everyone wore shorts, T-shirts, and flip flops and spoke to one another in both English and Hawaiian, as well as a smattering of Filipino and Japanese. It was not all that unusual that their instructor might show up at their school on a bicycle to observe the work they do.

When we stopped off at the first school, I was more than a little eager for the break. This was not because I was dying to get into the classroom to see how my students were applying their new counseling skills, but rather because I needed an excuse to catch my breath.

"I'll just be a few minutes," I called out to my friend apologetically, as if I was disappointed we had to interrupt our journey. "I just need to check on some teachers."

Both of my students had kindergarten classes next door to one another, and when I peeked in, I was proud to see that each of them seemed in command of her room. The little ones obviously felt great affection for their teachers and it was apparent that they were both excellent at their jobs. Still, I was a little surprised to find them making some rather simple mistakes in their responses to children that we had just practiced in class the preceding day. In one case, the teacher was asking a series of rapid-fire, closed-ended questions of a student, never pausing to let him get a word in. I could tell she was becoming frustrated by what she perceived as the student's reticence when, in fact, she was the one making it difficult for him to talk.

When we re-boarded our bikes and puffed up the next mountainside, I started thinking about how often I had witnessed a similar episode in which very experienced, skilled teachers, as well as beginners, fell into some bad habits when it came to responding to children in the classroom. I had a lot of time to think about this during the next 6 hours it took us to complete the journey, so I mentally checked off the common errors I'd seen again and again, even among those who had advanced degrees in counseling. They would interrogate students through a barrage of questions, each of which actually closed off the possibility of deeper-level exploration. They often misinterpreted silence. They reinforced approval seeking instead of creative thought. They structured things so that all communication filtered through the teacher rather than encouraging students to address one another with their ideas. In other words, all too often teachers seemed to ignore critical moments that would arise in their classroom and would continue on with their lessons as if the magical moments had not presented themselves.

Pedaling up and down the bumpy road, I formed a list in my head of all the instances I could think of in which critical incidents might arise—when a student says she doesn't know the answer to a question, when another becomes distracting, when the atmosphere in class becomes stale and predictable, when things just aren't clicking. In some cases, I noticed that teachers realized that something important was going on, but they seemed to feel at a loss about how to respond in ways other than their usual routines. It occurred to me at the moment I rounded a long, winding turn and was rewarded by the most spectacular view of the ocean surf crashing against a cliff, that one of the problems teachers might face is a lack of perceived options in the ways they could respond to certain predictable situations that arise.

For instance, I had discovered a long time ago that when a student says, "I don't know" to a question, it doesn't usually mean that he or she doesn't know the answer; rather, it often means that the person is reluctant to commit himself or herself or to risk being wrong. So when I counter that apparently indifferent response with the invitation, "Take a wild guess," I almost always get some answer, often one that is right on target. It's kind of like a "secret weapon" that I pull out whenever I need it. And I've got a hundred other ones I've collected over the years. So have you.

One of the truly amazing things about being a counselor is that we take for granted how fluidly and effortlessly we attend to aspects of human behavior that appear invisible to others. Consider your own favorite means by which you get others to do your bidding, even when in a "civilian" role. Think about all the apparently natural and skillful ways that you navigate through many interpersonal situations that others would find overwhelming. In the journey to finding your way as a counselor, you have also come closer and closer to finding your way as a human being.

Don't get me wrong: I think that doing counseling is the hardest thing I've ever tried in my life. No matter how long I practice, how much I learn, how much I read, how many workshops I attend, how many degrees I collect, how much research I do, or how many books I write, I'm convinced I'll never feel as thoroughly skilled and masterful as I would prefer. I'll never truly understand my clients to the extent that I would like. I will never, ever reach the point in finding my way that I will have arrived at my ideal destination.

I pedal along, huffing and puffing, trying to avoid the potholes and crazy drivers. Just when I think I have reached the top of the hill, I see there is an endless series of other steep ascents across the horizon. That's okay though. Whether riding a bike on a glorious back road or helping others on their own journeys, it isn't only where we are going that matters but also the enjoyment we take in the ride.

46
Learning to Blend Home and Work

Anne M. Geroski

t was dusk. The setting sun had cast its final show of colors in the sky and it was the end of a long, trying week for all of us. When it is a hard week for the parents, it is a hard week for the children. Feeling the relief that the weekend had finally come, my family and I set out for an evening stroll. An evening walk in the fall in the Northeast is a special kind of family counseling; the lack of direction in the conversation facilitates the connection among us.

The kids, ages 7, 5, and 4, were just ahead of me, running outside in excitement. I followed only a minute later. As I stepped out of the front door, my gaze was immediately drawn to the silence that emanated from the busy road in front of our house. A line of cars in both directions was stopped, and the headlights from the cars illuminated the reason for the strange eerie stillness that had evoked my attention. There in the middle of the road was Lillo, our family cat.

I rushed past the playing children, who didn't notice what had happened and ran into the road. There lay Lillo's body, still and perfect. No scars, no blood. He neither cried out in pain nor stirred in recognition when I called his name. A young couple had left their car and joined me on the road. Helpless, they stood next to me with quiet compassion, looking down at the cat.

I was suddenly overcome with the urge to do something. The couple offered their services to stand guard over Lillo while I went looking for a box. Not wanting to leave the road but also needing a cure for the tragedy that lay there, I turned and walked toward the house in search of some kind of offering to comfort Lillo. I was filled with competing emotions of fear, disbelief, and raw sadness. My memories of that moment are still a blur.

On the lawn, my daughter, the oldest, had stopped playing. I heard her scream, "Is he dead?" Her brother joined her; together they created a shrill chorus of fear. I picked her up and mumbled the truth in her ear—I wasn't sure if Lillo was dead. We walked toward the house and were joined by their Dad, our youngest son, and Lillo, lying still on a box top. The traffic flow resumed outside, and our world closed in as we confirmed that Lillo was, indeed, dead. With the final declaration, my middle son quieted, and the youngest joined in our tears.

What followed was the process of mourning. We brought our cat inside and sat with him in the living room. Through his tears, my 4-year-old asked if we could call the police and arrest the person who killed our cat. My daughter screamed out in anger, "Why did you make us move here in the first place? Why did you have to buy a house on such a busy street?" We acknowledged her anger and also reflected the pain and the sadness and the feeling of helplessness. No need to defend ourselves from her angry words—we, too, wondered who was responsible for the pain that we all felt.

Then my daughter's anger turned into sadness, and she articulated the existential question that we all were asking inside, "Why did Lillo have to die?" The middle child, in his predictable silence, climbed into the arms of his father where he knew that he would be safe from any further questions. He let himself be rocked into a sleeplike state.

Lillo was with us all that weekend, even after we buried him in the backyard the following morning. I was sure that some understanding would come to me from this experience of pain and sadness. Deep down, I guess, I believe that understandings always emerge from powerful experiences. For me, the understandings were both personal and professional. The blending of these two realms of my existence is something that I gave up resisting long ago.

Engulfed with pain and sadness, it feels shameful to admit that such pain actually fuels my passion for my work. I returned to my classes on Monday with newfound—if not still developing—insights about children, grief, and the process of counseling. I shared my story of Lillo with the students in my classes that week. In a theory class, I discussed how my children's cognitive understandings of this death experience were tempered by birth order. I told of how my oldest and youngest children seemed eager to give a final goodbye to Lillo, as if they understood that death was final. They sat beside Lillo's body that night and gently rubbed their hands on his fluffy long fur, as if they were communicating their sadness through caring for him one last time. They were creating a new schema of death.

In contrast, my middle son learns in slightly different ways. He was reluctant to touch the cat. When he did approach Lillo, his actions seemed motivated by obligation, or perhaps, curiosity. He gently touched the dead cat, and then quickly removed his hand, asking "What's in there?" It seems that all of the talk of Lillo's soul leaving, not feeling anymore pain, had ill prepared him for the solid form that his little fingers touched. "His bones and organs," I informed him, "they're still in Lillo." His new experience of feeling Lillo's bones intact further confused his understanding of the meaning of death. But in his silence and concrete questions, he grieved the death of our family cat. The next day, in his own private way, this silent child shared the news of Lillo's death with his friends through whispered accounts and invitations to see the place where Lillo was buried.

In seminar class, students cried in response to my story about Lillo. Recognizing this intensity, I let them grapple with their own meanings of my experience. The first student to speak apologized for her tears and confessed that she had been experiencing a lot of stress in her life. The others stared at her in disbelief and finally commented, "You always seem so together." Students seemed to find comfort in the knowledge that they were allowed to be human, and this shared knowing propelled the group to a new level.

Next, a student soberly admitted to the group that listening to children at her internship site recount stories of their difficult lives filled her with intense sadness and pain. We talked about how experiencing our own sadness helps us find empathy and that the expression of empathy pushed our group to a deeper level. In that deeper place, we were able to begin to make meanings of our experiences. Our own group process paralleled the process that my students will use in their client work.

We learned that empathy means to be with clients when they are in pain. Empathy means being strong and centered, capable of containing and directing, but also not controlling, not changing the focus, and not shutting down. The work of the counselor happens within a relationship of connection, not detachment; the counselor needs to feel with the client, but not for or instead of him. The relationship of caring is that intricate; the counselor is merely a conductor, guiding the sounds to create music.

Finally, another student in the seminar class thanked me for my story about Lillo. She told me that she was touched that I would share my story with the group, and she thanked me for all of the teachings that my children had given her. At that moment, my own meanings of the experience were validated; my home life and my work life truly are connected. Insights are not solely connected to either. This simple statement, one I have struggled to articulate in public, encapsulates my own journey as a counselor trying to find my own way.

This story about Lillo truly is a blending of my two realms of existence. My home so powerfully affects my work, and my work also deeply affects my life at home. My relationships in the home give meaning to the theories and practices I teach, and my presence that terribly sad night reflected the multiple layers of who I am—a partner, a mother, a counselor,

and a teacher. I hope I never become so highly trained or "skilled" that I lose the ability to feel with others. I also hope that I never become so learned that I lose sight of how my work informs my life and how life itself informs my work as a counselor.

47

A Man in a Women's Group

Jason Eckert

"No offense," one client said, looking at me, "but I don't consider you a man."

I always knew that as a counselor I would have to suspend parts of my identity. I did not consider that I would have to abandon my gender as well. Being the only married man in a women's group challenges many of my ideas of what masculinity is and greatly affects the kind of husband I am.

I have always been resistant to discussing my romantic relationships. I remember being in individual counseling for 2 years before ever mentioning my girlfriend (currently my wife) to my counselor. When I finally began talking about our relationship, I realized that I had not discussed it previously. What was my resistance? I wondered. Why did I not mention it before? Future discussions of her in counseling played a great role in my deciding to get married. Soon after, I began a new job as a counselor.

As an addictions and mental health counselor, I began running a group consisting of seven single women, all with a significant history of a substance abuse dependence currently in remission. All were diagnosed with a psychiatric illness that previously required hospitalization and currently required medication for mood and behavior stabilization. All have been physically, sexually, and verbally abused by men. All have provided me with great insight into the type of man and husband I am.

The group was formed 3 weeks prior to my wedding. At first, the women were concerned with my gender and the safety of the group. These fears were alleviated by a dominant figure in the group stating that she always wanted a women's group led by a man. Others agreed and my women's group began. During our second session, I announced to the group that in 2 weeks I would be taking a vacation that would require me to miss three consecutive sessions. I did not disclose my upcoming wedding. The next week a group member reported that she heard a rumor in the center that I was getting married. Immediately, I felt the temper of the group change. Questions about my marriage surfaced. Some I answered; some I did not. One stayed with me.

"What type of husband are you going to be," one client asked. I sat quietly.

"He won't answer you," another women said, and then began to talk about her history with significant others who treated her in a variety of ways.

What type of husband was I going to be? I might be able to avoid this question in the group but certainly not in my life. I knew I loved my fiancée very much. I knew I wanted to spend the rest of my life with her. I wanted to support her and be supported by her. I wanted to laugh with her, cry with her, and stand by her just holding her hand. But what type of husband did I want to be? Beyond these reasons, I did not know.

When I returned from my honeymoon, the members of the group seemed surprised. They reported fears, believing that the marriage would prevent me from returning. They could not articulate much beyond this basic fear. They also seemed delighted at the addition of a wedding ring to my usual dress. It would subsequently become the subject of many group discussions.

One group member said to another, "I told you he was the type of man who would wear a wedding ring." I felt pleased to be viewed as the kind of man who would wear a wedding ring.

The group continued for weeks in its usual fashion. The women continued telling stories of general life stresses with the occasional discussion of a here-and-now relationship. Some group members left, one due to illness, two who requested a schedule change. I wondered why the schedule changes were requested and concluded that my consistency and gentleness in style may have played a role in their desire to leave the group. Their relationships with men were never gentle or consistent. Remaining group members supported my theory when a new group member arrived. In describing the group to the new member, original members stated that this was a good women's group despite the fact that I was male. I began to see that my consistency and gentleness had begun to provide these women with some comfort and inner peace, perhaps more than my insights and interventions brought.

I wondered about this as a husband. I wondered if consistency would mean something in my marriage. I realized I wanted to be the type of husband who remained committed to the relationship.

It was not until 8 weeks later when I forgot to wear my wedding ring to work that my marriage came up for group discussion again. Toward the middle of the group a member asked me if I was in a rush that morning.

"What makes you ask?" I replied in confusion.

She looked smug and said, "You forgot your wedding ring."

Other members sang out as well.

"Did you have a fight with your wife?" one woman asked.

Before I could respond, another woman jumped in, "They're not fighting. They're newlyweds still in the love stage, making love all the time."

I reflected that the group was imagining what it must be like to be married to me. Members of the group then began to discuss how much they needed me. They stated that they enjoyed the group and always appreciated my feedback. Members again expressed fears that I would leave them and they would not be able to cope without me. I assured them that I was not leaving the group but was uneasy with their dependence on me.

I was again reminded of my marriage. I wondered how I was growing with my wife. Had I become overly dependent on her? I wondered if it was healthy to need her so much. Did I want to be the type of husband who always needed my wife? I know sometimes I need her, and sometimes I want her with me. I do get jealous and possessive, but I can be loving and supportive. I enjoy both the companionship and my independence. The group facilitated tough questions in me, ones to which I imagine the answers will unfold along with the development of my marriage.

The subject of my wedding ring did not cease. For many group sessions after its absence many of the group members would ask to see my ring before the group started. The symbol of my commitment to my wife seemed to become a symbol of my commitment to the group.

The focus of the women's group has begun to change lately. The members are expressing themselves to a much greater extent. They are discussing their relationships with men who abused them. They talk about histories of prostitution and the exchange of sex for drugs. They talk about their sexual orientations. Many discussed relationships that made them feel dirty and worthless, feelings that precipitated suicide attempts.

"I have never been able to say these things in front of a man," one group member said.

"No offense," another group member said looking at me, "but I don't consider Jason a man. I can say anything in front of him."

Later in the group I reflected that in fact I was a man but perhaps a different type of man than any of them had ever experienced. Reminding myself that I am now also a husband in perhaps a different type of marriage than I had ever imagined experiencing.

48

Walking in Maria's Footsteps

Marj Burgess

For a long time I had dreamed of creating a private practice. It seemed simple enough; it even held a certain mystique. In reality, I'm taking some of my lessons from a child, my daughter, who is 4 years old. We're both finding our way—together—and in some respects, the walk is similar. Attention is often given to what children learn from their parents, but as a mother, I am learning valuable lessons in finding my way from my daughter.

As I dreamed of having a private practice and imagined myself creating one, I enjoyed the luxury of time. While I lived in Brazil with my husband for 3 months, then 2 months more by myself in order to complete the adoption process that would unite the life of 8-week-old Maria with ours, I spent endless hours thinking . . . imagining . . . and creating an ideal. As the baby slept with me in our hammock and I listened to the breeze soughing through the palm trees, imagining myself back in Maine, I became increasingly concerned with details. How would my mothering affect my practice and vice versa? Would my husband be able to create a sufficiently flexible schedule to accommodate evening and Saturday clients and workshop commitments? How would I find a supervisor who was as wonderful as my previous one had been? How would I advertise the writing workshops that I envisioned? What would I do if I advertised and didn't get a favorable response? How would I create time for myself? For doing all the things I had always enjoyed? Crafts? Gardening? Painting? Most importantly, how would I enjoy and nurture my daughter and my marriage the way I desired if attention were also drawn part-time toward work outside my home?

When the adoption process became more difficult than I had anticipated, I feared that not only would I not be able to return home with Maria, but I also might not be able to create a private practice. As I worked through each obstacle in the adoption process and continued to mother Maria in ways that kept her healthy, I learned to trust myself quite differently from the way that I had before becoming her mother. Caring for her in a foreign country became a personal Outward Bound experience; I started to see the process as a metaphor for starting my practice. As I experienced not knowing the answers immediately and solving one tedious problem after the other, I came to believe while I was so many miles—literally and figuratively—from home, that a private practice would also be born, grow, and thrive in similar ways. Maria validated for me a belief that I could do it successfully.

March of the first winter we were home provided two uncharacteristically lovely days, the kind of days that we New Englanders value as evidence that we survived the winter intact. As I uncovered leaves around the emerging daffodils while Maria, unaware of chaos in the world, slept in her carriage nearby, I was reminded that I also must consciously choose to nap . . . literally and figuratively . . . for in the silence and peace of rest, answers bubble up. Insight comes. I hadn't realized that I had become so acclimated to the Brazilian concept of time until I returned to the States and said to myself, "Why are all these people rushing around?" Then, months later, I realized—sadly—that I also had readjusted to "the American way." Maria continues to live life at a pace that provides comfort and balance. I watch her daily, consciously slowing my inner drive. I hold her as my model of savoring the moments of life in a way that I also must have done at her age. A practice can't be hurried but must be built upon effective work done over time.

As I witnessed 2-year-old Maria explore her world by using a page magnifier to scrutinize the overwintering ladybugs in our loft, I experienced letting go of distractions and directing my attention to center. Her wonder at discovery was an invaluable lesson I relearned as I accompanied her wanderings. Never having learned any other way, she revels in the present.

Being with her is teaching me more to live the way she does, neither becoming concerned about the past nor worrying about the future. I watch her, my model, realizing that long ago before the pressure "to do" rather than "to be" was a part of my nature, I was like her. I hold the image, memorizing it to store like a photograph in the private place of my mind where dreams are kept. I promise myself to recall it when I feel pressure to attain a goal with a client rather than to be with her in the present time, feeling her pain as she recounts the detail. In this way I can be fully present with my clients.

Watching Maria master a skill has been invaluable in supporting my travels into private practice. She epitomizes an attitude that I emulate. Instead of expecting herself to know the answers immediately, she is content to explore and discover as she plays. She is patient but persistent. If she doesn't succeed at first, she tries again, calling out to no one in particular but anyone who will listen, "That didn't work!" A few minutes later, I hear, "Look! See what happened when I . . ." She hasn't internalized the need to "get it right" and has renewed my appreciation for exploration and discovery as I go about the process of attending to such details as advertising for workshops, creating experiences that are health-enhancing and personally enriching for workshop participants, and intervening in clients' lives as creatively as I can.

Maria plays. I watch her build a myriad of structures with blocks or Legos; experiment with clay, paints, and crayons; and play with stuffed animals and dolls, and I see her problem-solving skills develop. Her attitude of wonder and curiosity model a way of being that I admire. I watch her develop ideas and try them out in a playful kind of experiment, reveling in the discovery. Because of her, I have become more creative in my practice. In working to develop this shift in my thinking and the way I solve problems, I have become less concerned with the goal and more with the process, especially the enjoyment of the process. Because Maria has not developed an "inner critic," she is gentle with herself. Having her in my life has caused me to understand more fully how the inner critic becomes internalized and to reach back into my childhood, restructuring my thinking in ways that nurture my clients and myself concomitantly. My practice has become the recipient of these more playful, creative endeavors.

Maria has taught me to trust my intuition, an invaluable process for my practice. When I feared I wouldn't know what to do as a mother, she let me know, first with her cries and later with her words. As I developed my confidence as her mother, I came to trust that I would know what to do at various choice points along the way. This microcosm saw its parallel as my practice developed. When I had choices to make, I remembered that, like Maria, the practice would let me know what it needed. Last summer, for example, I moved into a larger office in my building, one that offered the warmth of a fireplace, skylight, and exposed beams. It was a big decision, one that needed to be right, one that was predicated upon the belief that a larger office would be more comfortable for writing groups. Never reticent to offer an opinion, Maria observed, "This is a good choice, Mama. It's much more comfy in here." By nurturing Maria and trusting my heart, I have nurtured my practice.

Becoming a mother and creating a practice has led me to greater understanding and insight, a spiritual walk, thereby enhancing my professional skills, as well as my personal satisfaction and enjoyment. In the East, they say, "When the student is ready, the teacher appears." With Maria as my teacher, the homework is delightful.

49
Rest Stops

Laurie Williamson

When working with clients or students I use an analogy of back-packing. When going into the wilderness, you learn to plan and prioritize. If you are carrying a 45-pound pack 20 miles, you learn a special appreciation for weight. The same is true for counseling. I've learned not to weigh myself down with excess baggage or lofty theories. Bring only that which you really need. Be practical. And, most importantly, be real. Be true to yourself.

In backpacking, I would always start the trip fully intending to make it to the top. But as the miles passed and I became weary under the pull of the pack, I would start talking to myself. "Why not just stop here? This is beautiful. It's all beautiful. Why kill yourself getting to the top? Let's rest here." After some water, a snack, and a stretch, I was ready to go a bit further. "Let's just see what's around the next corner. It's early. We can go a little further." One foot in front of the other, several more respite breaks, and eventually, I would make it to the top. It was always a glorious feeling to make it to the pinnacle. That's why people go there.

I have had many periods in my life where I was not sure I could go on. They were times and places where I felt so heavy, I was sure gravity had doubled. But with time and nourishment, I picked up and went on. I fully intend on making it to the top, but I will surely need another rest stop or two to keep climbing.

I have come far by some standards. I have my doctorate and enjoy my work tremendously. It combines three critical values for me: flexibility, creativity, and organization. The lifestyle of a counselor educator suits me well. I shake my head in amazement each semester that I teach graduate courses in life and career planning; my own career path resembles the zigzags of a steep mountain trail. I went to college my first year "just to see what it was all about." I had no intention of graduating. I had no real major. I didn't think I'd need one since I couldn't envision myself graduating. I first entered under the physical education program, which I thought sounded like fun. I had, however, never taken a physical education course, nor was I particularly athletically inclined. Why should that stop me?

The semesters and years rolled by until the end of my junior year, when the university demanded that I declare a major. During my first—and only—visit with an advisor, I discovered I had accidentally completed a double major in sociology and anthropology. These were two areas to which I was drawn.

I have come far by many standards, but the true test, a very steep section of the trail, was an unexpected challenge. The path required me to make many rest stops. Just prior to graduation from college I was diagnosed with kidney cancer. I was given a 50 percent chance of survival. I was scared to death. I withdrew from myself and others. I was hurt and angry. I hardened. I thought if I was tough enough, I could beat this thing—this cancer. I was determined to be strong. And so, at the tender age of 22, recently traumatized and totally unprepared for any specific professional activity, I was unleashed upon the world to find my way.

Interestingly, my first professional job opportunity came in the guise of medical social work. I thought a hospital was a fitting place to force myself to confront my health-related fears. But the fears did not come from the hospital. They came from deep within me. It didn't matter where I was or what I was doing, the fears were always there. I have lived and worked in international settings thousands of miles from home. Even the most sophisticated airport metal detector cannot identify psychological baggage—and it travels for free. It goes wherever you go. Little did I realize that I could not outrun or overcome my fears through confrontation, power, or strength.

Some 25 years and a second surgery later, I have come to learn that it is developing a softness, a giving in, that makes me truly strong. I have had years of therapy and dream analysis. I have tried antidepressant medication. I have developed skills in yoga and meditation. I have learned to look within, to breathe, and to trust. I have cradled and soothed my fears. My goals are to become quieter, warmer, and simpler.

My personal life, with many difficult challenges, has guided my professional life. I cannot really separate the two. How can I attend to others, if I am not attending to myself? I can not grow on a professional level unless I am willing to grow on a personal level. The most difficult job I have had is learning to live with myself. Learning to be my own best friend and not my own worst enemy. I have had to learn to forgive myself and to truly enjoy the company I keep when I am alone. These are life's most difficult learnings.

I am frequently besieged by students who want to be completely prepared upon entering the field of counseling. They want to have all the answers and a recipe to fix all that ails society. It is at those times I feel most like a hypocrite. It is awkward for an educator to admit, but most of my expertise has not come from the classroom but rather from "on-the-job-training," or perhaps more accurately, "being-in-life training."

My third or fourth foray into counseling for depression occurred while I was a doctoral student. As it happened, another doctoral student from my program was doing her internship at the clinic I attended. The primary therapist was reluctant to continue the intake session due to confidentiality issues. My response represented a giant leap in my recovery efforts. Previously, I fiercely protected my privacy and guarded my story. I was now able to stand naked, without guilt or shame. I had nothing to hide anymore. I remember giving permission for the intern to stay, commenting, "Everyone has a story. . . ." We all come to learn our stories at different times and in different ways, but we all have stories that shape us into who we are.

It was so liberating to finally and simply accept myself. I let go of all the expectations I had associated with being ill. I had worked, studied, and traveled far and wide searching for some peace . . . and it was right inside me the whole time. It amazes me yet to think that it took so long to see the light. I was so busy fighting, pushing, striving; I would will myself well. Eventually, I exhausted myself and the walls came tumbling down. No more super strength left. Pain and anger flooded over me. It was a magical, cleansing, and healing time. It took me years to pull down the bricks of my defensive walls—one brick at a time—to just be me. Tired. Afraid. Alone. Ready to take a good, close look in the mirror.

I have come to refer to myself as a two-time cancer thriver. I have not just survived; I have in many respects thrived. I think having had cancer has propelled me to do and be more that I ever thought possible. It's just like climbing that mountain path. As a child I never doubted I would soar to the highest peaks. As an adult I have learned that the path is steep and, at times, very dangerous. Fortunately there are also rest stops; places where I can go to heal and dream again.

50
The Integrity of One

M. K. Tailor

Many who successfully exit the client–counselor relationship do so after gaining an understanding of the pieces of the self, learning what must be done in order to align such pieces and gaining support throughout the self-alignment process. My experiences as a client have resulted in the achievement of these goals, in the alignment of my own self, or what may also be referred to as integrity of the person.

The journey to finding my way was by no means easy. The costs were many, yet the outcome was peaceful. Indeed, it is the outcome that has shaped my potential as an effective counselor. For readers to understand my view of counseling, they must first become acquainted with my life.

When I was 6 years old, I realized that our family had a big secret. I could not say what it was exactly, but it had to do with my parents' relationship to one another. I also knew that I had many relatives who would have nothing to do with our family and that my mother's siblings were somehow also directly related to my father. It had not occurred to me that my father could do anything wrong, so the secret must somehow be acceptable. Years later, I understood the secret fully: My father, who was the legal guardian of his teenage niece, began molesting her at age 16. Within the next 2 years, the molestation became full intercourse. This is the relationship out of which I and my siblings were born.

By the age of 10, I realized that some people actually liked to be with their mothers. The thought surprised me. My mother's dealings with me were often mechanical and cruel; it wasn't so bad then when she began to disappear for most of the day during the following 2 years. It was my father who actually enjoyed talking to me, anyway.

Three months before my 13th birthday, my father died of cancer. He had successfully smoked and drank himself to death at the age of 61. My mother sent two of her friends to where I worked after school to tell me that he was dead. The shock was terrible: Not only was my humorous, reliable father dead, but now I was left with HER. My thoughts were filled with visions of being slapped around for the next several years, especially since I found that strange man in her bedroom and now knew why she was gone for most of the day. My father's death would be her inconvenience. Now her children were solely her responsibility.

The next 4 years were worse than I could have imagined. Instead of violence and neglect in the presence of an alcoholic adult who actively loved his children, I now had this same combination without my father and with an alcoholic stepfather to-be who saw me and my two sisters as possible sexual partners.

I remember my high school years in two distinct ways. One involves my popularity as a student leader: salutatorian, band captain, and "Most Likely to Succeed." The other lives in my memory as a series of sleepless nights, a drunken stepfather beating on my mother, breaking windows, destroying furniture, pouring beer all over the place, engaging in "pillow talk" with my sisters and me. But didn't everyone live like this?

My life irrevocably changed when I received a scholarship to attend a university. It was my escape. What I didn't realize at the time was that my life up to that point was a series of jagged, painful pieces that were only beginning to bring themselves into my consciousness, and the time had arrived when these pieces would refuse to let me ignore the gross maladjustment with which I had learned to live.

Defense mechanisms are designed as temporary devices, and once their services have been performed, they can turn against the very person they once protected. Once at college, in a new atmosphere absent of the chronic violence and neglect to which I had become so accustomed, I began to experience a deep depression accompanied by flashes of panic. I was miserable, and I made those around me miserable. I didn't understand what was happening and thought I was going crazy. I remember sitting in my dorm room at my desk and crying because I felt so bad, so hopeless.

The spiral of self-defeat encapsulated me. I didn't know how to tell anyone what was wrong. I knew other people would probably tell their parents, but that was not an option, so I fell into a deeper despair. My only salvation during these next 8 years for fighting the panic, depression, and suicidal thoughts was my love of academics and of music. When all seemed so unbearable, I could rest by attending a class or playing piano.

While driving around one day during my sophomore year, it occurred to me that perhaps I had learned to look at life the wrong way. Maybe growing up in an atmosphere like that of my family taught me the wrong things. The thought made me hopeful and was quickly followed by a second thought: Find someone to teach you the right way.

At this juncture, I found it difficult to make decisions wisely. For example, I attempted to circumvent my absence of parental support by clinging to my friends and/or their mothers. I did not realize that what I was doing was unhealthy for all involved, and I lost many friends during this period of my life. However, as the next 8 years passed, I began making more healthy decisions and fewer self-defeating ones.

The one healthy decision that I did make was to seek professional help. I did not attend counseling sessions consistently, nor was I easily persuaded to change my dysfunctional patterns. The longest that I attended sessions steadily was for approximately 6 months. (I would stop attending when I felt that I had "learned enough" and then return when I humbly realized I hadn't.)

As stubborn and foolish as I was in regard to my counseling and as blind as I was to my own character flaws, I seriously wanted to become well-adjusted. The desire to put myself in order and be in control of and responsible for myself was the strong undercurrent that helped me to trust professional advice in the face of my confused, conflicting emotions.

Although I am not yet a licensed counselor, I know that the lessons I have learned from my own struggles toward self-alignment will directly affect my view of myself as a client helper. Indeed, even as I continue to teach students who struggle as I did, I find myself both patient and firm with them. Both qualities must be present to effectively nurture healthy change; I know these qualities will be hallmarks in my future role as counselor.

The greatest quality I see as affecting both my teaching and future counseling involves not searching for obvious, measurable change in the student and/or client. I know that my own change was often elusive and certainly not linear. No, change is best viewed peripherally, and only in glimpses at that. Instead, my main focus continues to be whether I live each day as an integrated individual, able to answer to myself for my own actions. I believe that herein lies the secret of effective counseling: If one knows herself or himself and can balance self-acceptance with self-responsibility, one cannot help but be an effective catalyst for change within clients.

I do not search for change in others; instead, I expect that my own healthiness is contagious and will affect certain others in ways that I may never know. To me, such a thought is both exciting and motivating.

Part X

Finding Your Own Truth

51
Finding Your Own Truth

Jeffrey A. Kottler

Most of us were taught very early in our careers that there are experts who really do know what good counseling is and how to do it. The problem, of course, is that very few of these prominent counselors seem to agree with one another about which therapeutic ingredients are most important. At various times, I have been told that I should work on the relationship, correct cognitive distortions, interpret unconscious desires, reflect underlying feelings, excavate unresolved issues, construct alternative narratives, reframe problems strategically, deal with existential issues, structure specific goals, and a dozen other strategies I can no longer remember. In most cases, the mentor or advocate felt very strongly that his or her conception of good counseling was optimal and everyone else was simply misinformed, ignorant or even incompetent. Needless to say, I found this to be a bit confusing.

During a trip to Alberta, in which I was the one expected to give presentations on the essence of good counseling, I took a break to do some hiking in the mountains. As I made my preparations, I spoke with a number of people in the area, each of whom warned me that there was a good likelihood I might run into a bear and that I had better know what to do.

"Okay," I prompted, "Would should I do if I see a bear?"

"Back away slowly," the native Albertan warned me. "And whatever you do, don't make eye contact. Look at your feet."

Sounded reasonable to me. Hadn't I once read somewhere about following similar advice when confronting a mountain gorilla? Something about showing deference. This was another mountain creature I might face, so it seemed a logical strategy. Thus armed, I continued my inquiries about the best trails to visit.

The next person I consulted, a shopkeeper, also warned me about the bears. "You know what to do if you see one, don't you?"

I broke into a big smile. "Why of course!" I said. When I began to explain about the downcast eyes, she began laughing.

"You've got to be kidding," she snorted. "You don't actually believe that, do you?" Before I could formulate an answer, she continued, "Actually, what works best is to immediately fall to the ground, curl yourself into a fetal position. Cover your head. And whatever you do, don't move. At worst, the bear may swat you around a bit. Just try not to make too much noise or you might piss it off more."

Right, I thought. I could just imagine myself trying to stifle my screams as I was being ripped apart. Even if this did work, I'd prefer to die on my feet rather than just lying there waiting to see if the bear read the same books she did.

Some time later, while outfitting myself for the adventure, another long-time resident of the town asked me once again if I knew what to do if I should encounter a bear.

"Yeah, yeah, I know. Curl into a ball and wait patiently for death, or life, depending on the bear's mood."

"Well, there is some truth to that. Actually, though, you don't have to sit still."

I perked up considerably at this. "Yeah?" I asked wearily. "What then?"

"Bears, you see, can't run downhill very well. It is a little known fact that it throws off their gait. All you have to do is find a downward slope and run, roll, or fall as fast as you can."

I was skeptical by this point, and it showed on my face. "Come on," he urged. "Have you ever seen a bear running downhill?"

Come to think of it, I hadn't. Besides, this was advice I liked a lot. I'm a good runner. I *like* to run. There is no better way I'd rather get snatched by a bear than running for my life.

Later that day, I was again asked by someone about my knowledge of bear lore. This time I was grateful for the opportunity to show off my obscure piece of intelligence that bears can't run downhill.

The woman thought this was hysterical. In fact, she found it difficult to catch her breath. She called others over to show them an especially dumb tourist. Once she regained control, she explained that bears can most certainly run downhill. And besides, look at the laws of physics—a small body mass rolling downhill, and a very large, angry body mass moving down the same slope. Which do I think would make better time?

"Yeah," I challenged her a bit too stridently. "What should I do then?"

"Why, climb a tree, of course," she answered. "Grizzlies don't climb trees. I have a friend who was being chased once. He climbed a tree and the bear was enraged. The bear camped beneath the branches, pacing back and forth, for hours. When my friend urinated on him from his high perch, the bear finally went away."

Now *that* was something I could do easily under the circumstances. I was a little leery about this advice though. The only bear I really knew much about was Winnie the Pooh and as I recall he climbed trees quite often to get at the honey. Now there may be a difference between what you should do with a pooh bear, a black bear, and a grizzly, but I didn't trust my diagnostic judgment to tell the difference under the circumstances. For one I was supposed to throw a rock at it to chase it away, the other I was supposed to crawl into a hole. And what if I couldn't tell which kind it was? Should I throw a rock at myself?

The incredible variety of bear advice continued all day long. The more people I spoke with, the more suggestions I got—all of them different. Some people advised me to wear a bear bell, others to carry a gun, still others told me not to go into the mountains at all. Most amazing of all, each person was so confident that he or she was right and everyone else was wrong. When I presented each of them with contradictory data, my challenge was met with an unconcerned shrug. Each had not the slightest doubts about what I should do.

Does this sound at all familiar? It sure did to me. And I felt immediate relief realizing that it isn't just some members of my profession who are so sure they are right and everyone else is wrong. There seem to be so many people trying to find their way in the world by convincing themselves, and others, that there is no other truth except what they have discovered personally.

Fortunately, I never ran into a bear that day. It was a good thing, too, because I'm certain I would have just froze, overwhelmed with all the choices available. The bear would have had some story to tell her cubs that night. A story about some guy she met who, alternately, hit the ground, ran downhill, climbed a tree, and urinated on himself. I'm sure I would have tried them all.

To this day, I'm not sure what to do with a bear. That's all right, though, because I'm not always sure about what to do with most of my clients. And when I talk to people about the essence of counseling, I may think I know what is most important, but I now remind myself that the world is filled with experts who believe they have found truth. Many of them got snatched by bears.

52
Doing Time on a Llama Ranch

Dan Gregerson

There's a story told in my family about when I was in fourth-grade Sunday School class. Like typical 10-year-olds, my fellow classmates and I were being rambunctious that day, and in order to calm us down and make a point, the teacher went around asking each child, "Why do you come to Sunday school?" The responses ranged from silent shrugs to "because my parents make me." When it was my turn, the answer was, "I'm here because I'm preparing for the ministry."

I grew up the son of a preacher, determined as far back as I can remember to be a preacher myself. I never really questioned that path, just followed it blindly through college and seminary and finally to the point where I was ordained in the Lutheran church. This was the first of three stages through which my life would progress. Each period reflected a different philosophy of life, and during this first stage, if asked what my philosophy of life was, I would have said: "The meaning of life is to serve others."

I received my first call to some rural churches in central Idaho, when after working my whole life up to that point to reach this destination, I looked around and said whoa, what the heck am I doing here? It was painfully obvious, to me at least, that parish ministry was not where I belonged. Sunday service was like putting on a one-man play; I used to get terribly nervous. I would practice over and over to get everything perfect, then as soon as it was done, by Sunday evening, I started worrying again about next week. I used to tell my friends in high school never to call me after 10 o'clock at night. When the phone rang in my house after 10, it meant someone was dead. I remember feeling sorry for my father, shivering in his underwear while murmuring comfort in the dark at the hall phone. Now the late night phone calls were my responsibility. I lived in dread that at any time, the phone might ring and it could be a parishioner saying, "my wife just died" and I would have to deal with it right then. What could I say? What if I said the wrong thing? One of the most important moments in this person's life, and so much was riding on what I came up with off the cuff. True, I had been given some skills in ministry, and the one time the phone actually did bring me the voice of a woman whose husband had just died, it turned out to be one of my most rewarding experiences. But I lacked such things as the ability to live with the anxiety of feeling "on stage" all the time and the patience to put up with endless discussions about trivial matters like where to put the piano in the sanctuary, while ignoring all the starving people in the world. Crucial skills necessary in order to do that job, live that life, and be happy.

You may be wondering how anyone could have overlooked that fact for so long. What kind of moron goes through 4 years of college and another 4 years of seminary without seeing that it was a mistake? Surely there were warning signs along the way. Well, my only answer to that is the opinions of others can be a very powerful influence. Think about every casual conversation you have ever had when meeting someone for the first time. What is inevitably one of the first questions asked? "So, what do you do for a living?" I wish you could see the expressions on people's faces when I would reply, "I'm training to be a minister." It was a combination of shock and fear, usually followed by a confession of the last time they went to church. But there was also always an element of admiration in their response. I heard comments like, "Wow, I could never do that," or saw the warmth in their eyes, heard the veneration in their voices as they told stories of a special member of the clergy who helped them or their family through a crisis. More than anything, I wanted to be that hero for someone, and it was hope of receiving that kind of admiration that drove me on for so long, ignoring the warning signs along the way.

But once I accomplished the goal of becoming ordained, I had to face the fact that I had been living my life not to serve others, but to please others. I had chosen this profession, not because it was what I wanted or felt comfortable doing, but because others told me it was great. I'd be rich if I had a nickel for every time I was at a party in college and someone handed me a beer and with it, like a garnish, the inevitable comment "Man, it's so cool you're going to be a pastor!"

It became clear after a short time in the parish that living one's life to please others wasn't the ticket to happiness; it was like trying to fill a bowl that has no bottom. There was never enough admiration to make me like myself. Years later, I would learn to call this "trying to meet an internal need through external means." Back then, all I knew was it didn't work. So I said screw others, I'm going to go live for myself instead. From now on, my philosophy would be, "To thine own self be true."

To that end, I left parish ministry and went to work on a llama ranch in Helena, Montana. Nice shift, eh? I was sick of working with people, so I decided to go work with animals for a while. The truth was I had spent so much time worrying about what others wanted me to do, I didn't really know what I wanted to do. It was a question I had never asked myself.

Working on the ranch, I did find a kind of peace. The quiet and simplicity of life was very appealing. Each morning hiking to the barn through the crisp air, spreading hay around the feeders, and leaning leisurely on a fence to gaze at the snowtouched mountains was like drinking in medicine to soothe my soul. I cried the first time a sticky newborn llama fell directly from its mother into my cradling arms and laughed like a child just minutes later as it struggled up on wobbly legs. Months went by without needing to speak to another person other than the owner of the ranch. A curious change occurred in me then. I had always been the kind of person who considered it a great imposition to make small talk with strangers; if someone made a comment about the weather in the check-out line at the grocery store, I would give a minimal response, then subtly turn away so as not to encourage further familiarity. Now, I discovered a desire to talk with strangers. I had extra energy to reach out and delighted in the exchange. It no longer felt like they were taking something vital from me, but giving instead, and I could give in return without feeling depleted.

However, a void was growing in me. After about a year on the llama ranch, the thought occurred to me that when I'm on my deathbed and reviewing my life and all I've accomplished, if fixing fences and shoveling llama poop is it, I'm not going to feel fulfilled. Although I was content on the ranch, I wasn't doing good for anyone else. There was an emptiness about that. It wasn't enough just to live for myself; life had to have more purpose than just surviving. As mentioned earlier, I had been given some skills and it seemed wrong not to use them.

That's when I remembered how rewarding it felt to help the woman whose husband had died. On the basis of that experience and others like it, I decided to go into counseling. Back into a field that involved serving others, but I'd learned something along the way. I had learned that I needed my time of seclusion in order to be able to help people.

Remember back to your philosophy 101 class, they might have mentioned a guy named Hegel. Hegel was a German philosopher, a forerunner to Marx, who came up with the Hegelian dialectic. The dialectic says that ideas evolve from a thesis, to the opposite or the antithesis, and then the two are blended together to become the synthesis.

That's exactly the way my philosophy of life had progressed. You will recall that during the first stage, it was "The meaning of life is to serve others"; then it became "To thine own self be true," but in the end, and this is still true today, I believe the meaning of life is "To thine own self be true *so that* you can serve others."

Spirituality is a very broad, all-encompassing concept, but at its most basic a system of spirituality seeks to answer one question: what is the

233

meaning of life? Well, for me, the meaning of life is helping others. But that is not possible without self-care. I had learned that life was more fulfilling when I was helping others, but in order to do this, I had to be able to go home to the ranch at the end of the day to recharge. This is how self-care and spirituality are interconnected. Spirituality without self-care leads to a sacrificial existence filled with misery and resentments (like when I was in the ministry). Self-care without spirituality leads to a meaningless existence and depression (like on the llama ranch). Balance is the key, or as my father is fond of saying, "Moderation in all things, especially moderation."

It is not selfish to take care of yourself; quite the contrary, it is a necessary ingredient in serving others. If this step is ignored or denied, we simply burn out after a short time. We run out of energy, our spirits fail, and then you gotta go do time on a llama ranch, not being any help to anybody.

53
Discovering My True Self

Laura Vaccaro

I believe my life experiences and the roads I have traveled were meant to prepare and lead me to this place called "Counseling." As I embark on this new journey, I recall the many challenges I have had that have helped me grow, develop, and strengthen my identity. Through my graduate program, I've come to recognize the parallels between my own development and the stages of development described in various identity development models used in counseling. A clear picture began to emerge of how the learned values and beliefs of others influenced what I thought about myself and the world around me. I was also able to pinpoint specific times in my life where I experienced pain, conflict, or confusion, attempting to live in accord with those values and beliefs—even though I knew deep down within me that they were wrong.

I grew up in the suburbs of northern New Jersey. Our house was similar to all the other houses on the block, and just about every family had a mother, a father, and some number of children. You might say I was a good Catholic. I went to church almost every Sunday and attended catechism, so I could strengthen my faith and make my sacraments, communion, and confirmation. Like most little girls, I assumed I would meet Prince Charming, make the sacrament of marriage, buy a house in a neighborhood with other similar houses and have some number of children. It was a cycle that all seemed to make perfect sense. Who I was and where I was going were all mapped out for me by the societal, religious, and family values that I had received. As I approached adolescence, I realized I had to find another way. I could no longer fit into what it meant to be White, feminine, and Catholic. It seemed that almost everything I was taught to value and believe was somehow incongruent with what I truly felt about myself and the world.

My foundation began to crumble during an argument with a neighborhood friend when I was 8 years old. In her anger and frustration she lashed out, "You lesbian!" Even though I had limited understanding of its meaning, that word cut right into the core of my being. I continued to wonder about it for quite some time and remember feeling especially annoyed that she chose to call me that word as opposed to a "jerk" or "stupid." The years that followed were characterized by denial, fear, and confusion. I started to abandon the activities I loved that were predominately associated with what boys do—playing softball, climbing trees, and going fishing. I wanted to be like other girls. I didn't want to be this thing called "lesbian." As I got older, my friends were interested in boys, and I was interested in my friends. In eighth grade I exchanged a kiss with my very best friend. It was too much for either of us to bear. We became passionate adversaries toward each other and then went on to become nothing to each other.

About a year later I found myself covertly shuffling through the card catalog searching for answers. I always sensed there was something different about me, and I wanted to know if the difference was this thing called "lesbianism." On that day in the library, the fragmented puzzle pieces of my identity began to merge together. The answers I so desperately sought validated the deepest fears I held about myself. I started accepting that I might actually be a lesbian and left the library feeling very shaken and distraught. After that day, I never looked at the world or myself in the same way. I no longer fit into the mold that was cast by my family, my religion, or society. To be a lesbian meant that I was now very different, perverse, and somewhat twisted. My self-esteem plummeted as I began to feel intense shame, guilt, and alienation.

I took this new knowledge about myself and buried it deep down so no one else could see it, except for me. Because of the many negative messages I had received about homosexuality, I knew better than to turn to my family or my religion for support. That type of support would only have reinforced my self-hatred and feelings of perversion. Looking back now, I realize how vital it would have been to have a counselor. Someone who was open, accepting, and empathic—who would affirm my newfound sexuality and help me work through the shame, pain, and confusion I was experiencing. Unfortunately, at 13 I didn't know anything about counselors or where or how to reach out for help. Instead I relied on my own inner sense of strength and faith in God to find my way. Although I had a strong desire to embrace this new identity and connect with other lesbian and gay people, I also felt a deep need to find someone somewhere to validate my worth as a human being. To let me know I was okay, that I could still love and be loved for who I was. For the first time in my life, I understood and completely experienced my own internal sense of homophobia.

The years that followed were challenging and difficult. Like many other teenagers struggling with their lesbian or gay identity, I often lost hope and contemplated whether or not I wanted to go on living. I charted a course of self-destruction by abusing alcohol and drugs. My body survived, but my spirit had died. Feeling alone and depressed, I often turned to God. I recall many painful occasions, sitting on steps outside locked church doors, desperate and at times intoxicated, praying, questioning, and crying out for His help. I was able to eventually persevere because of my strong faith in knowing that I was never truly alone and in believing that I was placed here in this world, in this way, for good reason.

Later I substituted my frequent substance abuse with abusive relationships. When the pain became too great and the desire for positive change escalated, I called a local therapist that was listed in a gay newsletter. Twenty-four years of my life had past. Yet, through all the pain, I managed to earn a bachelor of science degree, get a good job, and support myself. I focused on my educational and professional life because it gave me a sense of pride and accomplishment that was lacking in all other areas of my life. My new lesbian therapist introduced me to my next abusive partner just hours after my first session. Two months later I observed this "therapist" dancing oddly in a gay bar in Asbury Park—only to find out she was high on cocaine. My next straight therapist spent much time trying to link my sexuality to the lack of love I had experienced in my relationship with my mother. A number of years had passed, quite a few therapists, and a lot of money. Although I gained some awareness and worked through painful childhood memories, not one of those therapists, gay or straight, addressed the issues relating to my homosexuality. The internalized homophobia I experienced continued to undermine my self-esteem and cripple my ability to have positive, rewarding relationships.

Thirty-five years of my life have now passed. I have since come out to my family, friends, and some coworkers. My family has struggled with a coming out process of their own as they confront their own internalized homophobia and stereotypes about lesbian and gay people. A few years ago I started an open support group for lesbian women in my town. I'm happy to say that we meet twice a month in a Lutheran church that has not only acknowledged who we are but has also gone out of its way to embrace us. The group has been especially valuable to women who are just tolerating or coming to accept their homosexuality. Many of these women are looking for the same validation I so desperately sought in my youth: to be accepted, to know that they are okay, and to come to a realization that they don't have to live a life characterized by guilt, loneliness, and self-hatred. Group participants also seek to fulfill their social, sexual, and emotional needs by connecting with others who share common ground. Having a safe space to reclaim their sexual or affectional identity helps these women heal deep wounds that have resulted from living in a society that condemns homosexuality and perpetuates homophobic attitudes.

I don't believe it will ever be easy being homosexual in a heterosexist world; however, finally embracing and owning my sexuality has been empowering and self-affirming. I have found that judgment, guilt, and hatred directed toward the self is far more damaging than that which may be experienced from others. Challenging the limiting and self-defeating beliefs I internalized about homosexuality was not only healing, but it also opened the door for me to confront other values and beliefs I held regarding religion, family, relationships, people, and just about every other aspect of who I was. This self-exploration enabled me to move away from the fear, hatred, and judgment that often grounds our values and beliefs toward becoming a more empathic, accepting, and loving person. As a future counselor, I believe I will be less likely to instill my values and beliefs on clients, while encouraging them to find their way to their true selves. My experiences as a client, however, have pointed out a desperate need for truly competent professionals to work with lesbian and gay people. Presenting problems for this population are often a result of the alienation, guilt, fear, shame, and self-hatred that is rooted in homophobia. By using lesbian or gay identity development models as a backdrop for counseling homosexual clients, I hope to facilitate a process of healing and self-acceptance. I have also come to realize the importance of taking social action to confront discrimination and negative stereotypes against homosexuality and to help provide insight to other counseling professionals regarding the multiple issues and challenges confronting lesbian and gay people.

Well, I never did meet Prince Charming, get married, or have children. I did, however purchase a home in a nice community. A community where all of the homes are diverse, just as diverse as the families that are living there. I even had the opportunity to run into the girl from my youth who I had kissed for the first time. She greeted me with an uneasy smile, stretched out her hand, and proudly displayed the engagement ring on her finger. She too had found her way.

54
I Didn't Go There

Linda Chassman

I found that keeping an open mind and a vulnerable heart is both necessary and dangerous in working with people with chronic addictions. It is through their actions, perceptions, and sorrows that we learn of the world that they know. But in so doing, we come close to being with them, feeling the pain as they do. Getting this close to a suffering human being can be heart-wrenching. Learning to detach is a necessary tool to be an effective and long-lived counselor. But can we be so detached that we don't even realize that we are no longer even attached to ourselves?

Inviting heroin- and cocaine-addicted clients into my little office was frightening at first. I dealt with my initial fear by realizing that what scared me about them also scared them about themselves. Just as I had used my anger as a defense against my parents, the world, and myself as an adolescent, so these drug users use their anger and "druggie" persona to defend themselves against a world that they could only perceive as painful. Their creation of themselves served not only to defend them against me, and the other "normies" who would not understand them, but also kept them from truly knowing themselves. These were individuals who were afraid to give up the only security and control they had known. Their drug kept them warm in their emptiness and allowed them to avoid looking at their despair. They were injured inside, afraid to face the memories and the pain. The real threat was to be drug-free and then to have to remember the past they meant to forget.

Working with these chronic drug users was my training ground for working with people labeled as personality disordered. The emotional seduction of the pain of these clients tapped into my most basic desire to be wanted and needed. The pain of connecting with a suffering human being is tremendous, especially when they use that love to replace their drug. They needed me to nurture them, to protect them, to fight for them—to be their all-perfect mother, their superhero. Not only did I become that, but I also became what I had envisioned myself to be as a counselor.

The gratification I received in my relationship with my borderline clients had its blistering side. In allowing them to use me as their need-gratifying object, they at the same time had to sabotage me. Their fantasy, and mine, was spoiled with the first glimpses of reality—that I was a mere mortal. And I saw how this was not just about them but also a recreation of my own relational patterns. I had to accept the reality that my sense of self-importance only fed their fantasy of being insignificant. So, I did the only thing left: I surrendered and let them teach me.

My clients taught me that becoming their idealized object was temporarily satisfying but a therapeutic "set-up" for them to later devalue me. My supervisor advised me to become "neutral" with these challenging clients and to "listen" with the ear of empathy. As I became more proficient in this "listening," I heard many terrible tales of lives they had lived as children and the tragic lives they had created for themselves. I heard my young clients describe years of childhood torture, mental abuse, endless stories of parents who left them, parents who gave them drugs, parents who had sex with them. I heard their tales of raping women, torturing animals, stealing from their mothers, being raped in prison. Through questioning, they told me their recollections of the physical abuses, the nightmarish relationships they had with parents and spouses and children. I could confront them, make insightful interpretations, be the "listener" and the facilitator who could establish a basis for healing. But I never asked about the sexual abuse. I never probed about who, and how, and what it was like, what they thought, what they felt when it happened, even how they felt about it now. I didn't go there.

Is the cliché true that we try to heal others because we need to be healed? Is it possible that we can heal ourselves through our work with others? Sadly, I learned that I could not heal myself through helping others, but also I could not help others in the areas for which I had not yet been healed.

Several years after leaving my work at the residential drug program for a position as an administrator at a community counseling center, I re-entered counseling myself to save my marriage. After my marriage ended, something compelled me to continue the process. Perhaps it was a sense of inner knowledge that in time my secrets would be revealed. And in time they were—when my own past history of sexual victimization slowly came to surface. As I reluctantly allowed the memories to surface from my unconscious, it was as if I was discovering an entirely different me. I was at once so helpless and fragile and yet at times felt murderously angry and desperate for relief. Finally, I knew what it felt like to allow the ghosts out. I knew how it felt for the pain to take on a life of its own and to lose my sense of control. I knew how much I needed to trust my counselor, to hang onto him as he held onto the small sliver of the me I had known. It was a journey that took me to an unknown destination and, in the process, turned my world upside-down.

Through working with the difficult clients I had faced at the drug program, I had learned to lovingly coax out the demons in my clients in almost every circumstance. However, I could not deal with the pain of their sexual abuse because I was not yet ready to deal with my own. I helped bolster their defenses with cognitive platitudes and my own denial. I held them back through my own unknowing. This was an area for which they would not heal, at least not with me.

At times, I feel that I did a disservice to those clients whom I did not allow to work through their sexual abuse histories. But mostly I believe that the strength of my own personal work now contributes to my deeper understanding as a counselor. After several years of treatment for my own sexual abuse, and years more of postgraduate study in the area of treatment, I consider myself a highly qualified specialist in this area. While I do not always disclose my own history to my clients, I am keenly aware of how strong the defensive structure can be from such a devastating assault. I have immense respect for the psyche as protector and defender. My clients know I will be there for them. And if I can't be, I will be honest enough with myself to seek understanding of my own blockage. One important lesson that I learn so many times anew is that I can never "know" it all, that being a counselor is an evolving process of self-discovery.

Perhaps the greatest lesson I have learned as I find myself as a counselor is that my ears can listen, my mouth can speak, but only my heart can genuinely be with someone. To allow ourselves to connect at this level is to give the greatest of therapeutic gifts, to truly show clients in pain that they are not alone. When we invest in the knowing of ourselves and find our own deepest truths, even those that are most painful, we become the counselor that we dreamed of being and the one that our clients deserve.

55
Using Intuition to Find My Way

Stephanie B. Palladino

Throughout my professional life, first as a high school teacher and later as an elementary school counselor, I have used my intuition as a guide. My ability to tune in to the feelings, behaviors, and motivations of others and to shape my behavior accordingly is like an old friend who can always be counted on when called but who is sometimes ignored nevertheless. This skill is not something I was taught in graduate school, and in fact it has never been articulated to me as a useful tool per se for educators to possess. Yet I am convinced that intuition should be at the top of any list of attributes that are necessary for counselors to successfully find their way. This sixth sense provides the scaffolding upon which highly successful counseling stands. Without it, the interaction between counselor and counselee falters, even if the counselor's comprehension of the basic tenets of school counseling is strong. The combination of a solid understanding of the principles of school counseling, a well-articulated plan of action, and a fine-tuned intuitive sensibility results in a skilled professional who will use her abilities to their best advantage for the benefit of all those with whom she works.

As a child, my intuition many times proved burdensome to me. From very early on, I felt deeply the emotional temperature of the adults and children around me, yet more often than not I was incapable of controlling circumstances, so the emotional equilibrium would be maintained. The sense of helplessness that I experienced as a result was painful and confusing. My childish egocentricity was often at odds with my reality, after all; since I was the center of my universe, it followed that I should be capable of orchestrating the behavior of others as well as my own. Most of the time this did not occur and I was left feeling disappointed in myself and let down by those whose behavior I had been incapable of shaping.

Throughout my adolescence, my intuition often caused me to feel estranged from my peers in a way that was not at all comfortable. The additional layer of sensitivity I possessed prevented me from relating superficially in many situations. I felt like an outsider much of the time. I became a fly on the wall observing myself in the process of relating to my peers. This metacognition was an unwelcome companion that set me apart in a way that was quite painful during a developmental stage when more than anything else I yearned to blend in with the group in every way.

My intuition has accompanied me into adulthood, where it has proved to be more of a blessing than a burden in my professional life. For several years as a high school Spanish teacher, I had the task of motivating and encouraging my students to participate actively with me in the process of learning a foreign language. I worked hard at my lesson plans and made full use of each minute of class time. Above all else, my own enthusiasm and energy level set the pace for my students' learning performance. My intuition guided me in calibrating that pace on a moment-by-moment basis, depending on a variety of factors that never remained constant. When I ignored my intuitive sensibility, more often than not my rhythm faltered and my teaching became awkward. When I heeded it keenly, exciting teaching as well as learning took place.

It was through this teaching experience over the span of 11 years that I made the discovery that what interested me most in the classroom was not the subject matter, but rather the rapport I was able to develop with my students. In a variety of teaching situations over those years, regardless of the distinct ages, backgrounds, and intellectual abilities of my students, or the type of institution in which I taught, I had little difficulty in developing a positive ambiance in my classroom. It is my belief that my intuition was a significant factor in this success. My perception of the students' needs, desires, and capabilities shaped my teaching style and guided my demands and expectations of them, both on an individual basis and as a group. My intuitive barometer fostered a cooperative and respectful spirit in my classroom that benefited everybody, including myself.

However, it was not until I became a counselor that I experienced the satisfaction of making optimal use of my intuition. In contrast to my primary purpose as a teacher of imparting concrete knowledge to my students, as an elementary counselor my goal is to assist each student in navigating his or her journey of self-discovery. If all goes well, this journey will make possible the full use of his or her intellectual and emotional potential.

When I allow my intuition to guide me, the path of that journey emerges spontaneously as we work together. A certain amount of risk-taking is inherent to this process, as there is no preplanned route outlined in advance for us to follow. By this I do not mean that I have no plan of action. For each student, I establish an action plan that is clear yet flexible.

The outline of our experience is sketched by such a plan. A level of mutual trust is essential if I am to successfully guide my counselees along this mysterious path, for without it, no honest rapport would be possible between us. With all that in place, sometimes exciting things do happen. Let me give you an example.

Today I offered the students in third grade a chance to say thank you to someone of their choice. I reminded them that each of us, no matter how sick or healthy, happy or unhappy, lonely or loved, has someone in our life to whom we might offer our gratitude. Perhaps it is a family member at home, maybe a friend or teacher at school, or even a pet who offers us unconditional love. I asked the children to think of who that person or pet was in their life, and to ponder that question seriously and with attention. Then I passed out white oaktag paper, and asked them to make a card giving thanks to that someone. My only instructions included making sure to sign the card, and inside it to describe by picture and/or words specifically why that person was being thanked.

The children went to work quickly, folding the paper this way or that, cutting and trimming edges, writing and drawing messages of thanks—breaking open their creativity eagerly, turning lines into pictures and words. One 8-year-old boy thanked the turkey he would eat on Thanksgiving. It was such an honest message that it filled me with awe.

But it was to one boy, Justin, that I turned. As soon as my instructions were given, he announced defiantly that he wasn't doing this project. Now he had moved from his seat to the front of the classroom, where he fiddled with a scrap of modeling clay. He was looking at a calendar of the Saint Jude's Research Hospital that I had brought with me to introduce this project to the students.

Each page featured a child who had a chronic disease and was a patient of this hospital. In addition to their original artwork, there was a glossy photograph of the child, with a name, an age, a short message, and a disease—osteosarcoma, leukemia, other types of cancer, and many others I could barely pronounce. I had shown the children this calendar earlier by way of demonstrating that even children who faced tremendous difficulties in their lives had many people, as well as pets, to whom they were thankful. Each short biographical sketch, appearing to the right of their photo, mentioned their messages of thanks. Now Justin was studying the calendar page by page. He seemed more quiet and focused than I'd ever seen him before. My intuition told me that something of significance was going on for this child at that moment.

I approached Justin quietly, not wanting to pull him abruptly from his reverie. We talked briefly about the chronically ill child on the open page in front of him. My intuition told me to stay quiet—to listen for clues to the essential truth of that particular moment for Justin. After a few minutes, I gently asked why he wasn't making a thank-you card. I listened solemnly as he confessed that he had no one to thank. At home, isn't there anyone you might thank? I asked. No, no one, he replied with his head bent low. Justin went on to explain that his younger brother was a pain and that his mother always yelled at him. My intuition told me to prod further. I couldn't give up on this boy even though he had already given up on himself. What about pets? I inquired. Look what the cat did to me, scratched me here and here and over here too, he answered, while his pudgy fingers with dirt-encrusted fingernails traced each puncture up and down his forearm. I acknowledged his wounds with a few words of sympathy. Still I persisted, hoping to locate someone in his life to whom he might be grateful. Do you have a dog? I asked without much conviction. His face lifted slightly. His eyes met mine briefly. Yeah, Sparky, he confessed. Something told me we were onto something now. Well, do you want to make a card for Sparky? I eagerly suggested. Justin's eyes widened as he rolled this possibility around in his head. His fine motor skills were weak as his thick, clumsy fingers found it difficult to hold and manipulate writing tools. His confidence was already quite eroded by many failed attempts at pencil-and-paper tasks over the years. I had seen Justin give up before even getting started on many other occasions. I held my breath waiting for his response. Yeah, I'll make a card for Sparky, he announced flatly.

Justin wandered back to his seat slowly, his heavy construction boots dragging his thick-set body across the floor. But before even sitting down in his seat he asked the teacher if he could use the computer. I froze in place, praying her reply wouldn't sabotage Justin's newfound initiative after such a struggle to locate it. She quickly consented, and Justin positioned himself in front of the monitor. When I left the classroom, Justin had typed "To Sparky" at the top of the page. He was clearly on his way.

At the outset of our conversation I had no idea what the outcome would be for Justin and me. My intuition told me that this child might need more than the general instructions I had delivered to the students at the beginning of class. When I saw him studying the calendar, I perceived the connection Justin was experiencing with those chronically ill children—their vulnerability matched his in some mysterious, fundamental way. It was not necessary for me to question Justin on the details of that association; in fact, it never even surfaced throughout our conversation. Instead, I allowed my intuition to guide me in exploring Justin's personal reality with him and by giving respectful recognition to that reality. I was then able to coax him to take a risk, to allow his creativity space to express itself, and because of the mutual trust we had already established together, Justin answered that challenge.

56
Finding My Voice

Laurie Carty

I have struggled all my life to find, hear, trust, and express my inner voice. Expressing my voice has often left me exposed and vulnerable. It's risky and scary. I ask myself why speaking with my voice is so critical to finding my way. Couldn't I just find my voice and keep silent? Many life experiences have taught me that silence hurts more than disclosure. Writing this article is about breaking my silence and speaking with my inner voice.

My confusion over finding my voice began very early in my family of origin. I learned many lessons about being a girl. Girls were to be quiet, dependent, soft-spoken and deferential. Feelings were secrets never to be spoken inside or outside the family. Above all, never cause embarrassment to the family, even if that means supporting a lie. Growing up in my family made it very difficult to hear my voice. As a child, my voice sounded like a whisper and sometimes it sounded completely silent. This terrified me. I was the child who was too sensitive and too emotional. Most of the time my life felt out of control although I was constantly reminded that things weren't as bad as I thought they were.

There were other childhood experiences that silenced my voice and left me with unresolved core issues. In grade school, I was the only girl strapped every year for talking. My parents agonized over their lack of success helping me understand that girls did not rob apples, play baseball and football, or holler loudly while leading boys in a game of war. I have a deep voice that projects well. As an educator this has been helpful. As a child, however, my voice was a curse. I can still hear my father telling me that my escapades had to end. I was 12 years old and could no longer be tackled or tackle boys. I felt my life had ended.

Playing the adolescent dating game made hearing my voice almost impossible. It seemed that conflict within myself was constant. I wanted my relationships to be honest and open, but the social expectation demanded dishonesty and game playing. In order to have boyfriends I had to look good. I went on many crash diets as appearance seemed to count for everything. I wanted other things to matter in relationships. I wanted to have a voice that was heard. I wanted connection. I wanted to be more than somebody's doll. It was during my adolescence that I became aware that my culture sexualized and devalued my gender. I also became aware that men and women live in different worlds. I found this confusing. I still find it confusing both personally and professionally.

Dialogue between men and women as equals has not been my experience in male-dominated hospital and academic environments. Voices command, "Be a good girl, don't make waves, be only for others and do it in silence." These male environments do not support feelings, and the only voices listened to are those that are cognitive and logical. There is no room for expressing feelings except the expression of male anger. I have continued to struggle to have a voice when those in power do not listen. Hospitals and universities have rigid hierarchical power structures that support the traditional patriarchal model.

In order to be heard and taken seriously at work, I avoid using my feeling voice. I compartmentalize who I am. My logical voice speaks in my work environment. My feeling voice includes my heart and my soul. It is with this feeling voice that I talk with my clients and students. Teaching clients and students to listen, hear, and express their voices has helped me search to find my own voice. I try to create a learning environment where it is safe to be vulnerable.

I work as a group counselor and supervise students leading groups of young people. In this safe group environment, feelings are accepted and trusted. I teach others how to listen for their own voices and how to stop listening to the voices of others all the time. Students also learn how to listen to each other. They discover that the way to hear your voice is to speak it to someone who will hear it. Both speaking your voice and hearing the voice of another are ways to hear your own voice.

In the past 5 years, I have become aware of the cost I have been paying for being a good girl, not making waves, being only for others, and doing it in silence. The cost I have been paying is me. I had lost myself both at work and at home. I could no longer hear my inner voice. I had lost my way. I was counseling clients to find and express their true voices, but I was asking clients to do what I was unable to do. Clients believed that I had it all together, and the more I counseled them to empower themselves the more I felt like a hypocrite. These emerging insights were creating a war of loud voices inside my head. Because I was unable to resolve my turmoil, I decided to receive personal counseling. This was not easy. As a counselor, switching roles did not come easily. In fact, becoming a client is scary.

My counseling journey has helped me to take a number of actions to resolve my inner turmoil. I first became aware of needing authentic relationships to speak my voice and be heard. In order to do this, I need to have a voice. To have a voice, I need to express my feelings openly in my primary relationships. I became aware of my need to challenge two major relationships that would silence me. My relationship with my mother and my relationship with my husband. This decision terrified me.

I began the process with my mother. I expressed my feelings about how as a child I had felt disconnected from her and how I still feel that way. She would not hear me. I tried over a 2-year period to reach her. It was not possible. We now have a tentative relationship that is more honest than the illusion of a relationship of the past. What is most important is that I spoke the truth of my childhood. The family silence was shattered.

I then expressed my feelings to my husband. He chose not to hear either. There was no room for my voice and I was not heard. There had never been a relationship. Giving up my illusion of relationship with my mother and my husband left a huge black hole in my soul. To avoid filling that void with other dysfunctional relationships, I traveled more than 3,000 miles to a new environment. It was important to change my pattern. I needed to leave familiar ways of avoiding my issues. It is so easy for me to get lost in caring for others rather than caring for myself. I am really good at helping others, and helping has been my way to escape pain. In this new place, I began to hear my voice faintly. The voices of others who would silence me were not so loud. I began to hear my voice speaking just above a whisper. I chose to spend time only with those who would hear me. The more I spoke, the stronger my voice became. I became aware that most of my past conversations with others had been about talking without speaking. It felt like I was finally beginning to express my truth for the first time. I was beginning to hear what I needed to do to find my way.

I still continue my counseling journey. As a client, I have learned so much more than I ever did in graduate school. I have made many life changes. I have a different relationship with myself. In the past, I put the needs of others first and usually ignored my own. This made it difficult for me to hear my voice telling me what I needed to know. Now I look for ways to hear my voice, and I choose to do things that put me in touch with my voice.

Writing this article is part of my process of listening, hearing, and expressing my voice. As I have begun to learn how to listen to my own voice, I have learned not to try to control or make something happen. I have learned to trust myself and the process of hearing myself. I now know I must be true and honest with myself. My voice tells me I must be direct and honest in my primary relationships even when this is painful. Also I know I need relationships with friends who will hear me and whom I will hear. Almost all of my friendships have changed and this has not been easy.

Now I always listen to what my voice is trying to tell me. Even though at times the messages and meanings are unclear, I choose to speak rather than wait. The meaning becomes clear as I speak and express my true self. I continue to do this even when sometimes there is embarrassment and I feel vulnerable. I reach out to those who would not silence me and I promise to never silence myself. I hear my voice telling me what I need to do to find my way. My voice sounds clear and strong. Do you listen, hear, and speak your voice? What are the ways you have been silenced and the ways you silence yourself? Isn't it time you listened for your voice telling you what you need to do to find your way?

57
Son of a Counselor

Cary Kottler

It was a pretty normal Wednesday night during my sophomore year at college. My roommates and I had just finished a couple hours of studying and we were sitting on the porch of our off-campus house having a few beers and shooting the breeze. The hour neared 1:00 a.m. and our subject of conversation turned to times we had gotten in trouble as kids. One of my roommates spoke of the time he took out his parents' car when he was 14. He returned home to find his father standing in the driveway. Another friend was caught stealing baseball cards from a store. They both got in huge trouble, were grounded for weeks, and were denied any access to the outside world. Their parents were determined to make them pay huge reparations.

Then it was my turn. When I was 11 years old I had two friends over after school one day. My parents were still at work, and we were hanging out in the backyard. One of my older and more mischievous friends thought it might be fun to throw some eggs from my backyard to a house kitty-corner, about 200 feet away. Reluctantly, I retrieved some eggs from the fridge and we started launching our bombs. For some reason that only an eleven-year-old would know, the sound of the eggs going "splat" against our neighbors' house was quite satisfying.

We continued to throw various things on and off for the next hour or so, experimenting with different foods and household objects lying around. Suddenly the doorbell rang, and I was shocked to see a police officer at the doorstep. He had been called half an hour previously and had been standing in the neighbor's backyard watching the trajectory of the eggs and frozen foods sail over the wall from our house. Even though I was caught dead in my tracks, I still tried evasive action. I've learned being the child of a counselor not only teaches one to use high-level communication skills to help people but also to get out of trouble.

"No officer," I replied with as much sincerity as I could muster given the circumstances, "We've just been watching TV."

The officer broke out into a big smile. I suppose he loved not only catching someone in the act of a heinous crime but also someone trying to lie so feebly to escape punishment. There was no hope. Soon my parents returned home and were informed of my delinquency.

My college roommates began to giggle at the conclusion of this story when one of them spouted off, "I bet you didn't even get in trouble. I bet your dad said, 'So Cary, how does it make you feel to throw eggs at another house?'" Then another friend chirped in and said, "Yeah, then they probably asked you how you intended to accept responsibility for your behavior." My friends were obviously referring to the fact that both of my parents were counselors and educators. The way they so aptly anticipated my parents' behavior led me to believe that they had probably had a bit of counseling themselves. By now they were experts at predicting my parents reactions to different situations that I have encountered. They had already seen first-hand over the years we'd been living together that I spoke frankly with my parents, and they always listened to me and talked out my problems rather than getting visibly upset.

I laughed with them, feeling slightly embarrassed, but I was already used to this ribbing. It is a little unnerving growing up always hearing comments from people such as "Oh, your dad is a shrink." Another popular one was, "So does your dad always sit you down in his office and analyze everything you do?"

"Not really," I'd tell them defensively. I always thought my dad was pretty normal, just a little more intrusive and a little more understanding than most parents.

The truth is that I really didn't get in much trouble for throwing the eggs. I just had to give up my allowance for a while and sell some of my baseball cards to repay the damage. While I never got in too much trouble growing up, there were certainly times I let my parents down. Or at least it felt that way.

It is tough living with such high-achieving parents who make a point of emphasizing how much they value honesty, integrity, and curiosity. Even when they tried to hide their disappointments, I had learned over the years to become exquisitely sensitive to their moods and wishes. This is another one of those abilities the child of a counselor picks up along the way, a survival skill of sorts. Yet no matter what I did, break a window with an errant baseball, lie about where I'd been out late, or habitually refrain from keeping my room clean, they refused to ground me. It was almost like they punished me by *not* grounding me. Instead of sending me to my room, they would insist I talk to them about what I had done. There were times I would rather have been banished to my room for the week than spill the beans about how I was feeling or what I had done.

Many times I just longed to be yelled at or spanked. Then I could just be done with the situation and get on with things. Instead my parents encouraged me to find my own way.

When you are the child of a counselor, everyone in the family becomes a member of the Counseling Culture, whether you like it or not. Over and over I overheard my parents say things like, "I made myself upset over that," or the best one of all that I've used many times myself: "It's not about me; it's about you." And if that one doesn't work, then you try: "It's not about you; it's about me."

Certainly, being the son of counselors has been a rewarding experience even with the burdens of being hyper-aware of things inside me and around me. As a male adolescent it's somewhat rare to be very expressive of feelings. Yet it had always been expected in my family that I talk about what I was thinking and feeling inside. Even when I didn't know what was going on, I just made stuff up, violating one of my father's most important rules about the importance of being honest.

Like the children of counselors everywhere, I've picked up a lot of the basic skills and techniques over the years. As a result, my friends have always confided in me. They come to me for advice or tell me about a problem they are facing. Fortunately, I've paid enough attention to know that the one thing counselors are not supposed to do is give advice, so I just listen a lot.

My parents have always given me the freedom to make my own choices. Whenever I come to them seeking advice about some matter, rather than stating their opinions, they use that same basic counseling method of listening to me and helping me reason through the choices available. This was never more evident than in the college selection process.

Springtime of my senior year in high school I was faced with selecting my place of higher education. I was fortunate enough to have several choices available from some of the best universities in the country, so this was not an easy decision. Countless times I asked my father, "Where do you think I should go?"

I'm sure he was just dying inside to yell out a school of his liking. I knew when he was my age that he could barely get into any college himself, so he was definitely living vicariously through my successes. As much as he must have wanted to tell me where to go, he restrained himself. I think only a counselor has that kind of discipline.

As the son of a counselor, the relationship between me and my father was sometimes strained by his sentiments of "not really knowing me." I think this was largely due to the fact that he spent a significant portion of each day listening to people spill their guts. These clients would reveal the most intimate details of their lives, not something a normal 14-year-old is willing to do for his father. In comparison, my father felt that he didn't know me nearly as well as some of the boys my age he was seeing in counseling. From my point of view, I felt he was being overly intrusive, wanting to know the most intimate details of my life. Oftentimes I felt as though he was trying to turn me into a junior counselor, if not a client. One thing I learned from all this was how to be effective in telling him that some things were none of his business.

I tend to talk to my parents when things are going well, when I'm in a good mood and have interesting things to tell them. My more depressing moments are shared with my friends, just as they should be. Besides, with two successful parents, I am always concerned about letting them down in some way.

Because my parents are teachers and counselors, they are also pretty understanding of my troubles. In spite of my reluctance to do so, they want me to show my weaknesses, to tell them about my pain. This makes for a delicate balance between my feeling ashamed of admitting weakness and yet also wanting to take advantage of our open relationship. This has also prepared me extremely well for having intimate conversations with those I care about.

So there I was still sitting on the front porch with my best friends. I was acutely aware of being the son of a counselor. Their giggles died down after my story, and then it was another person's turn—he actually put ink in the coffee of his English teacher. Man, I should have thought of that one—it would have gotten me grounded for sure!

Part XI

Making
a
Difference

58
I Delivered a Baby

Joe Roberts

"They want you in obstetrics," the nurse told me when I entered the hospital geriatrics unit where I worked as a counselor. There was a young Mexican couple in the obstetrics room, and no one else in the hospital spoke Spanish. Group and individual counseling would have to wait."

Earlier that morning, the emergency room staff had called me at home to question the husband about how old he and his wife were, where their home was, and if they had health insurance. I had spoken to the husband on the speakerphone, and he gave me enough information to get his wife admitted to the hospital.

The husband and two nurses were waiting for me when I entered the obstetrics room. The girl lay in bed, writhing in pain. She gave her name as Anna Maria. The young man shook my hand firmly and introduced himself as Herman. The nurses advised me that the contractions were coming one minute apart, and I needed to tell the girl to push hard against the nurse's fingers.

"*Empuje contra las dedos,*" I told her.

Sobbing now, she pushed harder.

"Ask her if she has had other pregnancies," the older nurse murmurs.

"*Ha otras embarazos?*" I asked.

The girl shook her head and moaned something.

"She has pain in her hips," said Herman in Spanish.

"She has pain in her hips," I told the nurses.

"Tell her the pain now is natural so the baby can come out," the younger nurse says.

I told the girl that she would be safe now, and the pain is natural so the baby can come out. The girl nodded and turned her head away, biting her lower lip.

"You'd better get dressed in scrubs," the older nurse advised.

"All right," I said, and stepped into the dressing room where I put on the green paper surgical gown, shoe and head coverings, and surgical mask.

When I saw the girl again, she was in the delivery room, lying on the table with her legs in the stirrups. The younger nurse leans towards me and said, "Tell her it will all be over in a few minutes."

"*Casi*," I said to the girl. "*Toda va bien.*"

Her husband stroked her arm slowly. He was wearing everything but the surgical mask, so I called to him, "*Tu necesitas esto,*" patting my mask. He put on his mask.

The nurses squirted Betadine between the girl's legs. The surgeon was 75 years old and had delivered many babies. He nodded when he was ready. A nurse handed him a syringe, and he injected several places in the girl's thighs. He will not give her an epidural. Doctors in this hospital do not give epidurals.

"Tell her to raise her hips," the doctor muttered.

"*Levante las caderas,*" I told her. She raises her hips slowly.

"That's good. Now we're ready," the doctor grunted.

"*Esta bien,*" I said to her, stroking her forehead.

"Tell her to push hard once more!" the doctor shouted.

"*Empuje mas,*" I tell her, and she does. When I look down, the baby has come out. It is a boy.

"Congratulations. You have a son," I tell them in Spanish, but they are looking at each other now. Her husband squeezed her hand tightly.

When I see the girl the next day, her husband is absent. He has gone back to work planting trees for seven dollars an hour. The medical records clerk wants me to ask the girl what she has named the baby.

"Geraldo," the girl said.

Later that day, the hospital social services director asks me to tell the girl that Geraldo is eligible for United States citizenship and that he qualifies for Medicaid. I tell the girl, and she nodded at us with a blank expression, but when the nurse handed her Geraldo she grinned broadly.

My boss and I print up and frame a motto that says in Spanish, "Father is the head of the family, but mother is the heart" and present it to the girl on her last day in the hospital. She smiled and said, "*Gracias.*"

Suddenly, commuting 200 miles a day for 3 years makes sense. I am a part of the medical team when they need my skills. Back in the geriatrics unit, I pour myself a cup of coffee and sit down for the first time that morning.

59

Gardens and Thieves

Patricia Guest

Once upon a time, not so very long ago, a widowed grandmother graduated from a program in counseling, hoping that she could find a job helping people. She became very sad after she applied for counseling job after counseling job and no one would hire her. She began to think that something was wrong with her.

Only recently had she become aware that she had no self-confidence. As she contemplated this problem, the widowed grandmother suddenly realized that her heart was much larger than her head. She knew that there must be a balance if she were ever to become self-confident. She consulted a wise person who told her that an imbalance of head and heart could cause distorted thinking.

The widowed grandmother thought she could help everyone, even her family and close friends. Subsequently, as she had successfully "helped" all of her close relations, she noticed that she was alone. She was aware, however, that she felt very peaceful, calm, and serene in spite of being alone. In fact, as she embraced the peaceful, calm, and serene feelings, she began to withdraw deep within herself to seek the meaning of her internal imbalance. The wise person had told her that she could find relief if she spent as much time with her "self" as she did with others. So she decided to stop thinking so much about her imbalance dilemma and follow a childhood dream.

For years, the widowed grandmother had dreamed of planting her very own flower garden, but she always had been too busy. She told herself that now was the time if her fantasy garden were ever to become real. She would use the flower garden as a portion of her "self" time. She let her heart lead her to a small cottage by the edge of a woods with a perfect space for a backyard garden. She retreated here when she wasn't helping others. She began to create her fantasy garden by digging holes and planting her favorite roses, trees, shrubs, herbs, and flowering plants. Her fantasy garden took form, grew, and became real. Now, she impatiently waits each spring as she watches the color burst forth from winter's rest to bring her hope that the world will become as beautiful and peaceful as her garden.

Meanwhile, as the fantasy garden developed, so did an alternative sentencing program for social errants, with whom she spent much of her "other" time. It began one day when a beautiful lady—who, as it turned out, became a real-life "fairy godmother"—conferred upon the grandmother gardener the grand compliment of "what a wonderful counselor she was." The fairy godmother encouraged the sad, unemployed counselor and assisted her in setting goals so that she could use her counseling skills to help thieves who had been arrested for their first offense. Most people believe that thieves are scoundrels who belong in jail and are undeserving of a second chance at freedom. These people don't know that many of these social errants are college students who impulsively shoplift or choose to steal just for a thrill. The fairy godmother and the sad, unemployed counselor imagined that if a miracle happened, the social errants could become honest and not want to steal.

Shoplifting, breaking into houses and cars, and stealing money and properties are felony crimes. When people who shoplift, rob, and steal are caught and convicted of their crimes, they are known as criminals. Folks just don't like to be victimized by criminals. Many people believe that scoundrels who steal stuff will never change. Some people, like the sad, unemployed counselor and her fairy godmother imagined that if they could help the scoundrels understand why they chose to steal other people's stuff, then some of them just might become honest and socially responsible.

Before long, a miracle did happen. A knight with a vision listened to the unemployed counselor and her fairy godmother tell about their belief that scoundrel thieves could be helped. He gave the sad unemployed counselor an opportunity to see if she really could help the social errants become honest and not want to steal.

Excitedly, she began to counsel these scoundrels in a different, more cunning way than one would counsel non-scoundrel clients. She found that the scoundrel clients rejoiced when they were confronted with a "truth." From this epiphany they learned that manipulation was not acceptable in the counseling alliance. This became the essential foundation for the process of interrupting their unhealthy, compulsive, criminal thought waves. One by one, the scoundrels changed into honest, responsible, accountable taxpayers. As the scoundrels became more responsible by giving back all the stolen stuff, doing volunteer service in the community, and developing healthy thought waves, they began to feel better about themselves. No longer did they see themselves as scoundrels. By then, they knew that they could get what they wanted through their own powers, in socially acceptable ways, without victimizing other people by stealing.

Slowly but surely, the errant scoundrels learned valuable life lessons. How they felt and learned was influenced directly by their thought waves and behaviors. New socially responsible behaviors such as holding a job and developing relationships were really rewarding, and becoming honest with themselves was truly an adventure. As a result of these changes the court dropped the felony charges and bestowed the new title of ex-thieves on the former errant scoundrels. Freedom from the stigma of a felony conviction was the consequence of these changed thoughts, behaviors, and feelings. This freedom has spread into the far corners of the community, as nearly 200 of these transformations have occurred. The really good news is that only a very few of the ex-thieves have since been rearrested.

The distinguishing difference between errant scoundrels and ex-thieves is that there is no discrepancy in what ex-thieves say and what they do, that is, they walk their talk. On the other hand, errant scoundrels are likely to tell you one thing and do something else.

The busy counselor isn't looking for a job. She has found her way as a counselor. She continues to help first-time felony offenders pay back their victims and become socially responsible taxpayers. The proud counselor applauds her fairy godmother and the knight with a vision for success stories. She also applauds the many student counselors who have worked with her toward interrupting criminal careers of first-time offenders. Last, but by no means least, she applauds the real heroes: the ex-thieves who were courageous enough to face their internal demons and change their evil doings. She sees them in the malls, stores, shops, restaurants, and schools around the city. Chance encounters with the ex-thieves gives the counselor a very safe, secure, and peaceful feeling as she continues along her special way as a counselor by interrupting criminal careers at the first offense.

When the enlightened, wise counselor isn't spending her time counseling the offenders, she is either in her real fantasy garden, playing with her grandchildren, or going on "vision quests" with new friends. Her heart–head imbalance has equalized, a fantasy garden has become real, her self-confidence problem is in remission, and an alternative sentencing program has become so popular with first offenders that she has had to hire another counselor and recruit more student counselors to help her. Without her fairy godmother, the knight with a vision, the student counselors, and the errant scoundrels, this story might have had a different ending.

60
A Little Caring

Larry L. Gulick

Doug's quarrelsome reputation preceded him, so I was not surprised by his scowling countenance as he entered my sixth-grade class for the very first time. His round, freckled face gave no clue that he was an aggressive, impudent bully who had been intimidating the teachers and students in this elementary school since he was in the first grade.

A strain of mischievousness radiated from his short, husky frame, and as the school's only male teacher, I was supposed to make this impish kid adjust to a system he had controlled for his previous five school years. It was my first day in a new school district and only my second year of teaching sixth-graders, so I wasn't about to let Doug disrupt my other students from having a good experience in my class.

The first bell rang and my new students entered the room. They smiled and greeted each other and said hello to me. All but Doug. He gave me a cursory glance and sat down in a corner of the back row. No one spoke to him as the classroom filled. The last students in the room occupied the seats around Doug, who sat there glowering at no one in particular.

The second bell rang. As I was about to introduce myself, Doug blurted out "What's your name?" I told him, and asked him the same question. He gave a big grin and loudly announced his name. But when I asked him to tell me more about himself, he said, "No, let someone else talk first."

Doug liked to talk most whenever I was trying to teach. If his classmates wouldn't listen to him, he got their attention by hitting them with stealth paper wads. I put him in the hallway for punishment, but when he returned to the classroom he made sure that I heard him tell students near him that he liked sitting in the hallway. Within 2 weeks the other students started complaining that Doug was too noisy and asked to be moved away from him.

Frequent scolding only increased the paper wads, interruptions, and other distracting behaviors so I decided to move him to the back of the room. Far enough away, I thought, so he couldn't disrupt as many people, including me. He often would ask me to explain something just after I had given instructions to the class. After a while, I caught onto this little game and asked other students to explain the instructions to him. But this attempt to embarrass him just increased his questions, probably because this was one of the few times that other students would talk to him. I put him in a back corner of the room and tried to ignore him, but he just raised his voice to ask me to explain something again.

There was one more option that I thought might help keep Doug from being so easily distracted. So one day I told him that he would be able to listen better if I put his seat behind the wooden reading booth. This was a three-sided plywood wall that some students used when they wanted to work on something alone. Maybe now he wouldn't be able to sabotage my class so often. But this did not end the problem. After a few days of spitballs flying over the top of the "container," and Doug's loud voice complaining that he couldn't hear me, I surrendered. This turned out to be the beginning of the solution to helping my unhappy student.

I began applying some of the alternative ways of dealing with students that I was learning from my evening counseling courses. The substance of the counseling theories began translating into a practical way by preparing me to help Doug improve his interaction with others. So I started giving him attention before he did something wrong. It was then that I started becoming a more effective teacher.

When Doug entered the classroom the following Monday, I motioned for him to come to me and pointed to his desk, which I had placed beside mine. He protested that he hadn't done anything wrong; but I explained that he wasn't being punished, I just wanted him beside me so I could help him more. He gave me a puzzled look and sat down. That morning, for the first time, I asked him to take the attendance slips and the lunch money to the office. I didn't know it then, but this was the first step to healing Doug's relationships within the school.

The days passed and the more I asked him to do, the more his behavior improved. I was starting to give him the respect he needed. He became more interested in class activities, and his grades slowly improved. Teachers and students commented that Doug seemed easier to get along with; eventually, they also began to accept him.

From the time that Doug sat next to me, I started joking with him more and found that he listened when I put my hand gently on his shoulder. When he was given more responsibility, he responded by being more responsible. I had started to care for him, and it showed. I was learning the importance of showing that I cared for all my students. For Doug, and other students, demonstrating that I was interested and cared for them made the difference between succeeding and failing in the classroom—for them and me.

The school year ended and I completed work on my counseling degree that summer. I applied for a counseling position and began my counseling career, split between the middle school and high school.

This new role gave me the opportunity to continue working with some of the students I had taught in the sixth grade. School started and I asked one of my former students if she knew where Doug was. She said he moved during the summer but didn't know where. But I hadn't forgotten what I learned my last year of working with him.

As the new counselor at both schools, I worked with those students who needed extra time to adjust to their surroundings. I applied the same principles of caring that I had with Doug. Many of these students had not had positive experiences in their personal lives, and this carried over to their experiences with school. Consequently, they were often the "troublemakers," and teachers were happy to send them to me to see what "miracles" I might perform.

I was surprised by the reaction of some teachers in my interest in working with students who gave them the most problems. My association with these students gave me the reputation from them that I was more of an advocate for miscreants than as a helper for everyone. Slowly I began to learn that it was important for me to show teachers that I cared about their needs and frustrations as well. I was a champion to the administration but was perceived as an enabler for problem students by a few staff members.

So I expanded my role to include anyone who was experiencing a sense of "no one cares about my concerns." The more I listened to teachers about their problems, the more they trusted me to work with them on a common goal of helping students realize greater success in school and in life outside the classroom.

Teachers began inviting me to their classrooms to observe students who were having problems. I became a resource to help them with classroom behavior problems, and the teachers also talked with me about underachieving students and students who had problems making friends. The more I cared about their problems, the more they shared other concerns they had, personal and professional.

When an angry parent called, venting their frustration with their child's problems at school, I gave them the same respect I gave the students and teachers. I had learned to empathize with their concerns and offered to help them with their child any way I could. After all, I believed they were the true "experts" regarding their own children.

What had started as a better way to work with a single child with problems had evolved into a network of teachers, parents, and a counselor working together to help improve children's lives. I had learned more about the power of caring for individuals and was able to provide a better environment in which those students could learn, and teachers were given a better chance to do a better job of teaching—even with those students like Doug. By showing our students that we care, we show them that they belong.

61

Days of Our Lives

Carol Becker

This is my first year as a middle school counselor, so I am smack in the middle of "finding my way." After just 20 weeks on the job, I find it both stimulating and stressful. It's amazing to me that counselors at this level don't crash and burn after a few years. The frantic pace I keep reminds me of a drag race with its perilous twists and turns, weaving my way in and out of obstacles. It also reminds me of the environment that must be "status quo" in a hospital emergency room. Maybe some writer should come up with a sitcom called "Days of Our Lives, Counselor Style." It might go something like this:

It was 6:00 a.m. when the alarm went off, signaling that it was time to get up. I reached across the nightstand and punched the snooze button. "Just another 5 minutes please!" I thought. It was dark and cold, and I loved being snuggled in my "cocoon" of blankets. After a few more minutes of futile attempts at lapsing back into twilight sleep, I lazily stretched and sat up in bed. My mind clicked into gear as my body reluctantly followed. "Let's see, what to wear. I need to get into school early and organize my office. All those standardized tests need to be filed and sent home, my friendship group passes written out, and the progress reports . . . I haven't got a clue how to get through those! I still have a couple of parent phone calls to make, too."

I headed for the shower, did a quick 5-minute scrub down, and toweled off. Just 25 minutes later I was dressed, my hair was done, and my make-up applied. "Not bad," I thought. "Let's see, I'll grab a quick cup of coffee and eat a banana before I leave."

At 7:00 a.m. I was parking my red Toyota Corolla in the parking lot at Southwest Middle School feeling smug about the fact that I was early. As I casually strode in through the front door of the school, Marge, the principal's secretary was anxiously waiting for me, "Carol, could you come with me?" she asked nervously. As I walked with Marge down the hall, she quickly briefed me on the problem. "Listen, Helen is sitting in the spare office. She came to work in the cafeteria but fell apart emotionally, so I put her in here until you arrived. Her nephew was shot and killed in Birmingham last night." Adrenaline pumping, my mind instantaneously snapped into "counselor mode." As I approached the spare office, I spotted Helen hunched in a gray metal chair in the center of the room. I quickly went in and shut the door, pulled up another gray metal chair and placed myself in close proximity to her. "Tell me what happened," I said softly. As Helen recounted the gruesome details, I took a quick mental survey of Helen's current emotional status. Helen was definitely in shock. I patted Helen's hand and continued to listen attentively as Helen cried and choked on words as she recounted the details and blankly stared into space. After what seemed like an appropriate pause, I went over with Helen what she needed to do at this point and reiterated that I would be available to her anytime she needed me. Marge had offered to drive Helen home, so I urged Helen to go with her. I also suggested numerous times that she should call her doctor and get lots of support from family and friends in the coming months. I went out in the hall, found Marge, and the two departed for Helen's home.

Taking a deep breath, I checked my watch, "7:30 a.m.," I muttered. I already felt emotionally spent, and the school day had barely begun. As I approached my office, Connie, my secretary said, "Mrs. Carter and Ashley are here to see you." "Ashley must have been released from the hospital already," I speculated. Ashley had attempted suicide just 2 days prior.

"Hello, Mrs. Carter. Hello, Ashley, won't you come into my office," I offered. Unlocking the door, I quickly turned on the light and hung up my coat while they got situated. "How are things going?" I asked sympathetically. Mrs. Carter proceeded with a monologue about her ex, her job, Ashley, Ashley's friends, and generally how she was at her wit's end. I listened attentively while sizing up Ashley's nonverbal cues. It appeared to me that mother and daughter were miles apart on communication. Thankfully, Mrs. Carter stated that they were all, including her ex, going to see a therapist weekly. I murmured something sympathetic and reiterated, once again, that I would be available for Mrs. Carter and Ashley anytime they needed to work through something anxiety producing. Mrs. Carter appeared to be greatly consoled and left Ashley in my "expert hands" as she needed to get to work.

After Ashley went back to class, I realized that it was 8:00 a.m. and I was already late for a team meeting. "The Stanford Tests, phone calls, progress reports, and friendship group passes will just have to wait," I whispered to myself as I grabbed my teaming notebook and scurried down the hall.

Upon arrival, I quickly surmised that something was amiss. Tension was in the air. Two of the teachers were talking in low soothing tones to another teacher, Pam, who was extremely pale and appeared to be feeling ill. I approached and asked tentatively, "What is wrong?" She replied she had a fever and couldn't stop coughing.

Don't you think you should go home?" I asked tentatively. "I'm sure we can find a substitute for you. Your teammates will be glad to cover your class until the sub arrives," I added. At this point, Pam's teammates reiterated that they could handle her classes. While they were conferring about what work to cover, I called the main office and asked Marge to call for a substitute. Then, I called Beth, the nurse, who came down to help escort Pam to her office. Attempting to be reassuring I said, "Everything will be fine, just take care of yourself."

After double checking with Pam's teammates that all bases were covered, I excused myself and hurried down to another team meeting in the eighth-grade wing. Trying to compose myself, I took five deep breaths, visualized a relaxing beach scene for 30 seconds, and then opened the eighth-grade team room door. The team was in the midst of a parent conference, so I quietly made my way to the empty chair at the far end of the table. It was obvious from the ensuing discussion that the teachers were not too happy with the student's performance. After 10 more minutes of tense dialogue, I suggested that perhaps Dad could spend more time with Doug. At that point, the mother went into a tirade. "Yes, that's what I've been telling you all along! See, you need to spend more time with your son. I told you! I told you!" "Oh great," I thought, "now she's ruined any remote chance that Doug's Dad might have been willing to think about my advice." At that point the conference came to a rather awkward end. I, once again, offered my services to Doug's parents and told them to "call me anytime."

For the next 2 hours, I saw a steady stream of kids. Some of their concerns were related to Ashley's suicide attempt; other students had academic concerns, teacher problems, or student conflicts.

At noon, I made my way out to the lunchroom with a brief pit stop in the bathroom. As usual, the seventh graders were sitting around tables piling their trash high in the middle, chasing each other in between tables, or lining up to go into the gym to play basketball. Thankfully, a few students were just sitting around talking quietly. I spied Casey pursuing a couple of his friends with a full garbage bag of lunch trash. I quickly intervened by pulling Casey aside, talking to him calmly and asking him to evaluate his behavior. After another half hour of "guard duty," I made my way slowly back to my office. "I've got to eat something," I thought, "I'm about shot for the day." I pulled out my yogurt, apple, and soda and was just about to have a few minutes of peace and quiet, when Ben from In-School Suspension (ISS) stuck his head in my door. "Carol, do you have a minute to see Harold? He's in ISS and says he wants to talk to you."

"Sure," I sighed as I pushed my yogurt aside. Harold came bounding into my office and plopped himself down beside me. He proceeded to elaborate about how his life "sucked," his teachers "sucked," and his mother "sucked." After working him through his issues, including doing some visualization about how his perfect day would look and relaxation techniques, I escorted Harold back to ISS.

By then, my yogurt and soda were lukewarm, but I scarfed them down anyway. Scanning the office with a hopeless gaze, I realized that standardized test, progress reports, friendship passes, and phone calls had still not been addressed. I decided to tackle a few phone calls. After talking to three parents regarding their concerns, I again offered my services. "Call me anytime. I'm here for you," I urged.

After school, I did some grocery shopping and other errands, ate a quick dinner and slowly made my way up the stairs to bed. By 8:00 p.m. I was propped up in bed reading a Sue Grafton mystery. The soothing sounds of Yanni filled the room. After an hour I put down my book and sleepily reached for the light. As I snuggled down under my comforter I mused, "I wonder what tomorrow will bring," and then I whispered a brief prayer, "God, I need a clone. Help me minister to those in need."

Working as a school counselor in a public school is one of the most challenging yet rewarding jobs. I am in a highly visible role supporting many people daily with a variety of needs. I have to be calm, reassuring, in control, wise, organized, well-spoken, well-educated, professional, friendly, and caring. I represent the "heart" of the building. But sometimes a little voice inside my heart shouts, "Hey, what about me?" I am still finding my way in learning how to take the time I need to process, refresh myself, recharge, and at times, detach. Perhaps this will be a lifelong struggle, and my focus for now will have to be one day at a time.

62
Hopping Along With a Friend

Elizabeth Witherspoon

Kids easily find their way to my office; it's the only one in the school with a baby gate. The sign on it reads "Ellie's Gate." Ellie is my co-counselor, my friend, my lop-eared rabbit, and a beacon to the middle-school kids and staff where I work as a new counselor. When my door is open, Ellie watches the gate, lies under my desk, or sits in a chair. When my door is closed, Ellie enters into the realm of counseling and gets to work.

As a graduate student, I knew I wanted animals to be a part of my counseling with children. I often discussed this desire with my fellow counselors in training and my professors. Although I had no pets at the time, I imagined myself counseling with a dog at my side. During a session with my internship site supervisor, I shared my desire to incorporate pets into my counseling. She shared my enthusiasm for this endeavor and encouraged me to begin during my middle-school internship. The principal supported this idea and welcomed a pet into the school. Because I did not have a dog, I enlisted help from a friend's Welsh corgi. The dog confirmed my positive expectations of pet-facilitated counseling. She could sense my clients' emotions, and on videotape I witnessed her rapport with children. This experience motivated me to continue exploring working with pets.

My internship evolved into a job this past year. As a new counselor, I was nervous and excited. I spent the summer searching for the perfect therapy dog in the local shelter. Although I did find a dog, I realized it would take a lot of training with him before he was prepared to facilitate counseling. My rabbit, whom I had acquired through a friend, became the alternative choice but not without reservations. Ellie can be temperamental and shy around strangers, and she likes peace and quiet. With encouragement from my new colleagues, I decided to give her a chance anyway. With Ellie at my side, I started my counseling career.

As I expected, Ellie became a magnet for children. Word spread about the rabbit, and kids started coming by in between classes to meet her. In turn, I also became a familiar face to students so that when problems arose, they were comfortable coming to me.

In our co-counseling, Ellie's gift of connecting with children has emerged. I never know what she will do in our sessions, but it usually turns out to be right for the child we are seeing. In working with a severely depressed client over some time I was unable to engage him in any activity or conversation. In one such session, Ellie began circling this child. She received no response, not even a glance. The rabbit then jumped into his lap. He looked at her but still did not move. Ellie then jumped on his shoulder and tugged at his hair. The child clearly told the rabbit to stop it and set her on the floor. Ellie persisted until he began to stroke her ears and maintain eye contact with her. The response from this child clearly came as a result of the rabbit. I have seen Ellie evoke responses from several of my most unresponsive and hard-to-reach clients.

Throughout my week I am involved in conflict resolutions. Many of these are too volatile for peer mediation. In these sessions I have found Ellie to be a good source of tension reduction. During these times, Ellie may drag one of my stuffed animals around the room, hop on top of my desk, or try to get into a child's backpack. Her actions cause the children to laugh, comment to each other how funny she is, and get them relaxed enough to try to work out the conflict.

Many times when I am working on establishing a relationship with a child, mistrust and fear toward me and the process exist. Having my rabbit with us soothes the child and often produces a common bond with me—the love of animals. I have witnessed children being more comfortable talking directly to Ellie than to me. Many sessions begin with a discussion of pets, and it naturally flows from there. Children trust Ellie and that trust flows over to me. I have had a child tell me that kids can tell I am a caring and understanding adult because I relate to my rabbit so well.

The bond between Ellie and kids is strong. A child I see was preparing to undergo another reconstructive surgery on her face. She was feeling very nervous and frightened. Knowing how attached she was to Ellie, I gave her one of Ellie's photographs from my bulletin board for support. Later her mother told me that the child had carried Ellie's picture with her through the entire procedure. She could not wait to come back to school and tell Ellie all about it.

Ellie intuitively knows during a counseling session when not to be involved. In the times when her help is not needed she slips under my desk for a nap to keep out of sight. This may happen when a child is communicating freely or the child is engaged in play or art. She leaves that session to me.

Even the rabbit's timidity and crankiness is helpful in creating analogies for children about their feelings and behaviors. Ellie may be in a foul mood toward the end of the day just like my students. She needs quiet time alone like they do. She may feel quite angry and not want anyone near her but at the same time get upset if she is ignored. Children often behave in the same contradictory way. A key thing I try to show children is that no matter how Ellie acts or what she is feeling, she has my unconditional love. My hope is for my clients to feel our relationship is the same way. She lets each child know, as I try, that he or she is very special to her. The children know.

Ellie does wonders for me, professionally and personally helping me to find my way. My stress level feels a little less during the days when Ellie is with me. She adds humor and spontaneity between clients, which is a welcome diversion for me. Ellie receives numerous positive strokes throughout the day and I feel the effects. My rabbit helps me explore my creative side in counseling, which benefits me and my clients. My counseling style is the same whether Ellie is with me or not, she just adds more to the overall process.

Some days I take Ellie home when the day has been especially trying, and I begin to wonder if I can handle all that is involved with being a counselor. I start to feel disheartened and angry at the world in which kids have to live. I sometimes question my choice in a career. Then I look at Ellie who has heard all that I have heard and seen what I have seen, and her eyes tell me, "I know it can be hard, but we will keep at it." She reassures me as a counselor and I am ready for the next day.

I am not suggesting that every counselor needs to have a pet facilitate his or her counseling sessions. Each of us needs to find our own way as counselors. Ellie has helped me find mine. I hope you will find your own "rabbit."

63

Out of Place

Michael Taleff

It has been 20 years since I first entered the drug and alcohol field. Back then I really felt out of place, and sometimes I still do. In the old days, as I was trying to determine my counseling style, I attended as many workshops on this subject as I could. Yet, that is when I first felt as if I did not belong.

I could see the growth of a beguiling paradigm, and it was gradually taking over the minds of my colleagues. It smelled of dogma and seduced many into simply being "label-throwers" and "truth-finders." They became convinced that they had cornered a piece of reality as it applied to the dynamics and treatment of addiction.

Falling into this trap, many good counselors quickly became inflexible and stopped asking questions. They just tagged anyone who remotely resembled an alcoholic with the label. This was usually done carelessly and in the most casual, almost pompous, fashion. It betrayed the truth-finder in them—because they always made you believe that what they had to say was the truth, and it was never to be questioned.

This group of professional counselors gained a heightened sense of conformation and power by comparing their contorted counseling stories with others of the same stock. This was especially apparent in the many staff meetings I attended over the years. Clients were characterized in the most inappropriate fashion. The motif was one in which the addict was described as a "con-artist" and definitely someone not to be trusted. Inappropriate nicknames would be given to clients, while mocking jokes would fly around the staff room.

In this "golden age" of alcohol and other drug (AOD) treatment, programs developed schemes and schedules to offset this client motif. In particular, the loudest, the most confrontational, if not the most intimidating, counselor was a role model to emulate. It was said such counselors never took any guff, and that was the way all AOD counselors should be.

I recall one such person who had a bellowing voice, his share of false pride, and a magnificent strut. He had a back pocket full of handy insults and was forever calling clients disparaging names, all in the name of being honest. He had fallen into the dogmatic trap, lock, stock, and barrel, and was praised for his actions. He truly believed that there was only one way to treat addicts, and it was to be brusque and give no quarter.

If clients relapsed following this so-called treatment, they were the ones thought to be at fault. The program was never questioned, as the program was considered to have found the truth of recovery that the client obviously missed. To reinforce such thinking, the counselors would develop a set of rationalizations that shifted the blame to the client who relapsed. Some of these classic excuses included, "They have not hit bottom." "They are still in denial." Or, my all time favorite, "They have not hurt enough." It all seemed part of a "party line" to which you had to adhere or be ostracized. Anyone voicing a different opinion was seen as being duped by these people.

No matter how I tried to understand all this, it never felt right. I decided to voice my opinion, and it came with a price. I soon began to feel excluded by others because I questioned the party line. At other times, I felt I had to deliberately distance myself from these dogmatic professionals to save my sanity.

In contrast, I had always been taught that people are individuals and should be treated differently. Labels were of limited value and never had the ability to truly characterize anyone. As far as the truth was concerned, that was only something the AOD field thought they had. Truth, I felt, was too complex for any one idea, theory, or group to have.

Not believing I had the truth and not labeling people meant that I had to work hard to match the best treatment available to a particular client. That, in turn, meant that I had to stay "in shape." That was accomplished through continually reading, particularly the research literature. Laboring through such material can be conflicting if not bewildering. But it conditioned me to keep an open mind. More often than not, I had to swallow my own pet theories because they were not supported by the data. Yet, because of these episodes, I believe I have become more of a critical thinker as well as a questioner. An interesting question, as George Kelly states, is worth a thousand truths.

Through my actions, I have tried to let clients know I trusted them. Once that was established, we could then get down to the true business of recovery. This was evident in a case I completed a few years back. It involved a woman who had just finished one of those traditional inpatient programs. She was to follow up with outpatient counseling and I was to be her counselor.

On the day we met, my very first impression was of an angry individual. In a very hostile tone, she made it clear that she had not appreciated the method of treatment conducted by the inpatient program. She also made it clear that if I were to resort to that kind of therapy, she would not come back. She had thrown the gauntlet at my feet.

I decided to take up this challenge. I first asked her what type of treatment she had received. She seemed more than happy to tell me all the details of that experience. This "strategy" was very reminiscent of the approaches I had seen in my earlier inpatient career days. She had been confronted almost every day about her angry, denial-ridden attitude and was essentially told she would have to hurt more before she would be able to truly get into recovery. She was told her "best thoughts" got her into this predicament. That comment seemed to particularly infuriate her.

I carefully logged this growing list of complaints and made a conscious note to myself never to use such strategies with her. By first listening and not passing any judgment, I seemed to establish some rapport with her. She was not completely convinced that I was different from those other counselors but indicated that she would return for our next appointment. All that week, I tried to think of ways to see this case differently. The core question centered on how I could approach this individual in a novel and creative manner. I even reviewed the case with my peers in our weekly supervisory session. Their opinions were not that helpful. They saw her as terminally angry and in denial and strongly recommended that I confront her. I reported that this client had repeatedly told me that the confrontational approach contributed to her anger, so this case needed a different strategy. The consensus of that staff remained one of confrontation or else they believed she would relapse. Walking out of the room, I again had that old sense of feeling out of place.

I needed a different approach and hit upon a strategy that worked. I reframed her anger as a strength rather than a liability. In fact, I noted that it had helped her survive. I presented this interpretation to her in the next session and she warmed to the idea. Within a few minutes, she began to give me examples of how her anger had been a survival tool. As she continued to describe these survival episodes, her anger began to wane.

We soon developed an even better rapport and began to explore different ways she could use her anger in a positive fashion. She was determined that she was not going to fall into the prediction that the inpatient treatment center made of her relapsing due to the unresolved anger. Within a few weeks of this session, her inpatient discharge summary had arrived. It indicated that she had not hit bottom and predicted her imminent relapse. As I read that portion of the summary to her, she stiffened and said: "I guess I showed them." Then she laughed.

Toward the final sessions we began to review where she had been and we discussed her future. She reminisced about the first few sessions and how angry she had been. She let me know that one of the reasons she decided to stay in therapy was that she saw me as different from other counselors. I had not labeled her nor dared to predict how her life would turn out if she did not follow my advice to the letter. She liked that and felt trusted. In helping her find her unique way, I began to discover a little more of my own.

I have tried to transfer this attitude to the classes I teach. Sometimes it can prove difficult and other times it can be quite satisfying. A noteworthy reward came from a small graduate class I taught a few semesters ago. At first, the students were stiff and simply wanted me to give them easy solutions to the complex AOD problems. I resisted the temptation and encouraged them to find their own answers. We managed to gain a rapport and, through a process of critically analyzing the most cherished ideas in AOD counseling, the students began, at last, to question. The more they did, the more they became frustrated. Yet, it was a good frustration, because it led to more trips to the library. Soon I found that I did not have to lead the class. Each week the students arrived eager to share their latest discoveries.

What was even more apparent was the students' love of the work. The searching, reading, and analyzing of material was not drudgery; rather it was exciting to them. They discussed the issues in a thoughtful manner and without dogma. They began to formulate one tantalizing question after another. For each class they made new and spontaneous findings, not only about the literature but about themselves. In the end, there was not a label thrower or truth finder among them. They were beginning to feel the fire of true education.

Here, I mused, was what AOD education and treatment really personified: thoughtful people finding the best treatment available for their future clients. But there is a caveat. If they continued to be open and critical thinkers, they could evolve into a counselor in the truest sense of the word. That, in turn, could mean they might feel out of place. Despite the warning, they all were all willing to take this risk.

As this class ended, I knew I was making a difference with a future generation of AOD counselors. This is how I have begun to find my way and my place.

64
Learning From Disasters

Gary Koch

On August 24, 1992, the most devastating hurricane to ever hit the United States tore into South Florida with gusts reaching more than 165 miles per hour. Hurricane Andrew ravaged parts of Florida and Louisiana, killing 52 people. In South Florida alone, Andrew left 250,000 people homeless.

Unemployed at the time and resting from a hectic graduate school schedule, I wanted to do what I could to help. This opportunity seemed like a way I could be useful to others during a critical time of need and yet also help myself professionally.

I was able to arrange to go to Homestead, Florida, with counselors from a local mental health center. As we drove southward, I got my first glimpse of the magnitude of the disaster. The destruction was like nothing I had ever seen. There were piles of squashed cars, ruined appliances, clothing, and toys everywhere. My anxiety level rose.

The destruction was not the only thing that struck me. I was amazed at something that would stand out for me throughout this experience and for the rest of my life: the tremendous resiliency of the human spirit. One of the signs of this resiliency was the use of humor. Spray painted in black letters on the side of a house that had most of its roof torn off was "Half Off Sale." I have been told that disasters bring out the best and worst in people. I experienced much of the best in Homestead.

The first day we assessed the three tent cities in Homestead that were erected to house, clothe, feed, and care for the homeless. I remember starting my first walk around the second day thinking "What have I gotten myself into? What am I doing? What do I do?" However, this experience of disaster recovery taught me the true meaning of "self as instrument." In finding my way as a counselor, I learned how to use myself as my primary tool.

I found disaster recovery work to be exhilarating, but it's different than traditional counseling. First, there are no offices. Most work is conducted by mingling with victims wherever they congregate. Second, the working conditions can often mean sleeping on cots in tents, dealing with extreme heat and humidity, and consuming unappetizing and sporadic meals. Third, counselors must seek out clients as very few people seek assistance. Fourth, the disaster worker must be more self-sufficient. There are no secretaries, supervisors, or coworkers handy. Everyone is usually working in the field, so even when we tried to work in pairs, often we were separated. Fifth, flexibility of duties is a must. There is little structure. You do what must be done, whatever it is.

Why then would someone want to do this work? This is the most invigorating, exhilarating, rewarding, and challenging work I have ever done. I have worked in residential care with acute and chronic clients, performed in-home visits for clients recently released from the state hospital, led sexual offender groups, worked with sexual abuse survivors, worked with people with multiple personality disorder, and performed emergency crisis services. Nothing gives me such rewarding challenges as disaster recovery work.

When I think of my disaster recovery work after Hurricane Andrew, I think of Mary's quiet strength and smile. I think of Frank, who was usually found "camped out" in a lawn chair outside his tent, laughing with family and friends. The most significant experience, however, was visiting a counselor's relatives who lived in Homestead. I'll never forget their story. I can vividly remember them telling me how the hurricane sounded like a locomotive, how the ceiling started moving up and down like an ocean wave, and how they hid in a bedroom closet praying for their lives.

Few things have touched me as deeply or have been as pivotal in helping me find my way as a counselor as disaster recovery work. It has renewed my faith in humankind and my belief in a higher power. Do yourself a favor and become a disaster recovery volunteer. Not only will it make you a better counselor, it will change your life!

65

The Wizard of Ours

Wayne Schneider

As a counselor just beginning my career, I sometimes wonder about and imagine the vast number of roads one can choose while working with clients and even while working on oneself. The movie *The Wizard of Oz* portrays a girl, Dorothy, who has one road to follow; it is yellow and leads to one place—the Emerald City of Oz. Dorothy travels this road with her three friends, one searching for a brain, one looking for a heart, and one seeking courage. Dorothy herself is trying to find her way home, and she encounters a new family. In this family, members assist each other along their journey to find what each thinks he or she is missing. Is it possible that by listening with our hearts, trusting what seems logical to our brains, and finding the courage to pursue the decisions that we sense are right, we, as counselors, are traveling on the road to find our wizards?

I became a counselor for two reasons. First, I am exhilarated by the gratitude of the families and individuals I am helping. I know that I have affected their lives in some positive way. The second reason is that I believe this road we travel runs in both directions. In giving energy to my families and clients, I seem to learn as much from them as they learn from me. With this decision to counsel clients comes a commitment to my own growth. I am convinced that counselors are basically people engaged in the act of making suggestions. They just use subtle ways of making them. But how do counselors know that their suggestions will create desirable results? Dorothy had Glinda, the Witch of the North, to guide her and choose her road, but we as professionals have a more difficult task. Of course, it is more than essential to map out the family's journey toward growth and harmony. But the host of possible roads that ensures their safe arrival are so numerous. I often think of how difficult this task can be. Do I assist my clients on the road that they are already traveling, or do I try to direct them toward the road that I have in mind?

At times during group supervision, I can feel myself doubting the choices that I have made with my clients. This does not occur because of my own contemplation but is due to the words of others in the group. I think some counselors have the idea that there is only one road. With their professional opinions, they stand so strongly confident. I believe this stance limits our opportunity to find success. My point is, that with all these different views and paths, I have learned to see that when people are certain that they know the right road and are convinced that it is the only way, this may, indeed, not be the only road to follow. Just in case, I try something different. I am learning that when other counselors' hearts, brains, and courage take them in different directions, and down different roads, finding Oz is possible from many roads. Imagine that—thousands of roads all leading to the same place.

The Wizard of Oz has always been a special movie for me. I sometimes analyze the story. Could the color yellow of the brick road symbolize insecurity, lack of courage, or even failure to make decisions? Are the lion, the tin man, and the scarecrow dissociated parts of Dorothy? As counselors, our aim could be directed toward encouraging our clients to look within themselves for their yellow brick roads and journeys to find their own wizards. At the end of the movie, the wizard explains to Dorothy that she has had the power within herself to go home the entire time. *The Wizard of Oz* could be called the "Wizard of Ours," being that the wizard is inside of us all. As counselors, it seems essential that we first find our own wizards, before we aid our clients in finding theirs. It is possible to look together as a family, as did Dorothy and her friends.

When situations become difficult, and choices have to be made as to which direction to take, I have learned to use my brain and my heart and to have the courage to trust myself. The road might be yellow, but when we are hesitant, we think more. As I contemplate different counseling situations, the road seems to branch many ways. During those silent times, when the clients' emotions overflow, memories of past hurts and injustices are able to surface. At these moments I am not sure how I should behave. I do not recall from my introductory counseling class which is the best counselor etiquette. Do I sit there stiff, distant, opaque, and offer my clients a box of tissues, or do I cry with them and join in their sorrows? Do I embrace them, in the manner of most cultures and some members of the animal kingdom, when dealing with sadness and distress? It is difficult to make judgment calls in counseling situations.

My coworkers have noticed that sometimes during these sensitive counseling sessions, I cry more than our clients. Rather than cause embarrassment, this observation brings a smile to my face, as it is a sure sign that I am finding my own way as a therapist, a road that is comfortable for me. Understanding our clients enough to have tears for their situations lets them know how much we care. Usually the tears are happy ones of growth, which I find to be the best kind.

As a counselor, finding my way is a journey that will most likely never end. I may be confused when I get 26 different opinions from 26 different supervisors on the same case. But, as Dorothy had her obstacles, I will have mine. Although I may feel unsure of some decisions, one thing is certain, and that is the wonderful way I feel when I have made a loving and caring impact on another person's life. With all the decisions that come and go, I am satisfied to have chosen a career that not only allows me to help others but also gives me a chance to grow and learn more about myself. Life cannot possibly be more exciting. So, when we see lions, tigers, and bears, and the Wicked Witch of the West, we can accept this as part of the journey. Every obstacle and struggle is an opportunity for growth, and we can look inward to that "Wizard of Ours," which consists of our brain, our heart, and the courage to pull them all together, to find our own way.

66
What Matters Most

Jeffrey A. Kottler

I looked out into the audience and was astonished by how still everyone sat. I could see alternating stripes of white and burgundy in the shadows, the color of their uniforms. A single ceiling fan turned so slowly it seemed to be more ornamental than functional.

This was a nursing school in a remote part of the Kathmandu valley in Nepal. There were perhaps 150 young women packed into the room, each in their various stages of training. I was given one hour to tell them everything I know about counseling and everything they might need as part of their jobs working with the terminally ill, the sick, and the suffering. This was all part of my month-long assignment to promote counseling services in this part of the world, especially for reproductive health issues.

This is a country with epidemics raging everywhere—hepatitis, HIV, even polio. In remote villages I visited, many of the children have bulging necks, goiters the result of poor nutrition. If someone should break a leg, burst an appendix, or otherwise fall ill, the only help lies a 4-day walk away. Nepal has among the highest mother and infant mortality rates in the world. And so many of the problems stem from lack of accurate information, poor education, nonexistent medical services in rural areas, and very little in the way of counseling. So it falls upon the nurses to do more patient education, community outreach, and counseling.

In an article that appeared in *The Kathmandu Post* that very day, there was an announcement that the Nepalese Teachers Association had urged that the school curriculum be revised to include the subject of "girl trafficking." I am not making this up.

There is a belief among some HIV-afflicted men of their Southerly neighbor—India—that the only cure for their disease is to have sex with a virgin. Procurement agents are sent out into remote, poverty-stricken

Himalayan villages to buy or kidnap young girls, some as little as 10 years old, for the flourishing sex trade. The parents are told the children will be offered training and job opportunities that would never be possible in their own country. I suppose that is true in a way. When the girls return several years later, they spread the virus among their own people.

I compare the kinds of problems the nurse/counselors in this country will face compared to those I am used to treating: depression, anxiety, family conflicts, and such. It is not that we don't have our own problems with poverty and medical neglect in our country, it is just that in parts of the world where people earn a dollar a day the challenges seem absolutely overwhelming. How can one possibly make a difference?

Like most visitors to Nepal, I came to go trekking. This was not why I was sent here but it was the secret reason why I volunteered for the assignment. This would be an opportunity to hike in the Himalayas, take photographs, see interesting sights, maybe even visit a monastery or two near the Tibetan border. First, however, I had to take care of business—five straight days of seminars, presentations, and meetings with medical and administrative staff working in reproductive health. And then there are these lectures to large groups of nurses.

My job is to do what I can to prepare them. In one hour. I consider what I could possibly tell them that would make a difference and decide to promote the essence of what I think is most important—the relationships they develop with patients, their caring and commitment to helping. After all, this is what has helped me to remain centered about what is often so important—especially when I feel as confused and lost as I do now standing on this stage.

This is just part of what counseling is all about, of course. But what else can I tell them with a restricted vocabulary and limited time in a crowded, stuffy room?

The person who introduced me took a little longer than I expected, so now I have only 52 minutes—less than an hour to tell them everything I know about counseling, or at least everything they might need to know in their work.

I could tell them about active listening skills but there's no time or room to practice them. I could mention how important the placebo effect is; surely they'd know about that. I could introduce the technique of "looking for exceptions" in which they'd ask their patients to tell them more about what is going right rather than wrong. Because there are very few medications available and the people can't afford operations, words are about all they have to offer comfort.

Gee, there are so many things I could do or say, but I'm not sure how much English they really understand. I've noticed that the Nepalese smile a lot regardless of what is going on around them. Then there's the additional problem that I constantly get confused because they shake their head side to side when they mean "yes" even though it looks like "no."

I roam around the stage peering out into the audience, trying to read reactions to whatever I've done so far. Because there are no lights on in the room (to save money?), I can only see the first few rows. The girls are all holding hands, sitting on one another's laps, embracing one another as if these small comforts are what matter most. Then I realize that this is what nurses do best for patients. This is what counseling is all about to them. I don't even need the whole hour to tell them this. I finish up with a few minutes to spare, so there is time for a question.

"Please Sir," one of the few men in the room says as he stands at attention. I don't have any idea if he is a student or instructor. "I have heard there are eight stages of counseling. Could you please tell us about them?"

I feel panic welling up inside me, as everyone in the room looks at me expectantly. If I faint at least there are plenty of nurses around to take care of me, I think, trying to stifle a maniacal giggle.

Eight stages? I wonder which ones those might be? I can only think of six stages, maybe five, but . . . I look at my watch and see I've got 4 minutes left.

"Let's make it simple," I tell the questioner. "We don't have time for eight stages, so how about three? There's a beginning, a middle, and an end."

I think about telling them what might be included in each stage, but in just a few minutes, what difference can that really make?

I look out at their young, eager faces. They have the most difficult jobs in the world. They are underpaid, unappreciated, and face problems in their country that are so huge and widespread that their efforts won't put a dent in the poverty, disease, and suffering.

I see the man still standing, waiting for my answer. "Look," I tell him, "forget the stages. Forget everything I told you today. Just remember one thing." I stop for a moment, trying to decide what one thing that might be. What can I tell them that really matters? What can I tell anyone that will make a difference?

One week later I found myself in the middle of a trek in the Himalayas. I was feeling lost, still trying to find my way. During the preceding days as I walked over high passes, through isolated villages, past remote monasteries, over glaciers, I realized I had no idea where I was. Oh, I could see on the map that I was somewhere near the Tibet border, but this trek, this journey, had little to do with where I was at any moment in time, or even the destination—which would be to return in a circle to where I started.

The Hindus believe that there is no point in trying to change things—fate decides where we all end up. The Buddhists, on the other hand, believe that choice is possible, but one path may be as good as another. It doesn't matter so much where we do our good deeds, or even the method we choose to do the.

I feel so helpless, like my life's work has meant so little, that doing and teaching counseling in developed, affluent regions of the world means so little compared to the work that needs to be done in places like this, in places where the children are sold as sex slaves, where these may even be the lucky ones who at least will get medical care.

I have been walking for close to 2 weeks, sometimes up to 20 miles in a day, none of it on level ground. I am exhausted, filthy, limping, and sore, lighter by 15 pounds. For a few minutes each morning, just when the sun rises, the clouds clear for a few minutes during this pre-monsoon season. There, right in front of me, are the snowy walls of 23,000-foot Himalayan peaks. The mountains are always there, of course, but they remain invisible, enshrouded in mist, except during these magical moments when the curtains part.

I hear the sound of children playing, distracting me for a moment. I give one last longing look toward the mountains before they are swallowed up once again in clouds. I walk toward the sound of laughter and see two little kids, perhaps 4 and 6 years old, playing soccer with a dirty, deflated tennis ball. I sit down and watch them for a while until they invite me, through gestures, to join the match, me against the two of them.

We have to be very careful because, like every other plot of level land in this region, there is only about a fifty-foot span before the cliffs drop off in every direction. In spite of our vigilance, the littlest boy inadvertently kicks the ball wildly, and it goes sailing out into space. The two of them walk over to the edge and stare out into the clouds as if hoping that someone out there will throw the ball back.

When the boys turn around, I can see the little one is crying, his older brother doing his best to hold back tears as well. This was their only toy, a precious distraction from the family's daily work of hammering stones all day to make concrete or sawing logs into boards.

I don't know why I had thought to do this but a lifetime ago, when I first packed for this trip, I had thrown a tennis ball into my pack. Maybe I was thinking that it would give me something to do during one of the times I might be lounging around. That I hadn't stopped much to rest, nor found any level walls to bounce the ball against, was the reason why it was still bright yellow and perfectly unblemished.

I signaled the boys over to me. The little one was shy, but the older one shuffled over with downcast eyes. He had started crying as well and his nose was running. Once I reached into my pack, the younger boy ventured over as well, his curiosity getting the best of him. When I pulled out my hand, displaying the brand new ball, the kids looked at me with a stunned expression. I think for a moment they wondered if